GORO CRATER

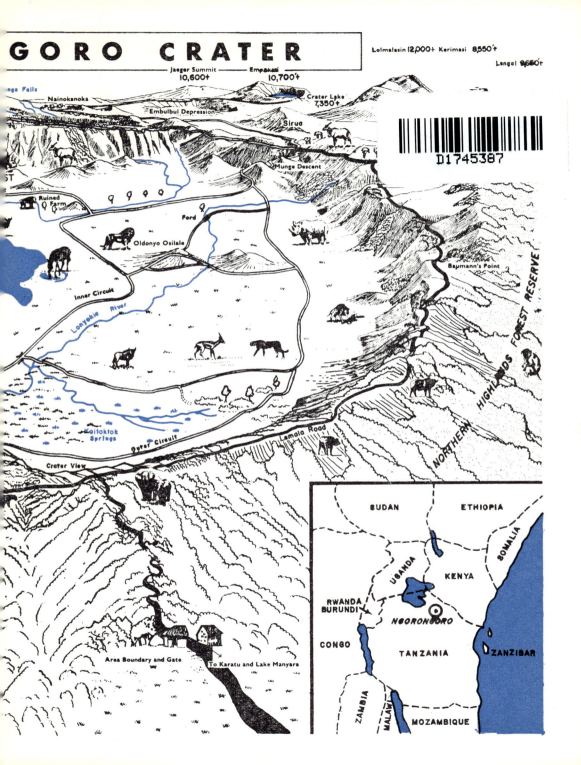

Loimalasin 12,000+ Kerimasi 8,550+

Lengai 9,650+

Jaeger Summit 10,600+
Empakaai 10,700+

Crater Lake 7,350+

ngo Falls
Nainokanoka
Embulbul Depression
Sirua

Munge Descent

Ruined Farm
Ford
Oldonyo Osilale

Baumann's Point

NORTHERN HIGHLANDS FOREST RESERVE

Inner Circuit
Lonyokie River

Koitoktok Springs
Outer Circuit
Lemala Road

Crater View

Area Boundary and Gate
To Karatu and Lake Manyara

SUDAN   ETHIOPIA

UGANDA   KENYA   SOMALIA

RWANDA BURUNDI

CONGO   NGORONGORO   ZANZIBAR

TANZANIA

ZAMBIA   MALAWI   MOZAMBIQUE

A SURVIVAL SPECIAL

Ngorongoro – The Eighth Wonder

Survival Books are published in close association with Anglia Television's
Natural History Unit who make the 'Survival' series of television documentaries
on wildlife

SURVIVAL BOOKS

Edited by Colin Willock

ALREADY PUBLISHED

*

The Private Life of the Rabbit
R. M. Lockley

Birds of Prey
Philip Brown

Living with Deer
Richard Prior

Town Fox, Country Fox
Brian Vesey-Fitzgerald

Birds in the Balance
Philip Brown

Grey Seal, Common Seal
R. M. Lockley

S.O.S. Rhino
C. A. W. Guggisberg

A Wealth of Wildfowl
Jeffrey Harrison

The Hedgehog
Maurice Burton

A Continent in Danger
A Survival Special on Australian Wildlife
Vincent Serventry

Man Against Nature
A Survival Special on New Zealand Wildlife
R. M. Lockley

Ngorongoro – The Eighth Wonder

HENRY FOSBROOKE

A SURVIVAL SPECIAL ON AFRICAN WILDLIFE
Editor Colin Willock

ANDRE DEUTSCH

FIRST PUBLISHED 1972 BY
ANDRE DEUTSCH LIMITED
105 GREAT RUSSELL STREET
LONDON WC1
COPYRIGHT © 1972 BY HENRY FOSBROOKE
ALL RIGHTS RESERVED
PRINTED IN GREAT BRITAIN BY
EBENEZER BAYLIS AND SON LTD
THE TRINITY PRESS
WORCESTER AND LONDON
ISBN 0 233 96035 X

Foreword
by Prince Bernhard

When I visited Ngorongoro, accompanied by Mr Fosbrooke, in August, 1965, I was impressed by the far sighted policy adopted by the Tanzania Government and the practical steps being taken to implement this policy. Some problems which face conservationists concern the preservation from extinction of a single species; in other cases national parks are established to preserve an assemblage of animals, a famous national feature or beauty spot, or even a specific bird or plant. But at Ngorongoro an attempt is being made to carry matters a stage further: a policy was recommended by scientists, particularly the late Professor Pearsall, and adopted by the Government of Tanzania, whereby the interests of all those with a stake in Ngorongoro should, as far as possible, be reconciled and developed. There are many farmers who depend on the waters flowing from the forests of the Ngorongoro Highlands, there are the Masai pastoralists, who live within the Conservation Area; scientists can study the wildlife and its interrelation to its environment, students can learn about conservation, and visitors both local and overseas can find here mental relaxation and spiritual refreshment. The nation benefits from the revenue from tourism and can display its maturity by preserving the wonders of Ngorongoro for posterity.

Conservationists throughout the world are watching this experiment in multiple land use with keen eyes and will read with interest Mr Fosbrooke's description of the Area and its inhabitants, and his account of the first five years of successes, failures and difficulties overcome.

As President of the World Wildlife Fund, I welcome this opportunity of wishing the Tanzania Government continued and ever expanding success in this bold and well conceived venture.

BERNHARD, PRINCE OF THE NETHERLANDS

Contents

	Foreword by Prince Bernhard	*page* 7
	Introduction	15
1	The Approach to Ngorongoro	19
2	The Land	30
3	The Vegetation	41
4	The Agencies of Change	49
5	The Herbivores	73
6	The Carnivores	107
7	The Birds	135
8	Ancient Man	142
9	Tribal Man	155
10	Modern Man	174
11	Can Ngorongoro Survive?	219
	Postscript	227
	Bibliography	230
	Index	237

Illustrations

Colour plates   *Opposite page*
A view of the Crater from Seneto Track   16
A shoulder of Makarut from the air   17
The lake in Empaakai   32
Waterbuck   33
Fever trees in Lerai forest   33
The first wildebeest calf of the year   80
Rhinos in the Crater   81
Zebra   96
Ngorongoro is famous for its black-maned lions   97
Wild dogs and their prey   144
A very fine tusker   145
An early safari in the Crater   160
A Masai village   160
The last drop   161
Masai women   161

Black and white plates
Prince Bernhard photographs Horace, the placid rhino   48
The Gregory Rift   49
The Eyasi Rift   49
Nasera Rock   64
The Shifting Sands   64
Koitoktok Forest in 1921   65

The same forest in 1966   65
Clump of trees in front of Crater Lodge *c.* 1939   112
The same group of trees today   112
Massed wildebeest in Ngorongoro   113
Wildebeest with calves   113
Giraffe and calves   128
Two old buffalo bulls in the Crater   128
Zebra foal   129
Zebra live in family groups   129
Dr Leakey in Olduvai gorge   176
The grave of Michael Grzimek   176
Prehistoric *bau*-boards   177
Masai elders playing *bau* with a wooden board   177
Elephant family crossing the road   192
Cock and hen ostrich at nest   193
Sacred Ibis at Hippo Pool   193

Text figures

The Ngorongoro Crater   *endpapers*
Figure 1 Ngorongoro through the ages   33
Figure 2 Vegetation map of the Crater   43
Figure 3 Main vegetation types of the Ngorongoro
               Conservation Area   45
Figure 4 Southern Boundary of the Ngorongoro Conservation
               Area showing migration routes   63
Figure 5 Ngorongoro Crater showing prehistoric and historic
               sites   147
Figure 6 Growth rate of tourism 1961–1967   209
Figure 7 The Ngorongoro Conservation Area   216–217

Tables

Table 1 Stock in the Ngorongoro Crater, 1966   75
Table 2 Serengeti wildlife censuses 1958 and 1965   88
Table 3 Crater wildlife censuses 1958 to 1966   90
Table 4 A brief chronology   175

Table 5 Stocking capacity of the Area   191
Table 6 Stock units in the Area   192

The photograph of Koitoktok Forest in 1921 was taken by Major Dugmore, that of trees in front of Crater Lodge by C. H. J. Wood and that of the Olduvai gorge by Tanzania Information Services. All other photographs, except that of the 1923 Safari, were taken by the author.

Introduction

To the visitor, Ngorongoro suggests teeming African wildlife in an idyllic setting of scenic grandeur: to the archaeologically minded it is the gateway to Olduvai, home of man for 1,750,000 years: to the conservationist it presents an acutely controversial issue: to the financier a source of foreign exchange: to the student of nature a paradise for research: to the land-hungry, an untapped expansion area: and to the Masai, a home.

Put simply, it is an area which presents many alternative types of land use; some of these are complementary, some conflicting. The task which the Government of the United Republic of Tanzania has set the Conservator of the Area and his team is to conserve and develop the natural resources in the interests of the local inhabitants, of the nation and indeed of the whole world. This involves the encouragement of those spheres of land use which are compatible with the overall plan, the elimination of any which are in direct conflict with it, and the adaptation of those which can be made to work in harmony if some slight adjustment is made.

Forestry and tourism present an obvious example of compatibles, where a minimum of give-and-take is required. Certainly the tourist must refrain from throwing lighted cigarettes around, and from collecting specimens of plants, whilst the forester should site his lumber yards and camps so that they are hidden from the main tourist routes. But beyond that, the two activities can be carried out side by side without interfering one with the other. At the other end of the scale, it would be quite incompatible with the general scheme of land use to establish a cement factory on the floor of the Crater! But between these two extremes there are a number of difficult cases which could be most easily solved by the elimination of one use or the other, but for various reasons, historical, political or financial, this may not be possible. To find a workable solution in reconciling the apparently incompatible is the challenge that Ngorongoro presents to the planner and administrator.

This is basically what this book is about: it describes the various uses to which the famous Ngorongoro Crater and the fascinating country around it has been put in the past. Prior to the development of ecologically-oriented thinking and land use planning, the simple solution of single-type land use was adopted. If an immigrant German rancher wanted the Crater, the Masai were chased out and the wildlife shot out; if the foresters wanted, very rightly, to conserve the forests, the simplest solution was to declare reserves closed to all forms of intrusion. If a national park was required, the interests of the inhabitants had to be subordinated to the interests of wildlife.

These were easy solutions, but not the way to get the best out of the country in the service of humanity, as represented by the local inhabitants, the nation and the world in general. If the answer had been easy there would never have arisen a 'Ngorongoro problem': the measure of the difficulty in finding a solution is to be found in the numbers of attempts which have been made. Having described these failures and successes this book finally poses the question; 'Can Ngorongoro survive?' The author's answer is an optimistic one, provided certain conditions are fulfilled; just what these must be is set out in the final chapter.

In the past the spelling of Masai place-names has caused some confusion and controversy. Even the spelling of the name Masai is in doubt, some preferring Maasai. This is not a problem confined to this one area – it is a world-wide one which cartographers and geographers have as yet failed to solve. Frenchmen will continue to call London *Londres*, and Englishmen will refer to Wien as *Vienna*. So a little inconsistency is to be expected in this book. Luckily however, the present Conservator Mr Saibull is a Masai-speaker by birth, who has paid considerable attention to this problem. He has drawn up a list of spellings for place-names throughout the Area which I hope will become standard and eventually find their way into all publications and maps.

The early cartographers very frequently recorded the Masai name in full, for example *Ol doinyo l'ol Kisale*, meaning 'The hill of the Kisale', five words in Masai (for the Masai language has an article, not a prefix

A view of the Crater from Seneto Track, showing *Euphorbia Kibwiensis* in flower

A shoulder of Lemagrut from the air. The yellow flowers are annual weeds which sprang up after a period of drought, but were later replaced by palatable grass

as has Swahili) and five words in English. But why laboriously spell this out at length every time? Mr Saibull has dropped the article in many cases, but retained it in some: as he sensibly says: 'For some words the article seems to enhance the meaning and is indispensable: one has simply to try and decide which is correct.' Thus we have Oldeani for *Ol doinyo l'ol tiani*, (the hill of the bamboos) but Sirua, not Esirua or Losirua for *Ol doinyo l'ol sirua* (the hill of the eland).

I have only made two exceptions to Mr Saibull's list. Firstly, in regard to archaeological sites I have retained the conventional Olduvai and Nasera instead of Oldupai and Nasira. This for two reasons, firstly because the former names are enshrined in the law and it might lead to legal complications if new names were introduced before the law itself is changed: secondly, the accepted spellings are so well known to archaeologists that a change would only lead to confusion. The second exception is, of course, in the titles of published works: for example Dr Leakey's recent book is called *Olduvai Gorge*, whilst Professor Reck's earlier work is called *Olduway*.

The altitudes of the mountains, as quoted in the text and on the maps, are the latest available at the time of writing, though revised figures may have been published by the time this book appears.

The bibliography is a full one, but does not claim to be complete. Except for news items and popular articles in the press, I have included all the works from which I have drawn either by quotation or reference to recorded fact. I have not, however, in a book of this nature, thought it necessary to give the bibliographical reference in the text in the form now accepted in scientific writing.

The use of scientific terms has been reduced to a minimum, and even when using popular names I have not thought it necessary to make every reference specific. Once having established the fact that we are talking about the black rhino, *Diceros bicornis bicornis*, I then only refer to rhino, unless the context demands otherwise. But where no popular English names exist, particularly in the field of trees and grasses, the scientific name has necessarily been retained.

Thanks are due to many people who have assisted me in my attempt to make this presentation of the Ngorongoro picture readable and easily understandable, but at the same time up-to-date and scientifically accurate. First and foremost thanks are due to Prince Bernhard of the Netherlands, who has once again shown his intense interest in the preservation of wildlife and wild places by doing me the honour of

2

contributing a foreword. Special thanks are due to those who have read the text in full or in part, and commented thereon – Dr Hugh Lamprey and Dr Hans Kruuk of the Serengeti Research Institute; Dr and Mrs Leakey of the East African Institute of Palaeontology; Mr Hamo Sassoon, lately Conservator of Antiquities, Tanzania; Mr John Goddard of the Ontario Forest and Wildlife Service, lately of Ngorongoro and now working in the Tsavo National Park Kenya; Mr S. ole Saibull, my successor in office as Conservator of Ngorongoro, and particularly to Mr Colin Willock, editor of the Survival Series, to whose original suggestion the book owes its being. To these and many other colleagues and friends with whom I have discussed the many-sided problems of Ngorongoro, the book owes much. The opinions expressed are, of course, my own.

Thanks are also due to Mr Denis Herlocker, a Peace Corps forest officer for tree identification, Mr Jack Hibbs and Mr Jackson Banda of the Kafue Basin Survey, Zambia, for their work on the maps and diagrams, Dr Fritz Walther for permission to reproduce the delightful sketches which so enhance the appearance of the book, Mr C. H. J. Wood for lending me the negatives of a series of photos which he took at Ngorongoro around 1937 and which provide most useful evidence of ecological change, Messrs Caltex Oil (Kenya) Ltd for permitting the use of their map on which the end papers are based. Mr Putnam Livermore and Mr Paul Fourie made available to me their respective fathers' diaries. Mrs Julia Ditchburn most efficiently produced from my illegible scribbles draft after draft, which finally resulted in a clean manuscript.

Finally, I must record the thanks due to the late Mr Lazarus Mwanza, who, as Permanent Secretary to the Ministry of Lands and Natural Resources in Zambia, persuaded me to come down to Lusaka and afforded me a breathing space sufficient to complete the book.

LUSAKA December, 1968.

1 The Approach to Ngorongoro

I am writing this book about Ngorongoro at my home at Duluti in northern Tanzania. Volcanoes are basic to our theme, and here, 200 feet below the narrow rim on which the house is perched, lies a small volcanic crater, half a mile across and now full of water. This is Luke Duluti, a subsidiary vent to the massive extinct volcano Mount Meru, the peak of which towers nearly 11,000 feet above us (14,978 feet above sea level) and only ten miles distant. The fertile, well-watered lower slopes are inhabited by the Meru people, allied to the Chagga of Kilimanjaro, and by the Arusha, an agricultural offshoot of the Masai.

On most days when standing on Duluti's crater rim, or boating on the lake, one can see the massive snow-clad dome of Kilimanjaro, sometimes silhouetted boldly against the rising sun, or tinged with evening pink, the highest mountain in Africa, 19,340 feet above sea level, and particularly impressive as it rises in one majestic sweep from the surrounding plains which lie only about 3,000 feet above sea level.

These two giants of the volcanic world lie at the end of a chain of volcanos which stretch on an east-west axis across northern Tanzania, and culminate in the Ngorongoro highlands, land of the great craters.

At the base of Mount Meru, at 4,500 feet above sea level, stands the attractive town of Arusha, headquarters of the East African Community and jumping off place for a safari to Ngorongoro, either by road or by air. The journey to Ngorongoro is an education in itself, if one has been told in advance what to look for, as all one sees has much relevance to the problems of Ngorongoro and its survival as the Eighth Wonder of the World. For Ngorongoro is not an isolated phenomenon, either geologically or ecologically, economically or politically. It is part of a greater entity and its problems can only be understood by a consideration of its relationship to the whole.

Around Arusha itself one sees the close-packed homesteads of the Arusha and Meru people, surrounded by banana groves and coffee plots. Here the population exceeds one thousand to the square mile, a high rate for even an industrialised western nation. As one drives westwards, having passed some large commercial plantations of coffee, wheat and maize, the wide open plains appear. Here the efforts of the overcrowded Arusha to spread themselves can be seen; agricultural homesteads are growing up in an area which, by virtue of its low rainfall, is basically ranching country. These enterprising pioneers are tough – one may pass them carrying their domestic water supply on an ox-drawn sledge, or rolling it along the road in a 44 gallon oil-drum. But population pressure is forcing them to misuse the country and severe erosion is setting in. This is particularly noticeable when flying to Ngorongoro; the arid, overcrowded, and now eroded country immediately to the west of Arusha is in striking contrast to the green, well-watered and uninhabited country of the Crater highlands which so soon loom ahead. It is small wonder that the Arusha people, and many others, cast such covetous eyes on it.

Out on the plains, the home of the pastoral Masai, the whole string of volcanos can be seen, with the Masai names adding a lilting touch of poetry to the grandeur of the scene. Away to the east is Kilimanjaro, *Oldoiny' oibor*, the white mountain to the Masai, then Mount Meru, *Oldoiny' orok*, the black mountain. To the north of the road, stands forest-clad Monduli, at the base of which can be seen the administrative headquarters and the offices of the Masai District Council. Then comes Tarosero, named after a Masai clan, *Oldoinyo Purko* (a Masai sub-tribe), and Esimingor, the Masai name for wildcat. Away to the south stands the granite insulberg Lol Kisale (a Masai age-set name), whilst to the north, now hidden by the volcanic range but visible later, lie Kitumbeni and Gelai, two 10,000 feet 'table mountain' silhouettes, and finally Lengai, the Mountain of God, the most recent of all the volcanoes of the area, and still active.

All these lie to the east of the Gregory Rift, which confronts the traveller 72 miles from Arusha, an almost vertical scarp or wall unbroken as far as the eye can see to north and south, ranging in height from 800 to 2,000 feet. Lake Manyara with its small but game-packed National Park lies at the foot of the rift, whilst the massive Ngorongoro highlands rise tier upon tier to the skyline. The peaks can all be seen from the road, bearing attractive Masai names: Oldeani – Bamboo

Mountain – at the southern extremity, with the tip of Makarut just visible over its northern flank; then the forest-clad crater rim, rising on the north to Sirua – Eland Mountain – and Lolmolasin – the Mountain of Gourds – the highest point in the Conservation Area, just over 12,000 feet above sea level, or 9,000 feet above the base of the rift. At the northern extremity where the rift swings westward, a recent volcano Kerimasi – the Speckled Brow – juts out: between it and the rift can be seen the tip of the active volcano Lengai.

A study of this rift, named after Professor Gregory, the first geologist to examine it scientifically, shows that it was formed after the volcanoes erupted, as the volcanic material, laid down in successive layers can be distinctly seen. The abrupt edge and steep wall further indicate that it is a 'young' rift, which has not been in existence long enough for the sharp edges to be rounded off. Thus it contrasts with the Eyasi Rift, which lies further to the west.

A significant point to notice here is that other than at the height of the rains, no water runs from the upper plateau down the rift wall. Immediately after a heavy rainstorm waterfalls can be seen in the gullies, deep red waterfalls showing that they consist of surface runoff carrying soil in the manner typical of flash floods. But for the rest of the year the moisture collected by the forests which cover the eastern slopes of the Ngorongoro highlands finds its way into the ground. This is partly due to the very porous nature of the volcanic soils, partly to the existence of the forest, whose mulch and roots retain the water and lead it underground. It then appears at the base of the rift in the form of glorious gushing springs, which form into the rivers which run into Lake Manyara. But on their way they support the heavy ground-water forest on which the very existence of the Manyara National Park is dependent, and of course the irrigated cultivation of the inhabitants of Mto-wa-Mbu, the village at the foot of the rift.

The inhabitants of this village are a heterogenous group who in the last half century have built themselves up into a flourishing community. There is a regrettable tendency to decry such groups as the rejects from other tribes, but they are in fact the pioneers who have opened up new country and relieved the population pressure in their homelands. Like the pioneers of North America or Australasia their motives for leaving home were doubtless mixed and varied, but the end result is the same – the establishment of a new community to the benefit of themselves and others. Though the presence of this community adjacent to a National

Park raises problems, it also has advantages; with plenty of water and a tropical climate it can provide fruit and vegetables for the tourist and staff for Manyara and Ngorongoro.

Two problems of this part of the world should be touched on here, but luckily as far as Ngorongoro is concerned they can be very briefly dismissed. The problems arise through two very important insects, the mosquito and the tsetse fly. The very name of the village Mto-wa-Mbu means 'the river of mosquitoes' in Swahili. It has, however, been shown that malaria can be kept under control by the introduction of prophylactic, or rather, suppressive drugs into the salt sold in the shops. As one climbs onto the plateau and up to Ngorongoro the climate becomes less and less suitable for mosquitoes; if any are met in the accommodations on the rim of the Crater, they will not be malaria vectors.

The other important insect met with at Manyara is the tsetse fly. There are several species of this fly, all of which may carry an organism called the trypanosome. Again there are several species of trypanasome, which, transmitted by the bite of the fly, cause disease in domestic animals – trypanosomiasis or *ngana*, and in man – sleeping sickness. Wildlife is generally immune to such diseases, but is capable of acting as a reservoir of infection which affects both man and his stock. The chances of a visitor being infected are minimal, less than the risk he runs of suffering a motor accident, or of being charged by an elephant. It is, however, the presence of the tsetse fly that causes the Masai of Manyara to make their encampments in the clear country well out on the plains. The women are frequently passed on the road carrying their domestic water on their backs or on donkeys, whilst the cattle are watered at the river nearest to the edge of the forest.

Certain species of tsetse penetrate up the gorges to the plateau country at the top of the rift. It was this fact which drove the Masai out of these attractive grasslands and accounts for the fact that this potentially rich country was empty in the early 1920's. It is now largely inhabited by people of the Mbulu tribe – properly called Iraqw – with a group of coffee farms along the forest edge largely developed and owned by expatriates: to explain the presence of these two groups requires a short historical digression.

Ngorongoro was of course well known to the Germans prior to World War I, and to British officials, farmers and hunters in the early twenties. But the land through which the road runs from the top of the rift to the Crater was then uninhabited. In the mid-twenties German nationals were permitted to return to their previous colony, then a Mandate, but the previously German farms had been sold by the Custodian of Enemy Property, so that returning Germans had to find somewhere new to live. Who the originator of the idea was will never be known, but a number of these people settled on the lower slopes of Oldeani and started carving out coffee farms for themselves.

One effect of this move was to encourage the Iraqw people to move up from their overcrowded country to the south, first as labourers on the farms, and then as settlers in their own right on the neighbouring uninhabited land. A specially appointed Land Commissioner, Mr Bageshawe, recommended – and the recommendation was accepted – that all the land lying to the south of the boundary of the Northern Highlands Forest Reserve, already demarcated by the German Government, should with the exception of the alienated farms, be developed as an expansion area for the Iraqw tribe. There were, however, three major deterrents to settlement; firstly the tsetse fly which prevented the keeping of cattle, then lack of water, and finally the fear of Masai raids from Ngorongoro. But the tribal authorities, with the aid and advice of British officers, organised extensive self-help schemes whereby the empty lands were settled, slowly at first, but with increased impetus in the period following World War II.

When I first travelled along that road in 1934 there was not a sign of habitation from Mto-wa-Mbu to Karatu, whilst the big triangle of superb land lying between the rift and the forest edge, called Mbulumbulu, was entirely empty. With Government aid and encouragement the Iraqw folk were just beginning to trickle north, when World War II broke out. This involved the removal of the German settlers to camps, but at the same time increased the need for self-sufficiency. The Oldeani-Karatu-Mbulumbulu area had proved itself particularly suitable for the production of wheat, and attracted the attention of the Custodian of Enemy Property (who was running the vacated farms in the interests of Government), the non-German farmers in the area, and a specially organised official Wheat Scheme. In addition to encouraging production within the boundaries of the existing farms, the Government of the day permitted all these agencies to clear and plough on the land allocated by the Bageshawe Commission to the Iraqw people, on short term lease, the agreement being that the land should be handed back at the end of the war.

In spite of the pleas of those in occupation to retain the land, the

Government honoured its pledge to the Iraqw people and put the land at their disposal. The result was that one had a number of wheat growers, with know-how and machinery at their disposal, but no land and a large number of Iraqw folk with a large area of ready-cleared wheat land awaiting cultivation, but lacking machinery and know-how. Common interests brought the two parties together, the wheat growers working the land for the Iraqw and sharing the profits. From their spare profits the Iraqw bought machinery of their own, and increased the area under cultivation. In this way the country benefited by the establishment, almost without effort, of a settlement scheme which generated its own capital for future development. It was the existence of suitable land, the fortuitous availability of equipment and know-how, and the industry and intelligence of the people which permitted this growth to take place with a minimum of Governmental interference and investment: if any of the planned resettlement schemes subsequently instituted by Government had achieved but half this success, they would now be held up as the showpieces of East Africa.

This then is the history of the well developed land through which the tourist passes with its smiling Iraqw farmers, working their tractors and combine harvesters, for the benefit of themselves and of the national economy. And what, it may be asked, has all this to do with Ngorongoro and conservation? Take one glance at the country, or at a map, and the answer is obvious; no water, no farms! The whole area is dependent on the forests of Ngorongoro for its water supplies. There are no natural springs in the area – the water flows down deep underground and gushes out at the bottom of the rift. Boreholes are a most chancy proposition in this volcanic country. All that is left is the small streams, now in some cases piped, coming from the forest. The drive through the forest up from the wheat and coffee farms to the rim of the Crater, drives home the point; for from the road-embankments and the way-side ditches emerge trickles of water, on which all the lower agricultural development is dependent.

In the middle of the nineteenth century the early Christian missionaries working on the coast recorded and published hearsay accounts of the hinterland. These they obtained from the Swahili caravan leaders, who detailed their camping places, the length of the marches, and in some cases gave particulars of the country traversed. In such accounts, recorded by the Royal Geographical Society, are to be found the first published references to Ngorongoro, together with remarkably accurate maps, considering that they were drawn from hearsay accounts. One was published in 1870, another in 1882. Ngorongoro was described as a thickly populated Masai district with many villages in a country full of big game, where the caravans remained about 20 days to hunt and trade. From my knowledge of the country and of Masai history, many of their camping places can still be identified from the names in the, not unnaturally, somewhat distorted records of the missionaries. 'Nduwai' cannot be other than Olduvai, and 'Simangoli' Esimingor, while 'King Sakis' marks the home of the mid-nineteenth century Masai leader, Segi.

The information on these maps is not only of historical interest, but equally of ecological significance. Where the camp sites are adjusted to conform to modern cartographical positioning they, and the notes which accompany them, reveal the pattern of land use of one hundred years ago. The western limit of Masai occupation at that time coincided with the western edge of the Serengeti Plains; beyond that there was an area given over to the hunting tribes, and then the route broke through the bush to an area of agricultural settlement commencing at Nata and extending to the shores of Lake Victoria. This is very similar to the land use practised till recently when hunting was first restricted under the Game Ordinance, and the Masai were moved from the western Serengeti out of the National Park.

This period of the early caravans was broken by the epidemic of the disease called rinderpest which decimated both wildlife and domestic stock. The unhappy position of the Masai at that time is recorded by Dr Baumann, the first overseas traveller to leave a record of his journey through this area in 1892. He arrived at the Crater on 18 March, and subsequently travelled across the Serengeti. His account has been translated in *Ngorongoro's First Visitor*, No. 1 in the booklet series issued by the Conservation Unit.

Thereafter, during the German period of colonisation up to the outbreak of World War I, numerous German scientists explored the area. The most outstanding was F. Jaeger, who left a very full account of his researches. Professor Jaeger revisited the Crater shortly before his death in 1966 and Dr Grzimek quotes him as observing considerable recession of the forest. This subject will be considered later in this book when vegetational change is discussed in the light of photographic records.

Adolph Siedentopf, a pioneer settler in the Crater, was visited by a

German archaeologist, Professor Reck, on several occasions and he has left a record of his impressions in his book *Oldoway*, published in 1933. There is also a short book in German recording the life of Siedentopf.

In the early British period we are particularly fortunate in having several accounts of the Crater which was visited in the early twenties by the occasional hunting party. By a happy coincidence on two occasions different members of a party have left their separate accounts which can thus be checked one against the other. The 1921 party was a colourful mixture of incompatible personalities thrown together by chance on a Union Castle liner. T. A. Barns, accompanied by his wife, was a keen naturalist, concentrating particularly on entomology, but interested in all aspects of the natural history of the country he traversed, including the geology. In this connection he invited the famous Professor Gregory, after whom the eastern rift is named, to write an introduction to his book. The other section of this party comprised Sir Charles Ross, inventor of the Ross rifle, accompanied by 'an American Diana whom we will call D.L.'. Also in the Ross party was Major Dugmore of whom Barns states: 'He had to join the expedition; he was never enthusiastic about it – possibly he was a little lacking in imagination – but, travelling with Ross, he could not well be left out.' Ross was also accompanied by his chauffeur Macmillan, but since in those days no car could get nearer to Ngorongoro than Arusha or Nairobi his duties must have been more in the nature of a personal attendant.

Barns has left his account of the visit in his book *Across the Great Craterland to the Congo*, whilst Dugmore's book describing the same safari is entitled *The Wonderland of Big Game*. Both these accounts give an impression of accurate observation, though there is an obvious clash of personalities in the conflicting approaches to wildlife by the various members of the expedition. Ross and his companion enjoyed their shooting, even to the extent of shooting a rhino right in front of the camp. Barns describes the incident: 'The very first day in our new camp produced a novelty, for a rhinoceros who marches up to within 250 yards of a large camp and lies down to sleep in front of everybody may be considered as such. Ross being absent at the moment chasing some other quarry, this fine old beast fell to D.L.'s rifle, to her unbounded delight.'

This incident, seen through other eyes, those of Dugmore, is recorded thus: 'On the evening of the second day after our arrival a poor old rhino, who had made his home in the Crater for many years, was foolish enough to come near the camp. He did not regard man as his enemy, for he had never been molested. Unfortunately, two of the party thought this an excellent opportunity for some easy shooting, and killed the wretched beast within sight of the tents. Not only was it an unnecessary thing to do, for there was no sport in killing an animal under such circumstances, but it prevented what would most likely have proved a splendid chance of obtaining some interesting film. It showed conclusively that shooting and photography of wild animals cannot be combined with satisfactory results.'

This party spent a fortnight in the Crater and each author devotes a chapter to it. From this and other accounts material will be drawn when specific subjects such as game numbers, lion and rhino are considered in subsequent chapters.

The next visitor was the leader of a filming expedition called F. Radcliffe Holmes, who left his record in a book entitled *Interviewing Wild Animals*, published c.1929. He does not give a date for his visit to the Crater, but it is subsequent to the Ross expedition of 1921 and prior to the Livermore expedition of 1923 (see p. 28). A character who appears on the Ngorongoro scene in these early days is a Captain G. H. R. Hurst, M.C. who lived in the ruins of W. F. Siedentopf's farm at Lerai. As no mention is made of him by Barns or Dugmore, whose accounts make it obvious that they camped at nearby Koitoktok, the evidence as to his presence in the Crater at the time is indeterminate. This party left the Crater by the Seneto Road and might well have bypassed Hurst's Lerai homestead by skirting the north, i.e. the lake side, of Lerai forest. If, however, Hurst had his establishment in the Crater at that time, although he himself was absent, it seems curious that none of the Ross party heard of the homestead or saw it. Holmes speaks of a hunting party which visited the Crater and shot up the lions during Hurst's absence. This might have been the Ross safari, but it might equally have been another of which we have no record. Hurst was, however, well established when Holmes came through: then by the time the Livermore expedition of November, 1923 arrived, Hurst had been killed by an elephant at Kilwa on the Tanganyika coast south of Dar es Salaam.

Colonel Hallier, who was Assistant Commissioner (i.e. District Officer) at Arusha at that time tells me that Hurst was squatting at Ngorongoro in the hope that he would be able to buy the Adolph Siedentopf farm from the Custodian of Enemy Property, but that he was outbidden by Ross who purchased the land. It was for this reason that Hurst went on the elephant hunt which led to his death.

In 1923 two American businessmen, Norman B. Livermore and Andrew Newbury, visited the Crater accompanied by J. A. Hunter as their professional hunter, assisted by A. P. de K. Fourie. Of this visit we have three records. Firstly Livermore's diary is a very valuable day-to-day account of the trip. A copy was kindly given to me by his son Putman Livermore whom I met in San Francisco in 1964. The period covered by their safari – on foot the whole way – from Arusha to Meatu on the western side of the Serengeti and thence via Sekenki and Mkalama to Tabora lasted 90 days and is covered by a 25,000 word section in Livermore's account of his expedition. He never allowed more than three or four days to pass without completing the entries in his diary, so in contrast to the other two accounts, which are reminiscences, we have here a reliable contemporary record.

The second account of this same expedition is to be found in Hunter's book *Hunter*. This was published in 1954 and consists of recollections, with, as far as can be seen, no contemporary records as a basis. This account, like his other writings, is obviously imaginative but gives interesting side lights on the expedition. In spite of inaccuracies, Hunter has a glib and facile pen and many of his descriptions are very quotable.

Fourie was a most interesting character of Afrikaans extraction who had served in the Boer War. He then came up to East Africa early in the German era, but after the arrival of the original voortrekkers. I use this expression for those who sailed up to Tanga under the auspices of the German Government and thereafter trekked up to Arusha. Fourie records that on this trek all their cattle died from tsetse and the German Government provided them with teams of Africans to pull the wagons! Fourie established himself near Arusha and went on several ivory hunts to the west, some trips taking him to Babati and Kondoa, now little towns on the Great North Road, others to Ngorongoro. He stayed in East Africa through World War I, worked for the Tanganyika Government in the Veterinary Department and wrote his recollections in 1947/8. He died in 1949 and is buried in Arusha. His manuscript runs to nearly 100,000 words and has never been published, but I have had access to a copy through the kindness of one of his sons, Paul Fourie. He visited Siedentopf at Ngorongoro in 1908. As in the case of Hunter's material, it is difficult to reconcile many of the incidents described with Livermore's contemporary and therefore doubtless more accurate descriptions; but one gains the impression when studying these records that Fourie's is the more genuine account and that mistakes are due to faulty memory and not, as in the case of Hunter to striving for effect.

The next few years are not so well documented, but by the late 20's and 30's the Annual Reports of the Provincial Commissioners and those of the departments concerned, e.g. the Veterinary and Forest Departments, provide records which can be drawn on. My own recollections commence in 1934 when in August I passed through Ngorongoro *en route* for Loliondo to take up my posting as Assistant District Officer in charge of the Loliondo sub-division of the Masai District, which, as now, included Ngorongoro and the surrounding highlands.

I have not attempted to place any subject or species in its wider East African setting. This is a book about Ngorongoro and as such must be confined to our experiences at Ngorongoro. But no area can exist *in vacuo*, so for this reason I have drawn on the literature of the immediately neighbouring areas, such as the Serengeti on the west; Manyara on the east; Loliondo to the north; and Mbulu to the south. For those who wish to follow up any particular aspect of conservation in its broader setting there are many books available, a selection of which are quoted in the bibliography at the end of this book. Many of these are right up to date, being published within the last year or so, e.g. Mervin Cowie's *The African Lion*; Rennie Bere on African elephant; the famous Elsa books by Joy Adamson; Guggisberg on lion, and the same author's contribution to this Survival Series, *S.O.S. Rhino*. Further, as research proceeds there is an increasing output of learned papers in the scientific journals on which I have drawn, without quoting chapter and verse in the text, but including them in the bibliography.

Whilst much is to be learnt from current and future research, the historical approach to the problems of Ngorongoro is equally important; how have the land, the vegetation, the wildlife, and the human inhabitants been treated in the past, and what have been the effects of such treatment? Considering the remoteness of the area we are lucky in having the amount of historical material which I have been able to unearth, and have now brought together for the first time. The significance of such material can only be appreciated after a detailed consideration of all the elements concerned, and to this we now turn our attention, commencing with the land and how it was formed, an exciting story in itself.

2 The Land

One's first view of the Crater is breathtaking. This is a hackneyed cliché, but a plain fact. After climbing up through the temperate evergreen forest, a mixture of high standing trees and evergreen scrub, the road emerges onto some open grassy glades, which come to an abrupt end.

When you get to the edge, there is the whole vast saucer of the Crater spread out before you, with a precipitous slope plunging down below you for nearly two thousand feet. As the eye follows the rim in the evening light, and it is usually evening when the visitor arrives, the forest-clad inner walls to the right are aglow with every conceivable shade of green, from the light grey-green of the lichen – old man's beard – hanging from the trees, to the dark green leaves of the evergreen trees.

The distant mountains are probably clear of cloud in the evening; Sirua and Lolmalasin, those old friends observed from the rift valley floor, here take on a different shape, whilst another ten thousand footer, Olmoti, rises up on the opposite side of the Crater. It looks like a table mountain, but as explained later, is in fact a crater or caldera, a smaller edition of Ngorongoro. Westwards for a considerable sweep, the grass-covered rim forms the skyline, with no mountains in the background; far beyond lie the limitless Serengeti Plains. The skyline is then broken by the rugged Makarut, and finally by the bamboo-and-forest-clad Oldeani.

Within the Crater, in the foreground is broken country, with springs and swamps to the right, and the soda lake and Lerai forest to the left. Beyond this lies the open central plain, where through binoculars a tremendous concentration of game can be seen at any time of the year. The visitor may have just come from Manyara, where from the hotel on the rift edge he has been able to pick out the elephants, the buffalo, even the zebra and the antelope with the naked eye, and to study them in detail with binoculars. Here at Ngorongoro the eye and the mind must be attuned to quite a different scale. At Manyara the game was about 800 feet down, and possibly about a mile away. Here at Ngorongoro, the game lies 2,000 feet below and anything from one to ten miles away. So the visitor should squat down on the springy turf, steady his binoculars on his knees, and see what careful study will reveal. Perhaps on the right, on the forested inner wall he may be lucky enough to pick out an elephant. The broken foreground will most likely yield some eland, a herd of waterbuck, and possibly a solitary rhino. The white edge round the pools, which at first seems salt encrustation, turns out to be waterbirds – spoonbills or egrets – whilst beyond, the short grass plains which appear bare to the naked eye are dotted with wildebeest, like pepper shaken out of a pot.

By now it is almost dark, and time to move to the accommodation awaiting at the various lodges, resorts and camps about six miles distant. At one point on the run along the rim of the Crater, the road passes along a narrow knife edge, where the ground plunges away a couple of thousand feet on either side. A stopping place is laid out at Oldeani View, where a vast expanse of unbroken forest sweeps up the mountainside till the timber gives way to bamboo near the rim of another broken crater. From this vantage point, can be appreciated the relationship between water supplies from the forest and farming activities; abutting on the forest are trim coffee plantations and below them, further out on the plains, the wheatfields, green, golden, or brown, according to season.

Sitting round the fire in the evening, someone is sure to ask what is the origin and meaning of the name Ngorongoro. Until very recently if I were asked I had to reply candidly that, in spite of continuing enquiry over more than 30 years, I just did not know. I always suspected that it had been inherited by the Masai from previous inhabitants of the area and so I had enquired from neighbouring linguistic groups whether any words in their language might be the origin of this name, but without success. I have recently discovered that it is a word of Kalenjin origin which has been dropped from the vocabulary for the last 150–200 years.

The Kalenjin ethnic group comprises the Nandi, the Kipsigis, and other smaller tribes in Kenya, whilst the Tatog (Barabaig or Mangati) of Tanzania, are an offshoot. Like the Masai the Kalenjin are

Nilohamitic pastoralists with a political organisation hinging on the age-set system, described in Chapter IX. It appears that in their cycle of eight age-set names there was in the past one variously recorded as Gorongoro, Kerongoro, or Korongoro. This name, however, fell into disgrace and was dropped from the cycle after the defeat by the Masai of the age-set bearing this name about 150–200 years ago.

The naming of a place after an age-set is not uncommon in East Africa. A conspicuous hill on the Masai steppe is an example: it is named Lolkisale, after a Masai age-set. There are numerous ways in which this name Ngorongoro may have come down to us. Perhaps the very defeat which led to the dropping of the name occurred in the Crater, and whilst the Kalenjin dropped it as a sign of shame, the Masai perpetuated it in celebration of their victory. Or perhaps the branch of the Kalenjin called Tatog, who now live to the south of the Crater, left the name when they inhabited the Crater highlands. The fact that they ever lived here is hotly denied by some Masai, as they feel acknowledgement of previous inhabitants may weaken their claim to the area, but until very recently, members of the Tatog group used to come back to perform religious ceremonies at trees which they regarded as sacred.

Or the name may have come indirectly through some of the Bantu tribes, Kuria and the like, who adopted and adapted the Kalenjin age-group system to their own use. These folk now live on the far side of the Serengeti and may at one time have penetrated over to the east.

So much for the name – now how did Ngorongoro come into being? Those who seek more detailed knowledge are recommended to read Dr Pickering's *Ngorongoro's Geological History* in the booklet series, from which the following information and the block diagrams in Fig. 1 are drawn.

The story is best started at a point – quite late in geological time – after the basic rocks had been formed in the sea, and a land surface, some of which can be seen today, had emerged. At this period the volcanoes of the Ngorongoro highlands did not exist, nor had the Gregory Rift, conspicuous at Lake Manyara on the drive to Ngorongoro, yet faulted. But another equally impressive rift occurred. Lying to the west of the country where the Ngorongoro highlands now stand (Fig. 1, Phase 1), it ran to the east of the Doinyoogol Hills which were even then in existence. The northern portion of this rift wall can be seen

The lake in Empaakai with a shoulder of Oldongo Lengai, active, and Kerimasi, extinct, in the background. There are flamingos on the water and round the edges

Waterbuck normally like trees, being frequently seen in the evergreen forest around the rim, or, as here, near Lerai forest on the crater floor with its yellow-barked acacia trees

Fever trees in Lerai forest killed by the rise in the level of Lake Makat, following a series of heavy rainfall years

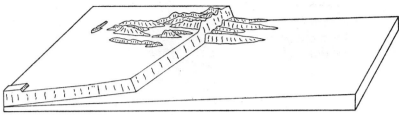

Phase I The Pre-Volcanic Era

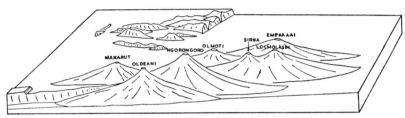

Phase II The Formation of The Volcanos

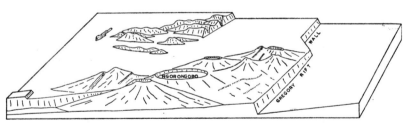

Phase III The Collapse of The Volcanos

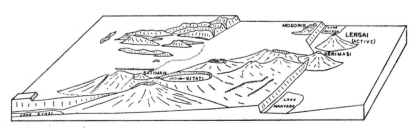

Phase IV NGORONGORO TODAY   DRAWN BY:- DR. R. PICKERING

Fig. 1 Ngorongoro through the ages

standing over the Salei plains where the Sanjan gorge breaks through; the central section is buried under the debris of subsequent volcanic action, but reappears in its massive grandeur running south-west along the western shores of Lake Eyasi. A most impressive view can be obtained – though it is apt to be hazy in the dry season – by driving along the Dulen road until the summit of the col between Oldeani and Makarut mountains is reached. The formation is, however, best seen from the air, where the difference between this and the Gregory Rift can be clearly appreciated. It is obvious that this is of harder rock than the Gregory Rift, and that it has been rounded at the edges and scored by gorges and gullies for countless ages.

This fault caused a weakness in the earth's crust, which permitted molten lavas to reach the earth's surface, probably along the elongated fractures caused by the rifting. There is no evidence of built-up volcanic cones from this period, such as occurred during the second stages of volcanic activity when Ngorongoro was created. Rather these were lavas of extremely fluid types, so that they could flow for great distances before they solidified. Dr Pickering tells us that these lavas, called 'flood basalts' underlie the Ngorongoro highlands, and extend eastwards across the floor of the rift valley as far as Kilimanjaro. Examples of these basalts can best be seen at the base of the Olduvai gorge: the stream has been able to cut through the subsequent softer deposits, but has been halted by the tough black basalt which forms the stream bed. This feature can be observed when crossing the gorge below the entrance hut.

The second stage of volcanic activity was after the floor of the rift valley had been covered with basalt. The flow from the elongated crack ceased, and instead individual vents appeared, seven in number, which account for Ngorongoro and its six attendant ten-thousand-foot giants (Fig. 1, Phase II). The evidence suggests that the lava welling up from the centre of the earth became more and more viscous. So instead of spreading over large areas as it emerged from these seven vents, it rapidly solidified and built up into dome shaped structures; this accounts for the fact that the Crater highland mountains are not markedly conical, as is the more recent Lengai. The mountains grew up to, and in most cases beyond, their present day heights; it is possible that Ngorongoro exceeded 15,000 feet at this time.

These viscous lavas, however, retained subterranean gases to a greater degree than the earlier fluid lava. Such gases could only escape by bursting out, thus causing tremendous explosions. Oldeani mountain is an example of how an explosion occurred and formed its breached crater. When approached from the east or viewed from the crater rim, Oldeani appears to be a complete crater or caldera like Olmoti on the opposite side of Ngorongoro. From the Lake Eyasi side, however, it is seen to be riven by a deep gorge; for this reason it contains no lake or swamp, but instead discharges its waters into Lake Eyasi down the rapid flowing Olbusare stream. To complete the picture of Oldeani, it is today clad with a magnificent unbroken stand of temperate evergreen forest on its south-eastern and southern slopes. At the point where the sweep of the mountain slope blends with the rim of the Crater, bamboo appears and is particularly noticeable on the west, where it presents a solid stand ending in an abrupt line where the vegetation changes to grassland. The mountain gets its name from the Masai word for bamboo: it is curiously enough the only place in the Area where bamboo is found.

Returning to the geological story, after the build up of the viscous volcanoes there followed a second phase of rift faulting. The main rift fracture occurred in a north-south line, forming the present Gregory Rift. As can be observed as one nears Mto-wa-Mbu, this rift is very different from the Eyasi scarp. The edge is abrupt, and the successive strata of volcanic material can be distinctly seen. This shows clearly that the volcanoes were formed first, and then had their easternmost 'toes' cut off when the rift was formed.

It was during this phase of faulting that the Ngorongoro volcano, having blown itself out so that it formed a hollow cone, collapsed (Fig. 1, Phase III). It is because it was formed in this manner that it is called a caldera, instead of a crater. The same applies to both Empakaai and Olmoti, and accounts for the fact that all three possess unbroken rims (save for one small crack in Olmoti, through which the Munge river falls).

There used to be much argument as to whether Ngorongoro was the largest crater in the world, until I appealed to Professor Tamura, the famous Japanese conservationist, to settle the question. It appears that the three largest caldera in the world are in Japan: Kucharo, 238 square miles, Aira, 218 square miles and Asu, 163 square miles. The first two have active central cones, and part of the wall broken: in the case of Aira part of the wall is sunk below the sea. Asu has an active central cone, and a gap breaks the west wall. The fourth in size is Taal in the Philippines, 150 square miles; this has a central cone with a crater lake within the caldera lake. Japan supplies number five on the list, Shikotsu, at 125 square miles, filled with a crater lake. Then comes Ngorongoro at about 120 square miles (rim to rim) followed by Idjen in Indonesia, 100 square miles and Bolsera in Italy, 90 square miles. Though there are bigger caldera than Ngorongoro, from the descriptions it appears that Ngorongoro is the *largest inactive unbroken unflooded caldera* in the world. Nowhere else can be seen the unbroken symmetry which is one of the most impressive features of Tanzania's wonder crater.

The wall of the Crater is in effect a circular fault and as is frequently the case with such breaks in the earth's crust, they permit molten material to well up. This accounts for the broken nature of the country immediately below Crater View, and more markedly for the rolling hills to the north behind Siedentopf's farm. The name of these, Nolkaria, means in Masai 'the hills of the red earth', indicating volcanic origin. The clinkery cinder-like nature of the formation can be seen at Silalei Hill, where it has been necessary to excavate road material. It is regrettable that a quarry had to be dug here, but it was only done after extensive exploration which showed that this was the only source of reasonable road material within the Crater. Even if there had been a conveniently placed supply outside the Crater, within reasonable distance (which there wasn't) it could not have been used, as no contractor would risk his lorries on the roads down into the Crater. So a scar on Silalei Hill is the price the visitor has to pay for the convenience of all-the-year game viewing in the Crater.

There are other minor geological formations worthy of note in the Crater. Kitati Hill, the small flat-topped circular hill (actually not flat, there is a shallow crater in the top) with abrupt sides, the shape of which has suggested its Masai name, meaning a woman's girdle. There is nothing to indicate what weakness permitted this miniature volcano to push itself up in the middle of the Crater floor.

Then the piles of rocks immediately to the west of Lerai forest are of interest, being the product of a geological phenomenon known as a lahar. The story here is that a lake formed on the Crater rim; the old bed of this lake is crossed by the road to the Serengeti just before it reaches the Dulen turnoff. One day in the distant past the wall between this lake and the Crater rim broke, and the whole lake debouched into the crater with a gigantic woosh! The retaining wall, the rocks on the Crater wall, the mud at the bottom of the lake, all glissaded onto the Crater floor. In course of time the mud washed away, leaving the piles of rocks which the Masai have termed Kung, 'the knee caps'.

Even on the Crater floor faults occur, which supports the contention that it is indeed a microcosm of East Africa; one such is to be seen running from east to west to the north of the Kaitoktok Springs. Indeed it is the *raison d'être* of these springs, permitting the water collected and driven underground by the forests on the inside of the east Crater wall, to well up to the surface.

The faulting which formed the rift wall and brought Ngorongoro into being also affected the shape of Makarut and Empakaai. Makarut presents a silhouette with a high central peak, 10,350 feet high, supported by two lesser flanking peaks, giving the mountain a pleasing symmetry.

Another of the big volcanoes, with a bit sliced off its side by faulting, is Empakaai, whose western extremity forms a distinct peak 10,569 feet high; it is separated from the main mass by a pass at about 9,500 feet. Near the top of the pass is an attractive spot called by the Masai 'The one watering trough', as the trickle of water will not support more. Here one finds temperate flowers, the gladiolas, the scabius, a wild arabis, and 'everlasting' flowers. At present it can only be reached by foot, but my recollection is that it should be possible to put a track through, at least to Land Rover standard in the first place.

What a trip a circular tour round Empakaai would be. For this is another of the Big Six which has remained intact, a complete caldera, five miles across, the rim ranging from about 8,200 feet to 10,700 feet. Its floor, at over 7,350 feet, is half covered by a lake two miles across, which is kept filled by small streams coming off the forest-clad inner slopes. As is natural with drainless basins, the lake is brackish: it is about 200 feet deep – this I know as I was the first person to take a boat there and plumb its depths to expose the legend that it was 'bottomless'. The inside of the Crater is a little Eden – short turf round the lake margin – which is characterised by dead, partly fossilised tree stumps, of which more anon. Then gurgling streams run through bush from the forest-clad slopes. There is enough flatland at the bottom to attract cultivators, and it has been a constant fight to keep this gem unsullied for the delectation of future generations. I have always held the view that, like Ngurduto near Arusha, this crater should be preserved inviolate from motor roads, but that unlike

Ngurduto a cabin should be established in the crater which the more adventurous visitors could visit on foot. What a place for youth groups tired of the town environment which will inevitably characterise the lives of many future Tanzanians!

However, to return to the rim: a circular tour coming up from Ngorongoro would lead through One Trough Pass; as the visitor emerges from this the country falls abruptly away, down a steady slope from 9,900 feet to 4,000 feet, with a precipitous drop to Lake Natron at 2,000 feet, its colour varying from pink to plum. To the left stretches the limitless Serengeti and below, the Sale Plains, backed by the harsh granite mountains of Doinyoogol. To the right the visitor has a unique view of the active volcano Lengai, its craters just about at eye level, and only twelve miles away in a direct line.

As the eye travels round the rim of Empakaai, a panorama of volcanoes would reveal itself, Gelai, Kitumbeni, Tarosero, and Monduli, with Kerimasi in the foreground and Meru and Kilimanjaro as a backdrop. More to the north could be seen Longido, topped by its characteristic granite rock – this marks the border post with Kenya – and Namanga, called by the Masai the black mountain, at the base of which the traveller on the Nairobi road finds refreshment. Our circular route round Empakaai, having followed the rim, and provided views inside the crater, would now swing westwards, over the watershed between the rift and the depression called Bulbul, and thence join the track back to Ngorongoro and civilization.

Looking even further ahead, it is possible to envisage a track running north from One Trough Pass, down to the plains where the magnificent Engare Sero gorge could be visited, with its almost sheer drop of over 1,500 feet. There one could look down on the nesting vultures circling in the up-draught, looking no bigger than pigeons or starlings viewed from the top of a skyscraper. This scenic route of the future would then descend the rift to the shores of Lake Natron, pass the base of the glittering, silver cone of Lengai, and halt under the shady fig trees of Engaruka where the ruins of the past would be visited. Then it would continue along the base of the rift, past the buffalo-infested swamps of Sitete, to join the main Arusha-Ngorongoro road at Mto-wa-Mbu. What a journey! But what country for road construction – descents from 9,900 to 2,000 feet through volcanic dust and blocks of lava. Tanzania's tourist industry will have to expand considerably before such a road could be justified economically, but if the present growth rate can be maintained, this dream could well be realised within a decade or two.

The Sirua-Lolmalasin block provides the highest point in the whole massif. Here there is some uncertainty about nomenclature, one school regarding the two as separate mountains, with separate names, the other – with Masai backing – contending that the block itself is called Sirua, the name Lolmalasin being restricted to the high eastern peak. The Masai name Sirua is straightforward, 'the place of the eland'; this antelope is certainly a climber, and has been seen on the saddle of Kilimanjaro at 15,000 feet. The name Lolmalasin is more intriguing: the literal translation is simple – 'the place of the gourds'. But why this name when no one grows gourds at that altitude? Sir Hugh Elliott considers that this name refers to the Giant Lobelia, an alpine plant growing in a small swamp near the peak of the mountain, and nowhere else in Masailand. But an educated Masai girl tells a different story, which she heard from her father. Down in the depths of the mountain there exists a spirit world, inhabited by Masai who live a life as on earth; they possess large herds of cattle, and at milking time the familiar clonk-clonk of two milk gourds banging against each other can be heard, hence the name 'the place of the gourds'. As with the lobelia theory, this also has a basic of physical fact, as in the still unstable area earth-tremors are frequent. They are heralded by a distant rumble, not unlike an underground train passing underfoot and the noise might well be said to resemble that made by two gourds knocking together as a Masai woman hurries across the kraal at milking time.

The three younger volcanoes should now be mentioned, Satiman on the southern flank of the Malanja depression, Kerimasi sticking out from the rift, and Lengai, standing in the valley near Lake Natron, just beyond the boundary of the Conservation Area (Fig. 1, Phase IV).

The eruptions of these have had, and in the case of the last named continue to have, a radical effect on the soils, on which in turn the vegetation is dependent. I recall that in the case of the 1940 eruption the ash was so heavy on the Sale plains, and the mountains to the west, that the grazing became inedible and the Masai of that part had to migrate. The fallout, which is carried westward by the prevailing wind, extended as far west as Banagi, and affected wildlife as well as domestic stock.

The fact that Lengai was liable to eruption was reported as early as 1882 by A. G. Fischer: it is also significant that on the Thornton and

Kersten map compiled in 1861–62 Lengai, in common only with Mounts Kilimanjaro and Kenya, is recorded as a 'sneeberg', a snow mountain. This confusion doubtless arose from a phenomenon which modern observers have recorded, that after erupting the upper section of the cone takes on an iridiscent silvery appearance.

One of the remarkable features of Ngorongoro is the number of salt lakes which lie within or around the Area. A sure way to spot Ngorongoro on the map is to pick up the triangle of three large lakes, Natron, Manyara and Eyasi; Ngorongoro lies in the centre. Then there is the salt lake in the Crater, which in a series of poor years dries out completely, and the lake in Empakaai, which in spite of its 200 foot depth is very brackish, and then Lake Ndutu, at the head of the main Olduvai gorge.

The reason for all these soda lakes is obvious if a drainage map of the area is studied. For it is covered by no less than eleven separate drainage basins, only one of which runs out into the sea; and this is via Lake Victoria and the Nile to the Mediterranean! The other ten are drainless basins, formed by volcanic activity and subsequent faulting. As the mineral-bearing waters have been pouring into these basins for millenia, evaporation has led to an accumulation of various salts. Lake Magadi at the north end of Lake Natron, just over the Kenya border, is worked commercially. Lake Eyasi has long been the source of eating-salt for the Sukuma people, who come over from their country on organised safaris. The Conservation Unit used in the past to get the material for its salt-licks there, but in the series of wet years it was impossible to harvest this salt. So instead the Magadi Soda Company, when I approached them, supplied a truck-load of salt on very reasonable terms. Lake Natron provides the *magadi* which the Masai chew with their tobacco, and Lake Manyara the cooking soda used by the neighbouring tribes – an interesting list of by-products, a large proportion of which have been carried down by water action over the years from the highlands of the Conservation Area.

So much for the land, on whose structure, conformation and soil the vegetation so greatly depends. But other factors, such as rainfall, wind and temperature, also play their part in determining what clothes the country wears.

3 The Vegetation

Vegetation is one of the most important factors in wildlife habitat, for it is from this that they draw their food supply and derive shelter and shade. There are, of course, other factors in the habitat which determine the types of wildlife that occur; water supply for instance, can be a decisive factor, its absence making large areas of country inaccessible to most herbivora, but still inhabitable by the thirst-resistant Grant's gazelle. Temperature is another factor, but in many species the heat retaining/dispersing mechanism obviously works well, as they exhibit a remarkable altitude range; elephants for instance seem equally at home on the tropical coast as in the temperate highlands of East Africa. Certain other physical conditions may be the major determinant; examples would be swamps and rivers for hippo, and rocks for klipspringers.

The remarkable range of vegetation types found at Ngorongoro is determined by many factors. The rule naturally is, the higher the cooler. That is why Ngorongoro is so attractive to visitors from temperate climes; they get sunshine and warmth without the discomfort of scorching heat or excessive humidity. At high altitudes, however, visitors should remember that less atmosphere lies between themselves and the sun; as a result its rays are more likely to cause sunburn in a shorter period than normal; sunbathers beware!

As the sun passes overhead twice a year, there is little choice between northern and southern aspects – one does not find sheltered valleys which the sun never enters, with a microclimate and flora and fauna of their own. Orientation in relation to the prevailing winds is however a most important factor. Northern Tanzania, in common with Kenya, enjoys two rainy seasons, which are dependent on the two Indian Ocean monsoons, the north east monsoon of November–December, and the south east monsoon of March–May. These carry inland moisture-bearing air currents which break when they hit an obstruction. On their journey westwards towards Ngorongoro the clouds may first strike the Usamburas, or the Pare mountains, then Kilimanjaro or Meru, and when they have precipitated much of their moisture, Ngorongoro may be lucky enough to get its share. Naturally the east-facing slopes catch most of this moisture; the western areas are in what is termed the 'rain shadow', that is, the region from which the rain bearing clouds are excluded by high ground to the east. The general picture is made clear by the way that the east face of Oldeani is covered with an almost unbroken canopy of forest – on the west face of the same mountain there is only bamboo, and that descends only to about 8,000 feet then turns into grassland.

The same pattern can be seen if we look at the Crater itself, which bears out the contention that it represents in miniature nearly all the features of East Africa. The outside of the eastern rim is not only forest-clad, but the inside wall also bears a considerable area of forest cover, whereas western rim, both inside and out, is grassland – with some scrub – and quite devoid of the evergreen forest of the eastern rim. The developed area around the lodges and offices is halfway between the two extremes – look westward and the country is obviously dry, even to the extent of carrying euphorbia and other dry-type vegetation, particularly conspicuous at Seneto. If you look east from the same site, you see evergreen forest, and in the early morning, the reason for its being there. With luck you will see, under a clear blue sky, a blanket of cloud flowing over the eastern rim in a constant stream; as the cloud falls into the Crater it disperses, like a Niagara or Victoria Falls of such height that the water disappears before reaching the bottom. When this phenomenon is taking place, one can drive from the sunshine around the Lodge towards Crater View and along the Lemala Road, and from inside this cloud observe how the festooned, moss-covered trees drip puddles where they overhang the road.

Over and above this misty precipitation the actual rainfall distribution is much heavier to the east than to the west; this, combined with other factors, such as soil types, the presence of groundwater, and the general topography, causes the Crater floor habitat to divide itself as shown in the map, Fig. 2, roughly as follows: short grass, 72 square miles; long grass and scrub, 19 square miles; Lerai forest, $1\frac{1}{2}$ square miles; swamp, 5 square miles; and salt lake, $4\frac{1}{2}$ square miles; making a

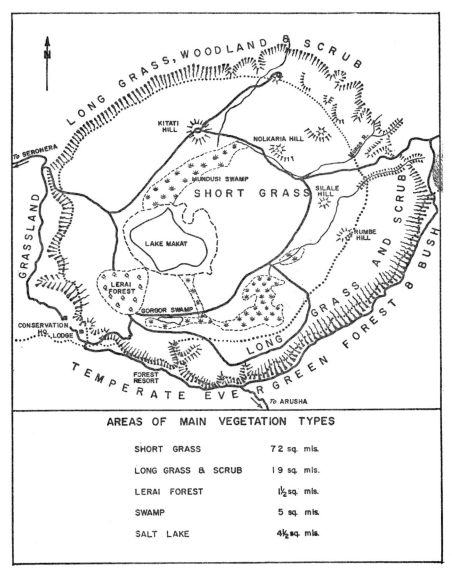

LONG GRASS, WOODLAND & SCRUB

To SERONERA

GRASSLAND

KITATI HILL

NOLKARIA HILL

Munge R.

MUNDUSI SWAMP

SHORT GRASS

SILALE HILL

LAKE MAKAT

RUMBE HILL

LERAI FOREST

GORGOR SWAMP

CONSERVATION HQ. LODGE

LONG GRASS AND SCRUB

EVERGREEN FOREST & BUSH

FOREST RESORT

TEMPERATE EVERGREEN

To ARUSHA

AREAS OF MAIN VEGETATION TYPES

SHORT GRASS	72 sq. mls.
LONG GRASS & SCRUB	19 sq. mls.
LERAI FOREST	1½ sq. mls.
SWAMP	5 sq. mls.
SALT LAKE	4½ sq. mls.

Fig. 2 Vegetation map of the Crater

total of 102 square miles. This excludes the inner rim of the Crater which of course must be regarded as crater habitat as far as certain species, for example rhino, are concerned. It is however, difficult to calculate the areas involved as the country is so broken, and it is not known for certain just how far beyond the edge of the rim the range of the various species concerned extends.

A refinement of the principle that the rain comes from the east, is that the short rains come from the north-east, and the long rains, usually about twice as heavy, come from the south-east. Thus there are areas with mountain conformation which get the full benefit of the short rains, but are in rain shadow in respect of the long rains; in consequence the short rains which they enjoy are usually heavier than the long.

All this affects the type as well as the distribution of the vegetation, determining both where forest occurs, and what type of forest it is. Species preferring drier conditions are naturally more common on the western side; a case in point is the East African cedar, the principal forest tree of Makarut, the westernmost mountain of the block, and it also occurs on the northern, i.e. the drier, slopes of Sirua and Lolmalasin. The Lodge area falls halfway between the moist east and the dry west and as a result has no cedar. Elspeth Huxley's description of the Lodge 'poised on the rim, surrounded by tall junipers which scent the crisp air with a fresh cedary mountain aroma' may be justified by poetic licence, but is ecologically incorrect. What combination of climate, rainfall and soil ordained that Oldeani, and no other mountain in the group, should carry such a large area of bamboo is not yet known.

The soils of the area are of course determined by the geology, but even here the prevailing wind has played its part, carrying the dust of the eruptions of Lengai to the west, and covering the Sale plains with their characteristic sand-dunes. Thus a combination of altitude, rainfall, soil and many other factors, including the presence of wildlife and man, determine the vegetation. I have attempted to compile a simple sketch map, Fig. 3, indicating the main vegetation zones: within such a broad framework many sub-divisions and graduations must obviously exist, but for an understanding of the land use pattern it seems sufficient to think in terms of two broad categories, highland and lowland, and then to divide each into four or five vegetation types. The highland area covers just over 1,000 square miles, that is, one third of the Conservation Area, and the lowland area about 2,000 square miles, i.e. two-thirds.

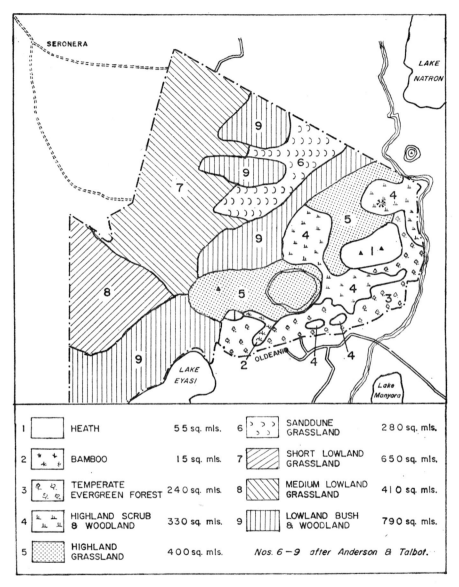

1	HEATH	55 sq. mls.	6	SANDDUNE GRASSLAND	280 sq. mls.
2	BAMBOO	15 sq. mls.	7	SHORT LOWLAND GRASSLAND	650 sq. mls.
3	TEMPERATE EVERGREEN FOREST	240 sq. mls.	8	MEDIUM LOWLAND GRASSLAND	410 sq. mls.
4	HIGHLAND SCRUB 8 WOODLAND	330 sq. mls.	9	LOWLAND BUSH & WOODLAND	790 sq. mls.
5	HIGHLAND GRASSLAND	400 sq. mls.		*Nos. 6 – 9 after Anderson & Talbot.*	

Fig. 3 Main vegetation types of the Ngorongoro Conservation Area

Starting at the top, the heathlands covered with erica (heather) types and aromatic ladslove occupy about 55 square miles, i.e. 5% of the total highlands. It is difficult to define the precise area occupied by the valuable temperate evergreen forest. The Forest Reserve covers about 320 square miles but in the nature of things some areas of heath, scrub, and glade are included in the Reserve, while some small stands of forest are outside it. The Reserve itself has been divided into detailed classifications – I have had the acreages and percentages computed from a map prepared by the Forest Division, with the following results: high forest, i.e. with tree canopy more than 50% complete, 27% ; low forest and scrub, 49% ; bamboo thicket, 4% ; heath, 10% ; and open grassland and swamp, 10% . This composition may be unsatisfactory from a forester's point of view – certainly from a lumberman's. But from a water conservation viewpoint it is very satisfactory; in certain conditions a hundred per cent canopy may favour rather than arrest runoff – plantations of exotic eucalyptus provide examples of this. But from the wildlife angle how ideal this mixture is: heathland providing habitat for species of animals, particularly birds, which could not live elsewhere; high-standing forest, scrub, open glades of grass and swamp, even bamboo for specialised species. What more could the wildlife conservationist ask for? It was indeed fortunate that, deliberately or not, the German foresters who surveyed the boundaries included such a variety of habitat within the reserve.

An overall analysis of the one thousand square miles highland block, shows its vegetation cover to be composed of 55 square miles of heath, 15 square miles of bamboo, 240 square miles of evergreen forest and bush, 330 square miles of scrub, and 400 square miles of grassland.

Subject to correction from the experts, it would appear to the layman that the distribution of vegetation in the highlands is affected more by altitude, rainfall and orientation than by soils. On the plains, however, where altitude variation is not so great, soil type is one of the major determinants, and, together with rainfall pattern and topography – gullies, stream beds, hills and the like – is largely responsible for the type of vegetation occurring in any particular area.

Drs Anderson and Lee Talbot have made a study of soil factors affecting the distribution of grassland types and their utilisation by wild animals on the Serengeti Plains. Excluding the soil and grass types found outside the boundaries of the Conservation Area, they distinguished four major types; I have calculated the square mileage of these and the percentages of the Conservation Area which they represent, with the results as shown in Fig. 3.

It is significant that in relation to the Serengeti ecological area as a whole, all the dune country and very nearly all the short grasslands and intermediate grasslands fall within the Conservation Area. Within the boundaries of the National Park lie the intermediate grassland type *Cynodon/Sporobolus* and two types of long grassland, *Pennisetum/Andropogon* and *Themeda/Pennisetum*. The bushland and the woodland is of course common to both the Park and the Area.

This section on vegetation cannot end without some consideration of introduced exotics, and the policy which should be adopted to them. Perhaps most conspicuous are the eucalyptus trees which mark the sites of the two Siedentopf farms in the Crater. Should they be removed as striking a false chord in the otherwise unspoiled Crater? Or should they be left as an interesting historical monument, and a reminder of the danger of conversion into farms through which the Crater has passed? If this latter view is accepted, it is logical that steps should be taken to en-sure that the trees are maintained in perpetuity, either by controlled felling and copicing, or by replanting, so that future generations may be reminded of the existence of these farms in the past.

Another similar problem arises over the sisal hedges, between the Crater wall and the Lerai forest; these mark the boundaries of cultivated plots planted in the squatter era of the 1920's and 1930's. It might be well to keep them as visible evidence of another danger through which the Crater passed, and yet survived; the danger of intensive peasant agriculture. And in this connection I wonder if some botanist can tell me if the watercress which grows in the streams here in such profusion is exotic or indigenous.

Another memorial to misguided endeavour is the eucalyptus trees planted on the rim of the Crater at Buffalo Ridge. From the inaugura-tion of the Conservation Area the Forest Department has continuously advised that the Conservation Unit should make itself self-sufficient in firewood by means of plantations of exotic species; otherwise over the years the indigenous forest would be eaten into, both legally and illegally, to meet the very pressing need for firewood – particularly acute in a cold, damp climate. Endeavours were made to establish eucalyptus plantations, first in the vicinity of Buffalo Ridge, and adjacent to Michael Grzimek's grave. The area selected may have been sound as to soil types and climate, but it certainly did not conform to the principles of optimum land-use. Such an area, through which every visitor to Ngorongoro, currently 25,000 per year, must pass, is patently better suited to game-viewing than to firewood production, particularly of such an aesthetically unpleasing exotic as the eucalyptus. Driving along of an evening one always sees waterbuck there – a most delightful welcome to the visitor. Buffalo can frequently be seen in large numbers attracted by the salt-lick maintained near Forest Resort. Elephant are frequent visitors, tawny lions lived here for a time, and bushbuck and reedbuck are often seen. Yet it was proposed to obscure the view with seried ranks of exotic eucalyptus which would not only render game viewing impossible, but so change the habitat that the species mentioned above would probably disappear.

It was buffalo, ignoring the electric fence, who defeated these efforts. When I diverted the foresters' attention to a less conspicuous area invisible from the road, the buffalo again triumphed, and I am pleased to note – in spite of the waste of public money – that the present Conservator now reports that plantation work is to be abandoned on the rim of the Crater in favour of Dulen, some 18 miles away. To my mind there is no question but that the very last eucalyptus should be eradicated from the Crater rim, even if a few remnants might remind future generations of this misguided endeavour.

Prince Bernhard in Ngorongoro Crater, August 1965, photographs Horace, the placid rhino.

The Gregory Rift was formed later than the volcanoes in the background and being recent, has still an abrupt uneroded edge.

The Eyasi Rift, of hard basic rock, was formed before the volcanic upheaval at Ngorongoro and has worn down to more rounded contours.

4 The Agencies of Change

There are many factors currently affecting the vegetation of the Area. In the previous chapter I mentioned volcanic activity, unique in Tanzania and rare in Africa. In a series of years without eruption the vegetation of the sand-dune area becomes stabilised; then a major eruption by Lengai covers the country with a fresh coating of ash.

The prevailing wind from the east not only deposits ash from Lengai, but keeps it constantly shifting. Wind erosion is a feature of dry flat country, and the eastern Serengeti is no exception. When roads are not metalled, each passing vehicle raises a cloud of dust, which blows down-wind, and so ruts are formed. Then the persistent breeze scoops out the ruts still further till the centre ridge catches on the sumps and differentials of vehicles, so that they must take another track – where the process is repeated. So the construction of good roads is not only a convenience to the traveller – it is also a sound conservation measure.

The vegetational map, Fig. 3, shows a large area as sand-dune country: but ground and aerial study reveals that many of these sand-dunes are to greater or lesser degree grass-covered. For them to have formed at all, they must once have been free of vegetation: this is possibly an indication of some minor climatic change – a swing towards increased rainfall – or perhaps of less frequent volcanic eruptions.

Just north of the Olduvai gorge examples of uncovered sand-dunes can be found, known to geographers as *barkhans* (from the Arabic word for sand) and to our guides and tourists as the Shifting Sands. These show the typical characteristic of a gentle slope to windward, up which the grains of sand are blown, then a sharp edge and a precipitous drop to leeward: the crescent formation is well defined.

From wind erosion, one's thoughts lead to water erosion, which may be the cause or the effect of vegetational changes, or more often, a

4

combination of the two. Some factor, say reduced grass coverage due to decrease in rainfall, causes accelerated sheet erosion; this means that the exposed land surface cannot support the vegetation it previously carried; runoff increases, gully erosion sets in, and so the vicious circle continues.

Before dealing with the local situation it is as well to consider the situation throughout Africa, and indeed throughout the world. If man clears and cultivates land, builds his houses and his cities, and then for some reason abandons them, in many parts of the world the scars which he has made on the surface of the globe quickly heal. How many civilisations are lost in the jungles of Central and South America, of India and Ceylon, Indonesia and South East Asia? Yet in other parts of the world it is not jungles, but the encroaching sands of the desert which bury the cities of the past. Why should this be so?

When forest and climate are equally balanced, the forest takes over and dominates when man departs. But when the cleared forest does not return, when clearing leads to degradation, then the vegetative cover is no longer in harmony with the existing climate. In other words, the forests grew up in a wetter climate than prevails today, and if they are cleared, burnt or die a natural death, they will not automatically return. That is indeed the general position throughout Africa. We are faced with a state of gradual desiccation; unless the climatic trend changes and wetter conditions prevail, the process will continue. But that is no reason for man to throw up his hands in despair and let the process continue unchecked, and even aided, by man. On the contrary, this critical state makes it all the more imperative to retard the process by every means in our power.

In this situation it is profitless to assess blame for events in the past. Too much energy has been devoted to pointing out how excessive grazing by the Masai, or excessive cultivation by the Rangi has caused the country to deteriorate. And in any case, does not the root cause lie in the introduction of modern medicine both to humans and animals? It is far more profitable to try to get the situation into perspective, and by historical, biological and ecological research, find means of correcting the situation in the future.

One hears a great deal of talk about soil erosion, much of it nonsense, especially amongst those who wish to appear knowledgeable about conservation. 'You must stop that erosion', I was so often told by visitors to Ngorongoro: but erosion is a world wide phenomenon. It is in fact the process whereby fertile land is formed from barren rock. Without erosion man would be unable to cultivate. In short, no erosion, no cultivation, no man.

Whilst most readers with any knowledge of Africa can no doubt point to areas where African agricultural methods are leading to erosion, few would say that the Vale of York is badly treated farmland. 'We do this so much better in England than the under-developed countries.' How many are aware that the Ouse brings down sufficient silt to justify the establishment of polders in the Humber estuary so that the waters of every alternate tide can be trapped and the silt precipitated so that, in time, it builds up into new farmland?

So erosion will always be with us. It would indeed be bad if it were not. What *is* unhealthy is *accelerated*, man-made, erosion: that is, erosion which removes top soil – and often sub-soil as well – at a rate whereby fertility is being removed faster than nature can build it up.

Having for two years been District Commissioner of a district notorious for its erosion problem, having discussed this matter with some of the leading experts on the subject, and having endeavoured, with some success – and admittedly some failures – to put the advice of these experts into practice, I listened with a tolerant attitude to the many experts who told me just how I should deal with the problem confronting me at Ngorongoro. The track coming down into the Crater from the Munge side provided a case in point. This had never been a constructed road with suitable side drainage, merely two wheel-tracks made by the vehicles taking the Lemala road to get into the Crater. These wheel-tracks had worn into a gully which was very conspicuous in September, 1961, when the delegates to the Arusha Conference visited the Crater. Numerous ideas were put forward by our visitors for halting this: wash stops at intervals made of sticks or stones, mitre drains, and so on. I listened, but put my faith in the recuperative powers of the Crater soils. The result is now apparent: the gully is completely grass-covered without any expenditure of effort or funds. It is, however, understandable that such experts were misled. Ngorongoro was certainly looking in bad shape at that time. We had been through a series of bad years. Local conditions luckily did not reach the nadir experienced in, for example, the Nairobi National Park, or the Longido section of Tanganyika Masailand, where wildlife and bovine starvation was distressingly apparent. But the vegetative cover in Ngorongoro had been nibbled pretty low and large areas of bare earth were visible. This brought forth jeremiads about dust bowls and gullies, and plenty of advice on how to remedy matters.

There are, however, no grounds for complacency when examining this problem. Accelerated erosion in and around the Crater may not be apparent at the moment, but the problem is none the less real for being latent. Pressures on the land have been heavy in the past. The deeply worn cattle tracks and the depositing of silt in the valleys of the Loirobi Plateau and elsewhere is evidence of this. The creation of these cattle tracks may have happened way back before the Masai arrived in the country, possibly through the passage of cattle year in and year out from settled homesteads to water and to grazing lands. Again, there may have been abnormal concentrations of cattle in and around the Crater: in times of drought the more adequate pasture and water of Ngorongoro have certainly acted as a reserve for the Masai of the surrounding areas more heavily hit by prevailing conditions. We have evidence that this was the case in 1892 when Baumann found that the refugees in Ngorongoro coming from the surrounding areas were in dire straits, whereas the local inhabitants were less badly off. The situation was the same in September, 1961 when some cattle, but greater numbers of small stock, had come in from the areas to the north. This is why the Masai think of Ngorongoro as having a special value for them, not only for the resident local Masai, but equally for those living up to 50 or 100 miles away.

But there is a weakness in this system of what we might call 'pastoral communism' whereby grazing is free and available to all members of the particular tribe concerned. For this means that the worst hit areas are eaten bare and more favourable places become overcrowded with stock and are speedily reduced to famine conditions. This weakness is not confined to Masai, or indeed to purely pastoral tribes. Some years ago the Government made a great effort to encourage the establishment of grazing reserves throughout Sukumaland where the villagers are mixed farmers. Each village or sub-chief's area was encouraged and assisted in the demarcation of these reserves where grazing was prohibited until such time as the authorities permitted the entry of cattle. These reserves were in effect haystacks, with the grass not cut but still standing. Naturally some chiefs and some villagers were more responsive to this suggestion than others. When the bad years came it was those who had failed to set aside such reserves who were the first to feel the pinch.

Under the communal system, the improvident ones flocked into the grazing reserves of the more provident, who could not refuse them entry. So when they in their turn needed their own reserves, all the grass had already been eaten. When asked why they did not refuse entry to the improvidents, the providents replied that one day, whatever they might or might not do, the improvidents might get good rain and the providents bad rain, forcing them to ask for reciprocal help from the improvidents. Indeed the rainfall in this part of Africa is so patchy, that there is little one can say in reply to such an argument. These are problems which must be faced when considering the pastoral development of the Conservation Area, and indeed the whole livestock industry of Tanzania.

Erosion in the Crater can and does occur: for example in the south west corner there is an area where a curious form of step erosion can be seen. This is no new feature: Barns in 1921 commented on it. Being in the driest corner of the Crater, it is unlikely to be caused by excessive runoff. From what I have observed I think it is more probably caused by the animals seeking some salt or mineral. This is not obtainable by licking the surface – the minerals have doubtless been leached in for some distance – and so the animals stamp out the shelves with their feet and then lick under them, causing an overhang which eventually collapses.

Another point where erosion is obvious is on the rolling downland behind the old (Munge) Siedentopf farm. Here it might well be that the concentration of cattle in the old ranching days triggered off the process of erosion, which has continued ever since. Certainly I have never witnessed concentrations of Masai cattle there though wildlife graze in considerable numbers.

Taken by and large the Crater is singularly free from accelerated erosion, considering its heavy stocking rate. This, as shown in detail elsewhere, amounts to about 5 acres per 1000 lb. stock unit. Equally for the Area as a whole, erosion is not a serious problem. There is one serious gully visible on Makarut mountain, which I have observed, and have photographs of, over the last 30 years. It is really surprising how little change has occurred in this period.

Occasionally, however, freak storms cause dramatic changes. In two separate places and in different years landslides have been observed on precipitous slopes. In the case of Empakaai it is remarkable that the landslides occurred so high on the slope, almost at the crest, before the water could have achieved much volume or momentum. Perhaps an uprooted tree or dislodged boulder set the process in motion. In the case of landslides in the Crater, on Kelerwani Ridge, it is significant how the bush-covered gullies withstood the impact of the water, in contrast to the other gullies which were swept clear by the storm and deposited a considerable amount of material on the lower slopes.

Another way whereby excess water affects vegetation is flooding: this is currently observable in the Crater, where the waters of the lake penetrated into Lerai forest, and killed off a large number of the yellow-barked fever-trees. It is a curious feature of these trees that they require a considerable amount of water, and so like lake-side habitat. Lake Babati on the Great North Road, and Lake Nakuru in Kenya provide good examples. But if there is too much water — if they remain waterlogged over one dry season — then they die off. This species is not of course unique in this respect: 'drowned trees' and/or the remnant stumps of evergreen species can be seen at Empakaai, or, very conspicuously, when one flies into Entebbe on Lake Victoria. All these examples indicate how fluctuating lake levels, by altering the habitat, may have serious repercussions on the wildlife.

For this reason I asked the hydrologists to consider the possibility of controlling the flow of the Munge river into the Crater. It appeared to me as a layman that the flow of this river into the Crater was the main cause of the lake level failing to drop in the dry season; this meant that when the next rains came the lake was already high, and continued to rise: in other words here was a cumulative process which might be halted if the dry season inflow could be cut off. It seemed a very simple operation to cut a furrow, with adequate gates and anti-scour controls, so that this dry season discharge of some five million gallons per day, could be diverted into the Bulbul depression in the northern highlands. I appreciated that on hydrological grounds the scheme might not be workable. It might be that when percentage runoff, evaporation rates, acre-feet and all the other technicalities were considered, the dry season flow was so small in relation to the total hydrological picture, that diversion would have no significant effect. But the 1966 Annual Report states that the scheme has been abandoned for another reason: 'Dr P. J. Greenway, of E.A.A.F.R.O., and an expert on plants, advised that the maturity age of Fever Trees is about 30 years. He examined the dead trees and considered that the trees would be dying, in any case, at their great age.' This seems to me a false deduction; what if the next flooding kills off the next crop of trees when they are five or ten years old? One might as well say it is futile to seek a cure for influenza because one particular epidemic happened to strike an old people's home and killed off a group of people who were about to die anyway!

Thoughts of flooding led me to study the new 1:50,000 map of Ngorongoro, recently issued by the Directorate of Overseas Surveys. This carries detailed contour lines, and it is interesting to note that if the lake level were to rise only 35 feet it would flood 20,800 acres, i.e. 32.5 square miles, or nearly one third of the Crater floor. The Koitoktok Springs, Hippo Pool, half of Lerai forest, and the Manduusi swamp would be inundated; the whole habitat of the Crater floor would be radically changed. So flood control should not be dismissed out of hand.

Fire, in the ecological sphere just as in the domestic, is a good servant, but a bad master. Too frequently, having been kindled as a servant, it grows into the master. Hunting people throughout the world have used fire to help capture their prey, either by driving animals out of thick cover by firing it, or more wantonly, by actually surrounding the prey by fire so that they are burnt to death. Fire may be used with more finesse for bringing on a crop of fresh green grass, which attracts animals to a spot where they are more easily killed. We have our hunters in and around the Conservation Area, the Hadza of the Eyasi trough, and the Masai-speaking Dorobo of the northern Serengeti: but if these folk do start fires, they have little effect on the grazing areas.

A very frequent cause of fire in the Conservation Area is honey hunting. Wild bees nest in hollow trees in the forests, in clefts of rocks, even in holes in ant-hills. Honey hunters collect the honey, lighting fires to smoke out the bees while they collect the honey. Frequently they fail to extinguish such fires, which easily spread to neighbouring vegetation, and start a forest or a grass fire. Honey production is taken a step further when hives of hollowed-out logs are hung in the trees, to attract bees. The collection of honey from these hives causes a fire hazard equal to that of collection from natural hives, whilst in addition trees are felled to provide the logs from which the hives are made.

In the past the Lerai forest was heavily festooned with such hives, but now it is forbidden to place them there: throughout the rest of the Area honey hunting and beekeeping is controlled by law; but it is difficult to put such laws into effect. This is not only because of the great distances involved and the fact that honey hunting is particularly a pursuit of the empty places: it is largely because the honey-hunter has the sympathy of the local Masai since honey is the raw material of the Masai's most popular alcoholic drink!

For a pastoral people fire is a useful tool: that is an accepted fact throughout the world. If grasses are consistently grazed they are at a disadvantage in their competition with the woody shrubs, which can speedily become dominant and spread throughout the grasslands. In some areas this bush encroachment can lead to the grass disappearing. This appears to have happened in the Kongwa area at the southern tip of Masailand: when the impenetratable thorny deciduous bush was cleared by the Groundnut Scheme, ancient excavated rain-ponds were revealed, indicating that this had been pastoral country in the past. There is also another hazard in bush encroachment: it frequently changes open country into suitable tsetse-fly habitat. This means the exclusion of cattle, and at times epidemics of human sleeping sickness.

If, however, the stocking rate of livestock is such that enough grass is left to support a fire, this scorches the woody shrubs and sets back their bid for dominance. Such fires also clear up old unpalatable tough grass whose value as fodder has been greatly reduced, making way for fresh growth. Another advantage of fire is that it burns up the ticks and keeps the rate of infestation within bounds.

So much for the credit side: on the debit side the main danger is of course that such fires get out of hand. One effect of this may be to denude the area of grazing; if the fire has been started in anticipation of the onset of the rains, and the rains are delayed, considerable hardship may be caused to the stock. But the more serious and permanent effect of uncontrolled fires is that where the grassland abuts on forest they cause irreparable damage to the forest. For the reader unacquainted with local conditions, but familiar with forest fires depicted on cinema and television screens, it should be explained that in general the forests of Ngorongoro are not of the type with terrifying crown-fires, setting alight fifty- or hundred-foot conifers like roman candles and burning out in a matter of minutes. Instead, the fires sweep through the grass to the edge of the forest and scorch the bank of scrubby vegetation which fringes the forest. This means that any tree seedlings or saplings in this fringe of shrubs are destroyed, and any chance of the forest extending or holding its own is lost. This is particularly dangerous when, as explained earlier in this chapter, the forest is out of balance with the climate. With the protective fringe removed, next year's fire – if conditions favour it – may creep into the forest itself, advancing through dead leaves and dry undergrowth, and killing the seedlings and saplings which would normally replace the adult trees.

So in general the situation is one of slow attrition rather than dramatic change. In the case of the dry cedar forests of the western slopes the situation may be different. In Kenya large areas of burnt forest indicate that fierce fires can sweep through and kill off in one fell swoop large acreages of cedar forest. Indeed there is evidence that this has happened in the past on the slopes of Makarut mountain. For there one can see considerable stretches of cedar forest as uniform as a well-tended plantation, all trees being of the same height and the same age. Here the implication is that a fierce forest fire has swept through and completely cleared the old trees; then a series of favourable rainfall years has permitted a uniform regrowth.

Another tree which exhibits yet a different reaction to fire is the mountain acacia, *Acacia lahai*. This is the umbrella-shaped thorn tree seen near the road on the descent into the Malanja depression on the road to the Serengeti: or on the Dulen road where considerable areas are covered with this species: or again on the Lemala road in the neighbourhood of the Munge descent into the Crater. This tree is to some extent resistant to fire, and is a pioneer into grasslands. It is first met as an annoying spiky growth in the grass if you are walking through it. After being burnt off for several years – with the roots surviving underground – some circumstance, perhaps less rain and less severe fire, finally permits it to 'get away' and form a man-high thicket. This again is subject to fire, which acts as a thinning agent, till finally a canopy forest develops. If the processes outlined above could be more thoroughly understood and thereafter controlled, they might provide a solution to a recurrent administrative problem, the provision of firewood for residents and visitors, mentioned in Chapter III (p. 47).

This brings up the subject of exotics in general. There is a great need for skilled landscaping and tree planting to cover the inevitable con-comitants of tourism – lodges, post offices, petrol pumps, administrative offices and so on. But why import, for instance, the delightful but alien jacaranda when there are equally attractive indigenous flowering trees growing within a mile or two? One is the *Hygenea abyssinica* with its pendulous clumps of flowers looking like bunches of rather pinkish muscatel grapes. A natural grove of these occurs on the Crater wall near the Forest Resort and I know of a single specimen growing at the side of the Lerai road. It requires no feat of imagination or of translocation to get these growing around the modern buildings, and that in fact was just what the early lodge builders did. Some of the *Hygenea* trees planted about 1936 are still growing round the lodge, but a number of them have recently died, after a very short life of only 30 years. Luckily the species is very easily raised by conventional forestry methods, and recent plantings have been from nursery-raised stock; perhaps their lives will be longer. Another delightful indigenous flowering tree is the Cape Chestnut, called by the Masai *ol arash*. Again specimens of this tree can be seen on the Lerai road; when in flower the whole tree is covered with mauve blossom, an entrancing sight. Although again easily raised from seed this is a slow grower and one must have patience if results are to be achieved.

A quick growing screen is provided by the *Crotelerea*, a leguminous bush with yellow flowers which grows about fifteen feet high. When nurtured in a garden it grows very rapidly; if one makes a road through grassland, the disturbed turf breaks out into a solid bed of *Crotelerea* seedlings. But when I tried stirring things up by a few plough furrows outside the fence of the dairy farm or the ill-placed eucalyptus plantations, I got no results whatsoever, not even when handfuls of *Crotelerea* seeds were scattered along the furrows. So here again there is room for research. The Masai elders say that where one now sees extensive areas of *Crotelerea*, there was once open grassland. Their view is, and they are astute observers of nature, that after a period the *Crotelerea* reaches maturity, dies off and the area reverts to grassland; then after a time it again dominates.

One introduction which might be justified in that it is at least indigenous to Tanzania (north of Kigoma on the shores of Lake Tanganyika) is the *Spathodea nilotica* or Nandi flame. This does well in the nursery at Ngorongoro, but the altitude is probably too high for it to blossom well: however even without the flowers it is a handsome tree and might well be persevered with.

Another African transplant which I tried is the Zimbabwe creeper, as I was anxious to cover an atrocity which I could not at the time afford to demolish – the hangar-like edifice which was originally erected to house the prisoners engaged on the construction of the Lerai road. I converted this into a cow-shed as I was anxious to get the experimental dairy farm established without delay and without undue capital expenditure – indeed a case of swords into ploughshares, or cells into cow-byres. The Zimbabwe creeper certainly grew well, but did not produce the mass of pink blossom which is its characteristic in its home habitat.

For the rest, I deplore the introduction of pines, cypresses and monkey puzzles: what is wrong with the majestic podocarpus or the delicate aromatic East African cedar?

We have digressed rather far from the subject of fire, but it is not entirely irrelevant to consider what species of trees should be used to restore the ravages of uncontrolled fires or to ensure an adequate supply of domestic fuel.

Fire can be a useful tool in wildlife management, just as it is in livestock production. Even in the case of the short grasses of the Crater floor it is noticeable how grass which has been burnt and reflushed is preferred by the wildlife to the unburnt stale grass. I have seen such areas grazed flat, whilst the adjacent areas of unburnt grass – of the same species, but at a more advanced stage of development – remain ungrazed.

Grass fires as already explained keep down the intrusion of woody shrubs into grassland, and it is obviously desirable to keep the Crater floor 'clean' and open. So where there is sufficient grass a late fire is preferable, because it will be fierce and hit hard the encroaching scrub. If, on the other hand, it is desired to 'thicken up' the cover, as on the Crater wall, an 'early' burn is desirable, that is as soon after the rains as it is possible to get a fire going at all. This will not be fierce, but will serve the purpose of removing the bulk of combustible material, and so obviate the risk of an accidental, uncontrolled 'late' fire which will damage the shrubs and set back the thickening-up process.

An even better agent for removing shrubby growth from grassland is the rhino. There is a low growing spiky shrub which grows on the plains on the Crater floor called *Pluchea monocephala*, a favourite food of the rhino. They can be observed rooting this out, and leaving the grass untouched, for all the world as though they were groundsmen engaged on weeding out plantains from a cricket pitch.

The firebreak running round the eastern foot of the Crater wall was established for the following reasons. Above the firebreak, early burns are desirable to encourage 'thickening up'; below the firebreak 'late' burns will keep the grassland clean. The long-term effect of fire control on these lines can be observed on the Crater wall just above the Lerai camp, where a well-used cattle track has acted as a firebreak over the years; the bush above the track is markedly thicker than that below.

Out on the plains other factors must be taken into consideration when working out a burning programme. Will a burn leave enough food for all the species concerned – taking into consideration the particular diet of each? Will it disturb certain species which may have taken up territorial positions during the mating season? Will it affect the cover for animals or birds? These and other points show how much observation and research is required before wildlife management can be adequately practised.

The Manduusi swamp, into which the Munge river spills before it reaches the salt lake provides wonderful cover for the rhino and lion of the adjacent plains. It also attracts the elephant who come down by night from the Layanai forest for a drink and a wallow in the mud. Not infrequently the odd elephant stays behind in the swamp for a day or two – providing an interesting sight for our visitors.

With these points in mind the authorities had kept fire out of this swamp vegetation which was last seriously cut back in the drought ending October, 1961. As other grazing was in such short supply many animals, including a considerable number of sheep and goats brought in by the Masai, had penetrated into the swamp – at that time dry – and eaten and trampled down the coverage. Then came a series of good years and the vegetation grew up. Without fire or grazing the mat of dead sedge became so thick that when a new season came round the fresh growth of vegetation just could not penetrate the mat. In particular the plant from which the swamp's Masai name is derived, Manduusi, was suppressed; this normally grows to about 12 feet and provides excellent cover for wildlife.

Then came an accidental fire: this completely cleared the vegetation, and left a desert of charred tussocks. But as the rains came on, and the swamp flooded again, the vegetation returned with a completely new look. The sedges were upright and clean stemmed, and the Manduusi grew to about 12 feet, making altogether a much more attractive habitat. The lesson to learn for the future is that, whilst such a fire is valuable, it would be even better if the swamp were divided into two by a firebreak, and the two halves burnt in alternate years, thus ensuring that some cover is constantly retained.

The control of pasture burning outside the Crater presents problems.

That it is advantageous in certain conditions is undeniable, but the fact is that the pasture experts have not had the opportunity to carry their research far enough to give us all the answers. For the point about any ecological problem in Africa is that there is no simple answer of general application. There are so many variables in each situation that the problem and its answer are never quite the same. So the solution which research has revealed in one place can seldom be applied unadapted in another.

One burning problem arises in connection with the tough tussock grass called *Elusine jaegeri*. When mature this is quite unpalatable to cattle, so the Masai try to burn it; but it is seldom possible to get a fire to sweep through a stand of this grass, so children have to carry fire from one tussock to the next. A fair proportion of the 'forest fires' which visitors so rightly deplore when they see smoke arising from the forest are not forest fires at all. The smoke is often caused by Masai illegally grazing in the glades inside the forest reserve, and burning *elusine* in this manner. There is seldom danger of such fires getting out of hand and they are probably advantageous rather than the reverse.

There has been much talk amongst the experts about the 'elusine problem'; the assumption is that the domination of this grass over considerable areas of the highlands has been caused by 'Masai over-grazing'. But the grass exists in profusion in glades in the forest not habitually grazed by the Masai, either legally or illicitly. I also know of a flourishing stand of elusine on the slopes of Mount Meru, ungrazed by cattle, but in an area carrying a considerable population of buffalo.

Elusine is also very persistent in returning rapidly where it has been eradicated either by hand or by chemicals. Dr Glover has explained to me, how in the Ngorongoro forest he had observed that the palatable Kikuyu grass had killed off the elusine, completely growing over the tussocks till all that could be observed was a hummock of the Kikuyu grass mantle. Now this is very valuable information, but all it tells us is that this *has* happened at a certain spot on the rim of Ngorongoro. But it was not happening elsewhere in other spots at Ngorongoro or on Mount Meru where there were no Masai cattle. Why not? Was the rainfall in one area better than in another, or had this happened only after a series of good years? Or was one area grazed by buffalo and the other not, and if so, why? So what at first sight seems an easy answer – keep out cattle and the Kikuyu grass will kill off the elusine – has considerable limitations. And in any case, do you want to kill off a coverage which at least had the advantage of a deep root system to guard the soils against erosion? What, furthermore, would be the effect of covering the large areas of the Ngorongoro highlands, now covered with elusine, by the more palatable and nutritious Kikuyu grass? An inevitable increase in the number of cattle would occur. This would be fair enough if there were any guarantee that the increased herds would play their part in the national economy – that more beef would come onto the market. But would it? Experience throughout East Africa indicates the reverse.   Equally would there be any guarantee that the herds would increase only to the numbers the pasture would support. Or would the increased herds trample out the more delicate herbage which replaced the elusine, and erosion set in, as in the very similar dry dusty country on the western slopes of Mount Meru?

On balance it would appear that the elusine, like the tsetse fly, is a blessing in disguise, keeping rich land locked up in reserve, until such time as man has learnt to use it without destroying it.

The effect of wildlife on its habitat can be considerable. A striking case much in the public eye is that of the elephants of the Tsavo National Park in Kenya. Another example occurs in the Murchison Falls National Park in Uganda, where a large area of open grassland is covered with the gaunt skeletons of great terminalia trees, killed off by elephant which stripped the bark off them.

The trouble is that a particular species may ruin the habitat, not only for itself, but for other species as well, both large and small. It is estimated that in the drought ending in 1961 the East Tsavo National Park lost some 300 rhino. As to the cause of death, Dr Foster considers that: 'The ultimate cause was probably lack of sufficient quantity and/or quality of food due to the massive destruction of the vegetation by elephants which concentrated along the rivers during the drought. With the resistance of the rhino thus lowered, they succumbed to a variety of proximate causes.'

That is an extreme case, but it is obvious that if the elephant (or flooding, or fire, or any other cause) succeeded in eliminating the Lerai forest from the Crater floor, the visitor would miss seeing many interesting species, so frequently met with in or near Lerai: first the elephants themselves, then waterbuck, bushbuck, baboon, vervet monkey and guinea fowl. It is true that these can be seen elsewhere in the Crater, but not in such numbers, nor in such an attractive setting.

So the damage caused by elephant to the forest, and in particular to the yellow-barked fever-trees, is watched with some anxiety. On the one hand it may be argued that if the elephant were going to eliminate this forest, they would have done so long ago. But that complacent approach ignores the fact that events are taking place outside the Crater, outside the Conservation Area, which have repercussions on the situation in the Crater and in the Area.

As elsewhere in East Africa increased agricultural activity is restricting the range of many species of wildlife, thereby increasing the density of population in the Parks and Reserves where they are unmolested. A case in point is the Serengeti National Park which had held no elephants for the last 30–40 years. But since 1955 when the first immigrant elephants were recorded, the population has increased till it now numbers over 2,000. Such numbers are doing considerable damage to the habitat, and pose a serious management problem.

A more subtle but equally important effect of development is that it may restrict migration routes. This has happened particularly between

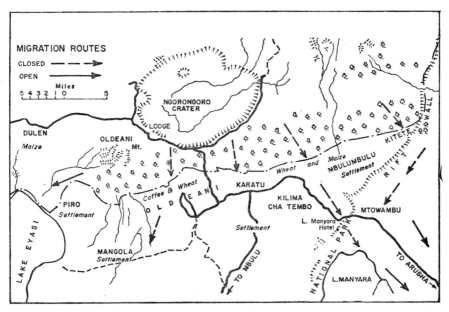

Fig. 4 Southern Boundary of the Ngorongoro Conservation Area showing migration routes

the forest of Mount Kenya and the Aberdare Range in Kenya. In the case of Ngorongoro the southern boundary has in effect been completely closed by settlement since the first German coffee planter arrived at Oldeani about 40 years ago. From these beginnings, Iraqw development has taken up the whole of Mbulumbulu, culminating at the apex of the triangle, where the Forest Reserve boundary meets the rift wall, where the Kitete scheme is located.

The map, Fig. 4, shows how all routes are barred save at the extreme west, near Lake Eyasi beyond the Piro settlement. When I pointed out that the only way of relieving the situation on the east – a small relief at that – was that a corridor should be left through the Kitete Settlement Scheme, I obtained general acceptance for the proposal from the Regional Development Committee. The following year an extensive wheat field had been ploughed and planted right across the proposed corridor!

When the uninitiated look at Lerai forest, they cannot believe that anything – least of all a wheat field about 30 miles away – can threaten its existence. But a few years ago who could have envisaged the devastation wrought by the encroachment of the lake?

At Manyara, hemming in by agricultural development and rising lake waters, have had very serious effects. Firstly, the plains species zebra and wildebeest, cut off from their open ground to the east, face imminent extinction in the Park. Furthermore, the remaining species, particularly elephant and buffalo, by being concentrated, are pressing so heavily on the vegetation that signs of accelerated erosion are becoming apparent.

Interference with migration routes may have very subtle effects; it may be that the migration was motivated by a regular visit to a salt lick to make up some mineral deficiency – perhaps a trace element. When prevented from making good such deficiencies from the previous source of supply the species in question might well seek its minerals elsewhere – perhaps in the bark of a tree – which it promptly strips and kills.

It is a natural human defence mechanism in the face of a potential disaster to say: 'It can't happen here!' 'It can't happen to me!' As far as the loss of forest in Ngorongoro is concerned, IT HAS ALREADY HAPPENED: look at the two photos facing page 65 of the fever-tree forest in the neighbourhood of the Koitoktok Springs. The first, taken by Dugmore in 1921, shows a solid block of forest, more

Nasera Rock, an outpost of the ancient rock formation on the Serengeti Plains, home of stone-age hunters, it is still used as a dwelling site by the Masai – note their huts on the right.

The Shifting Sands, crescent shaped *barchans* on the Serengeti Plains, piled up by the prevailing easterly wind from material recently thrown out by the active Lengai volcano.

Koitoktok forest, photographed by Major Dugmore in 1921.

The same forest from approximately the same position in 1966; note how the forest has thinned, not due to flooding as the land is too high, but more probably by man-made fire or elephant damage.

imposing even than Lerai. The second photo taken 45 years later, shows a few miserable straggly trees. Every visitor to Ngorongoro knows of and derives great pleasure from the Lerai forest, but who knows of the forest near Koitoktok? It has no popular name, and doesn't appear on maps, in fact it is 'the forest that was'.

No one knows the cause of the disappearance of this forest, elephant damage, or man-made fire. It certainly was not lake inundation – it is too high for that – nor yet agricultural clearing – as in the case at Mto-wa-Mbu. But whatever the cause, the forest has gone! Here is a case where the old saws have real relevance – 'Prevention is better than cure!' 'Better be safe than sorry!' 'A stitch in time saves nine!', or in Swahili, '*Usipoziba ufa, utajenga ukuta*', 'Neglect a crack and build a wall'.

In addition to the localised problem of the yellow-barked acacia in the Crater, no one yet knows in detail what effect the wildlife has on the forest in the national Forest Reserve. It has been pointed out above how the whole of the Oldeani-Karatu-Mbulumbulu development is dependent on the waters of this forest. If the closing of migration routes leads to wildlife overpopulation in the forest and its subsequent destruction, what then? Surely a few acres given over to elephant corridors, and a few pounds spent on fencing, or even the killing of some elephants, is a small insurance premium to pay for a water supply guaranteed in perpetuity.

The agency which brings about the greatest vegetational change is of course MAN. In some spheres man is too puny to be an effective factor in the situation – he cannot control the wind or the eruption of volcanoes. Nor can he control rainfall, but he can to some extent control the runoff. In the case of fire man, as hunter, pastoralist, wildlife manager, or cigarette-smoking tourist, plays a dominant role, though cases of fire being started by lightning doubtless occur.

The part of man the pastoralist has been touched on in the sections on erosion and fire. Here I would make one further point: it is the particular type of pastoralism being practised that maintains or degrades the vegetation. At its best the semi-nomadic pastoral system of the Masai, the system of transhumance, should not damage the vegetation; in many circumstances it most certainly does, but such damage does not approach the devastation caused when settled agricultural people take to livestock rearing and their herds increase beyond the carrying capacity of the land.

5

When the farmer has a fixed homestead, yet shares communal grazing, and a water supply possibly some miles from his farm, his cattle trek along the same route day after day, year in, year out, to grazing and to water, and then back home again. To economise in manpower, usually a group of neighbours take turns at herding, so instead of a few cattle going in one direction and a few in another, a considerable herd is built up, with consequent increase in the damage it does.

There is also much talk of 'the African', maintaining large herds of cattle to 'buy wives', or as a status symbol, or in place of a bank account. These indeed are some of the motives, the last named, the bank account, assuming today more and more importance. In the developing money economy numerous teachers, clerks, messengers, and other employees seek a means of saving, and of investing their gratuities on retirement. If they put their money into a savings account they get a miserable 3% or 4% interest. If they put it into cattle or smallstock they get between 50% and 100% per annum: disease or famine may wipe out their capital, but with a high return in sight the risk is worth taking.

The Masai also accumulates cattle for a number of motives; to increase his status, to ensure an adequate milk supply in the dry season, to have sufficient bullocks for bleeding purposes, to permit sales sufficient to supply his household with maize meal, cloth, cooking pots, and so on. Also over the years the numbers of Masai have increased – there has been a steady build up since the disastrous dispersal of the tribe around 1890.

Equally there has been a tremendous contraction in the area available for grazing. The Germans decreed that the Masai should be confined to the area south and east of the Arusha Babati road. This would have deprived them of Ngorongoro and the Serengeti, and the Longido and Kissongo areas. The British when they took over after World War I relaxed this ruling, but permitted a gradual attrition to continue. The eyes were picked out of Masailand, the farms around Kilimanjaro, Meru and Mondul mountains for instance. All these, to be farms at all, had to be placed on a water supply – which meant that the water no longer flowed down to the plains nor was available for the cattle coming up to the highlands.

Thus the Masai lost not only in area, but in type of country, which prevented them from practising their traditional pastoral methods.

Ideally they move out to the plains, lock, stock and barrel, during the rains. There many depressions and water courses fill up which enable the Masai to get water both for domestic and stock use, and in this way they are able to use grazing which otherwise would be out of reach from their permanent water. Thus the cattle tap new grazing, and perhaps make up diet deficiencies, even trace elements, missing from their normal diet. But the advantage of the system is two-fold, as not only does the grazing round the permanent water get rested, but a surplus of fodder accumulates. This rest takes place at seeding time, so that the permanent pasture is given an opportunity to renew itself. So the Masai, having been pushed further and further out into the semi-desert, are unable to practise their traditional pastoralism, the country deteriorates, and the ignorant exclaim: 'Aren't the Masai dreadful, look at the way they are ruining their country!'

An even greater danger than pastoralism in the wrong place at the wrong time, is agriculture in the wrong place. There is much talk about the utilisation of 'marginal land'. It is insufficiently realised that what is marginal to one crop or one system of agriculture is not necessarily marginal to another. Mechanised agriculture on a large scale by individuals or co-operatives growing cereals or beans may be profitable in a 'marginal area', for the profits of three or four good years can carry the loss of the occasional failure. But such country will not successfully carry subsistence peasant agriculture, because in the absence of adequate storage, or a fat bank account, each crop must produce enough food to tide the family over till the next crop comes in.

Examples of both well-placed mechanised production and badly-sited peasant agriculture can be seen on the road between Arusha and Ngorongoro.

Within the Conservation Area, there are few places where the individual peasant cultivator is likely to be successful. The Serengeti plains are impossible and also the scrubby western slopes of the highlands. The east-facing slopes which catch the moisture could support such cultivation, but they are rightly designated as forest reserve, and fulfil their obligations to the nation by providing water for the development area below them. There are odd pockets of land, in the neighbourhood of the Kerimasi and Olmoti mountains, which could support families. But such pockets are usually in water courses where once the cover is removed to make way for crops, accelerated erosion soon sets in.

In any case small pockets of cultivated land are completely unsuited as a pattern of agriculture in an area where wildlife is plentiful. For this means that for the protection of a patch of maize producing half-a-dozen bags of grain, numerous animals may be shot. By law anyone can protect his property and kill wildlife which raids his farm: this situation is liable to abuse if many small plots are scattered indiscriminately over the countryside.

When the Masai take up cultivation on their own account or by hired labour, there are still further dangers, for the plot-owner will be unwilling to move away from his crop just when it requires weeding and protecting – that is in the middle of the rains. Thus for half an acre of maize one may find a thousand head of cattle anchored down on the permanent pasture just when it should be resting.

There are many false impressions in circulation about agriculture in Masailand. A good stand of maize or tobacco may mislead the uninitiated into thinking that part of the country is suitable to large-scale crop production. But the good-looking crop may well be planted on the site of an old cattle kraal, where the fertility of the surrounding country has been concentrated in the dung. It is rumoured that the advisers looking for suitable sites for the Groundnut Scheme were misled in just this manner in the Gogo country round Kongwa.

Solutions to Ngorongoro's problems can be reached by applying the principles of optimum land use and weighing up alternatives. Some types of land use are obviously incompatible with each other, e.g. factory development and national parks, or market gardening and wildlife. Others are completely compatible, or can be made so by very minor adjustments. Tourism and wildlife are compatible, tourism and forestry if tourists refrain from throwing lighted cigarettes out of their cars. Forestry and wildlife do not always go well together in harness, as anything from rabbits and squirrels to elephant and buffalo is liable to cause damage in plantations.

But the type of forestry practised at Ngorongoro, protection not extraction, is 99% compatible with both wildlife and tourism. It is significant that it was only when the Conservation Unit started growing its own firewood that it became necessary to introduce barbed wire fences – not exactly a tourist attraction!

The degree of compatibility is maybe less in other cases, but it can none the less be achieved with a little give and take on both sides. Pastoralism and wildlife is a major issue in the Conservation Area, and a problem with numerous facets. If pastoralism means a highly developed dairy industry, it is obviously incompatible with wildlife and tourism. This explains the fact that large areas of the Kenya highlands have been denuded of game, and any attraction for the tourist now lies in the sunshine and scenery, the birds and the lakes, the fish (introduced trout) in the rivers and in the more artificial features such as golf courses, tennis courts and swimming baths.

But with open range ranching as practised by the Masai, the area of conflict with wildlife is minimal. Cattle and predators present some problems, but it is quite remarkable how lions and Masai have learnt to live together. Provided there is sufficient wildlife, lions do not trouble cattle much. Many of the cases which occur I feel sure are accidental. A lion which never ate an ox in its life is lying up in a thicket; a Masai herdsboy just happens to drive his cattle right in front of the lion's nose: the temptation is too great, out jumps the lion and there you have a 'stock raider'. The local Masai turn out in their customary manner, and fail to track down the lion concerned. But they do come across a couple of lionesses and half a dozen cubs, which they promptly attack and kill.

But this need not happen and indeed does not frequently happen today. The Masai usually report a 'stock raider' and leave it to the Conservation Unit to deal with the menace. It has occasionally been necessary to shoot a confirmed stock-raiding lion, or to trap and remove rather than shoot a goat-eating leopard. The incentive to leave it to the Conservation Unit to deal with, rather than follow the traditional 'self-help' method, would be greater if a compensation scheme were adopted, as in other parts of the world, whereby compensation is paid for stock losses suffered at the hands – or rather at the teeth and claws – of the protected carnivores.

Another source of friction between wildlife and cattle occurs at watering points. In normal years, in the Conservation Area, this is not an issue, but in time of drought the Masai may fence in and even guard overnight their precious diminished water supplies, to the detriment of wildlife. Difficulties can occur when a new dam is developed by or for the Masai: unless this is well fenced it can, for instance, attract wildebeest in large numbers, so that they impinge heavily on the local pastures: more important, the permanent water supply provided by the dam may mean that the wildebeest stay all the year round in country which should be rested.

Agriculture introduces an incompatible element into a conservation area such as Ngorongoro. I have mentioned above the
dangers which arise from the cultivation of small scattered plots of
maize throughout the Area. The Conservation Unit, charged with the
dual task of 'conserving and developing' the natural resources of the
Area, had neither a mandate nor a wish to *prohibit* the Masai from
cultivating. But there is a right place for everything, and it was considered that the Dulen area – which incidentally did not fall within the
old boundaries of the Serengeti National Park – was the most suitable
site for the 'granary of the area'. Several of the non-pastoral families
were successfully moved there, and were given help to establish
themselves. But our endeavours to get the pastoralists to club together
and establish a co-operative maize-producing unit had not succeeded
by the time I handed over. I hope that my successor will be successful
where I failed.

The story of man's impact on the vegetation of Ngorongoro is not
one of consistent degradation. There are signs that the sand-dunes are
grassing over in the Doinyoogol region; there is evidence of large scale
regeneration of cedar forest on Makarut mountain; the spread of
Acacia lahai in the highland grasslands is not fully understood, but is
doubtless occurring. These trends may or may not be due to man's
indirect intervention. This chapter may appropriately end with three
instances of direct intervention.

The first may be seen from the Lodge: if one looks down on the
country between the base of the Crater wall and the Lerai forest, one
can see the delta-like formation of the Lairrataat stream, which splits
into four branches; these disappear into and support the existence of the
Lerai forest. I have a photo taken around 1937; it shows that the
courses of the streams are practically clear of trees. This was the time
when a score or more of 'squatters' lived at Lerai, and their houses and
farms can be vaguely discerned in the photograph. Doubtless they were
responsible for clearing the vegetation from the streams, either for
firewood, or because the trees harboured birds which destroyed their
crops. Today the streams are lined with trees – an attractive habitat for
wildlife. Such regeneration is doubtless the direct result of Government
action in removing the squatters when the National Park was
established.

An equally striking example occurs in the grounds of the Lodge.
The panorama of trees and shrubs was photographed first about 1937,

and again from the same spot in 1966. The photo facing page 112 shows the changes – one tree has been lost, but another has grown to counter-balance this. Fire control, brought about by the presence of the Lodge, is probably a factor in this situation.

In another example, this time of a single tree, both man and nature have played their part in bringing about change. The tree concerned was a magnificent evergreen around which I laid out the administrative rest house, office, and dispensary, in 1936. The tree is still there but now largely dominated by a parasitic fig, distinguished by its aerial roots and broad glossy foliage through which some of the branches of the original tree can be seen protruding.

So this is not all a tale of woe, and as I pointed out at the beginning of this chapter, the fact that the forest, at any rate round its margins, is out of balance with the prevailing climate, is no reason for despairing apathy. Rather it is a challenge to the authorities to ensure its survival for as long as possible; experience shows that it can be done; expediency demands that it must be done.

Of course, there are those who argue that it is wrong to interfere with nature, that the habitat should remain uncontrolled, and allowed to change without interference. But this argument overlooks the fact that nature has been interfered with in any case. As one example, as soon as the Oldeani farms were established, or the Mbulumbulu settlement scheme developed, the movement of Ngorongoro's wildlife was re-stricted, as illustrated in Fig. 4. So if habitat must be controlled in Ngorongoro, here are some suggestions for the Crater.

Firstly, we must clear up the dead timber in Lerai; there is a constant demand for firewood by the Lodge and others on the Crater rim. Even charcoal burning, if discreetly carried out, might prove feasible.

Secondly, if and when the lake recedes sufficiently, we should try to re-establish the clump of cover on the Koironyi island, and in particular try to restore the yellow-barked fever-trees which grew there. There are other places where the acacia should be encouraged; round the Seneto spring, where photos show very little change since 1922, and along the swamp beyond Hippo Pool, where the single existing tree could well be supported by some additional planting.

A commendable effort was made by some Peace Corps volunteers to plant fig-tree stumps along the Lonyokie stream, but various animals found them convenient rubbing posts, and they never had a chance to establish roots. I developed a technique of iron railway sleepers ('ties' in

America) as signposts which proved reasonably durable – something similar to support young trees might well be devised, though care must be taken to avoid the appearance of a city park.

These, of course, are minor amenities, like the planting of ornamentals round the buildings on the rim. I must once again emphasise that the major vegetation cover depends on the control of fires and stock numbers, both wildlife and domestic.

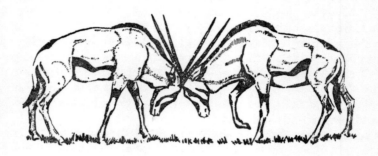

5 The Herbivores

The attraction of Ngorongoro's wildlife lies not only in numbers, but also in variety. In Ngorongoro we have a microcosm of the East African plateau with its long-grass areas, short-grass plains, fresh-water swamps, saline lakes, temperate evergreen forest, gullies filled with lush gallery forest in the east, and dry euphorbia in the west. All this lies within a radius of half-a-dozen miles from the centre of the Crater. If you set your compass at 25 miles and draw a circle you include alpine moorland at 12,000 feet, portions of the Rift Valley at 3,000 feet, lakes, waterfalls, limitless plains, shifting sands, and even an active volcano. So in an area of such topographical contrast it is no surprise that the wildlife, being dependent on its environment, reveals an equally spectacular variety.

The absentees, the species not to be found in the Crater, are of equal ecological interest. Conspicuous by their absence from the climatically suitable Crater are giraffe and impala. Both are found quite close on the western slopes and in the Balbal depression, but not in the Crater itself. It has been suggested that giraffe could not climb down the Crater walls, but apart from the fact that giraffe could obviously walk down any of the well-graded cattle tracks on the western wall, an old Masai recalls seeing a giraffe, which was resident in the Crater for some time many years ago. The reason for the lack of giraffe is the absence of their favourite browse trees, particularly *Acacia tortilis*, *A. mellifera* and *A. seyal*. Similarly the impala is not to be found, as its favourite habitat, open woodland, and no doubt the foods that go with it, does not exist in the Crater. Thus the frequent suggestion of introducing these two species into the Crater is undesirable, on ecological as well as aesthetic grounds. The basic satisfaction gained from a visit to such places as the Crater arises, I feel, from the evident harmony between all the elements which go to make up the overall picture. That is why there is more satisfaction in seeing an eland or rhino in Ngorongoro than in a zoo, and why all jarring notes should be avoided: there must be no buildings in the Crater, roads must be as inconspicuous as possible, bridges should be a simple plank without handrails or whitewash. Equally, any animal out of its ecological context is incongruous: and in any case, why should we repeat for the tourist what he has already seen elsewhere? Each park should surely preserve and develop its own individuality.

Biomass, a term which we must now introduce, has been defined as 'the weight of a population of organisms per unit area'. The basic idea is not new; farmers and ranchers have long thought in terms of so many acres per beast. From this developed the idea of a stock-unit, which has now been standardised as a one-thousand-pound animal. Smaller breeds of cattle, and of course sheep and goats, were written down *pro rata*: average Masai cattle count as two-thirds of a unit, i.e. 666 lbs. and sheep and goats as one-tenth, i.e. 100 lbs. The same process was then applied to wildlife; thus a 2,000 lb. rhino would represent two stock-units, a 660 lb. antelope two-thirds of a unit, or a 100 lb. gazelle one-tenth of a unit.

The concept of biomass can be illustrated by the Crater wildlife census which is compiled from time to time by aerial counts kindly undertaken by the Tanzania National Parks and the Serengeti Research Institute. The total of each species is then reduced, according to average weight per animal, to 1,000 lb. units. These can then be added up, giving the total wildlife biomass in relation to the area of the Crater.

Such a figure, however, ignores one important factor, the domestic stock, which utilise the same area and largely compete with the wildlife for the available grazing. So, to make the count complete, the cattle, sheep and goats of the Masai must be included. These of course are counted by a different method, house-to-house visits by enumerators who count the stock as they leave the houses in the morning or return at night. This gives much more detailed information than an aerial count of domestic stock could possibly reveal. One not only gets an accurate count, but also details of the age and sex of the beasts, and of the ownership. The domestic stock can, like the wildlife, be reduced to 1,000 lb. units.

The result of such an exercise in relation to the 1966 census of wildlife and domestic stock is shown in Table I. From this it will be seen that the total stocking rate is 9,269 stock units: converted into biomass, i.e.

TABLE I

Stock in the Ngorongoro Crater, 1966

	Total	Weight factor	1000 lb. units	Percentages
WILDLIFE				
Wildebeest	10,438	9/20	4,697	50.5
Zebra	4,040	3/5	2,424	26.2
Hartebeest	67	7/20	24	0.3
Eland	320	$1\frac{1}{2}$	480	5.2
Waterbuck	85	7/20	30	0.3
Gazelle: Grants & Thomson's	2,100	1/10	210	2.3
Rhino	109	3	327	3.6
Hippo	34	$2\frac{1}{2}$	85	0.9
Total Wildlife			8,277*	89.3
DOMESTIC STOCK				
Bovine, mature	1,295	2/3	863	9.3
Bovine, immature	203	1/3	68	0.7
Small stock	294	1/10	29	0.3
Donkeys	48	2/3	32	0.4
Total Domestic Stock			992	10.7
GRAND TOTAL			9,269	

* This figure differs slightly from that given
in the 1966 Annual Report – 8,310.

weight per unit area, the figure is 113,000 lb. per square mile. This compares with 125,000 lb. per square mile in the Manyara National Park, where fears have been expressed that the heavy stocking rate is leading to habitat degradation. Conditions there are however very different from Ngorongoro, the altitude being about 2,500 feet lower, with consequent difference in vegetation. The Park wildlife is being hemmed in by a rising lake level and by cultivation, resulting in an excess of elephants, and at the same time the near-extinction of the wildebeest and zebra. Converted into a formula more acceptable to husbandry-men, the Ngorongoro figure represents one beast to 6.7 acres and at Manyara one per 5.1 acres, both figures comparable with the best paddocked pasture land of the Kenya highlands.

Of the total stock of Ngorongoro, the Masai stock comprises 992 units, i.e. 10.7 %, and over the previous five years has varied from 20.3 % to 8.0 %. Such variation may of course arise from several causes. When the Masai percentage increases it does not necessarily mean there has been an influx of cattle from outside; it might well result from a temporary exodus of wildlife just at the time that the count was taken. Again, variations in the number of any one species cannot be taken as a genuine rise or fall in that particular population. For instance, our figures show that wildebeest have varied between 14,000 and 8,500, but the high total may have been calculated shortly after calving and before the new crop of youngsters had been reduced by inevitable losses. Or perhaps when the low count was recorded, a large proportion of the Crater wildebeest were in the Balbal.

So this concept of biomass must be treated with considerable caution as there are so many variables which do not necessarily apply in the same degree to all the species in the total population. Furthermore, the climatic conditions prevailing at the time of the count can be responsible for a biomass range from a very considerable figure to nil. The eastern Serengeti is a case in point, which at one season will be black with wildebeest and later completely devoid of wildlife. However, if treated with caution the biomass figures can provide a useful thermometer to gauge the ecological health of an area. They are obviously of greater value when applied to one particular area than when used to compare one area with another, since then the variables become greater and so lessen the value of the figures.

Before dealing with individual species let me explain that this book is not intended as a detailed description of all the species of wildlife found in Ngorongoro. A check list enumerating the 115 different species of mammals is published in the booklet series as *Ngorongoro's Animal Life*, with explanatory notes by John Goddard. In addition, there are several good, reasonably-priced publications on East African wildlife so anyone wanting to know the average weight of an eland cow, the period of gestation of a lion, or the range throughout East Africa of Chandler's reedbuck, is advised to consult one of the many books available.

A further point concerns the number of species not mentioned in this book. For example, out of a check list of 115 species there are 27 of the order *Rodentia* (rats and allied species), and 15 species of bat. It is not because they are uninteresting that they are excluded, but firstly they are not easily observed by the visitor, and secondly they lack the same striking ecological impact of the larger species. A possible exception is the mole rat; its ecological significance is not fully appreciated, but it occurs in such numbers in the highland grasslands that its burrowings must at least make the country more absorbent of rainfall and less liable to runoff. What further effects these rodents have on the grasslands is yet to be investigated.

The wildebeest is the dominant and most conspicuous animal in the Crater; as shown in the table they number over 10,000 and form just over 50 % of the biomass.

The wildebeest is probably best known for the spectacular migrations over the Serengeti plains. Readers of Dr Grzimek's *Serengeti Shall Not Die* and other books on East Africa will recall that something in the nature of 100,000 head of wildebeest yearly stream over the boundaries of the Serengeti National Park and drop their calves on the short grass plains which lie largely within the Conservation Area. There is much speculation as to why these migrations take place. Nutrition is one of the factors frequently considered. There may, it is suggested, be some trace elements in the grasses of the eastern Serengeti which are lacking elsewhere, though Anderson and Talbot after a study of the soils and correlated grassland types concluded that the growth stage and palatability of the grasses are equally important motivating forces provided that water is available.

Another factor might well arise from the predator/prey relationship. The wildebeest can obviously be more closely approached by predators where the grass is long, making the young calves particularly vulnerable: hence the mothers instinctively seek the short grass areas to drop their calves. However, further research into these theories is still needed.

In the Crater itself the behaviour of the wildebeest is very different. We do not get any large-scale migrations, though at certain seasons the Ngorongoro wildebeest spread out westwards in considerable numbers as far as the Balbal, and marked animals from Ngorongoro have been seen as far west as Leakey's camp at Olduvai. The Serengeti wildebeest certainly spread further eastward than this, so the two groups must at times intermingle. It is uncertain, however, whether any Ngorongoro wildebeest has ever attached itself to a Serengeti herd and returned to the west. Only the finding of a beast marked in Ngorongoro will prove this. Dr Watson of the Serengeti Research Institute, who has studied the Serengeti wildebeest in detail for several years, claimed that he could tell the difference between the Ngorongoro and the Serengeti wildebeest when he met them on the plains by their 'flight distance', i.e. the distance at which they took fright and ran away, when approached in a Land Rover. He contended that the Ngorongoro wildebeest were so used to Land Rovers that they permitted a close approach. Certainly in the years that I have been associated with Ngorongoro I have noticed a taming down, not only of the wildebeest, but of all forms of wildlife.

The social life of the Ngorongoro wildebeest has been studied in detail by Dick Estes. He found the bulls to be extremely territorial in nature. Each pegs out his claim to territory, resents the intrusion of other bulls and attempts to attract as many females as possible into his territory. The antics of the animals at rutting time are most interesting. Having amassed a reasonable harem of ten or twelve cows, the territorial bull will rush around the group in frantic circles keeping his herd together and at the same time driving off any intruders. There is not, of course, enough land in the Crater for each bull to have his own stamping ground. The surplus form up into bachelor herds and it is from such herds that the challengers derive.

A remarkable feature of the wildebeest is its capacity for carrying a disease, malignant catarrhal fever or *Snotsiekte* which does not affect the carrier, but can be passed on to cattle where it produces very severe, usually fatal symptoms. The peculiar feature of this disease is that although the capacity of wildebeest to act as a carrier is passed on from generation to generation, only for a very short period is an animal an active carrier, namely from birth to some six months of age. Its bodily secretions befoul the grazing, and any bovine contacting such secretions is liable to infection.

The repercussions on Masai grazing are immediately apparent. For several months of the year large areas of grazing where the wildebeest calve, or where they migrate to after calving, are unusable by the Masai as pasture for their cattle. This fact was well known to the Masai long before the details were discovered by veterinary science. The Masai traditionally avoid the wildebeest grazing grounds from the time that calving begins till the calves have shed their brown juvenile fluffy hair;

from experience they deduced that the disease was carried by the after-birth and by this fluffy hair when it dropped onto the grass. This is not in fact correct, but birth and the coat change do mark the beginning and end of the period of infection as determined by veterinary science.

But as yet the solution to the catarrh problem has not been found; it cannot be eradicated from wildebeest and cattle cannot be immunised against it. The only way is for the Masai to continue to avoid the grazing grounds as they did in the past. But they feel a sense of grievance about this. Their argument is: 'We agreed to keep our cattle out of the western Serengeti; i.e. the National Park. Why cannot the National Park keep its wildebeest out of our grazing grounds on the eastern Serengeti?' Logical enough, but physically impossible. Not only would it be ecologically unwise, but the cost of an effective barrier would be quite prohibitive.

A small scale experiment was undertaken by the Conservation's pasture research officer, working with Nuffield Foundation funds. The suggestion was that it should be possible to fence off the entrance to the Angata Kiti plains, lying between two parallel ranges of the Doinyoogol mountains, thereby preserving the grazing for cattle. It was argued that if the fences went some distance up the steep flanking mountains, the wildebeest would be deterred by the steep and rocky terrain from out-flanking the fence. But when this scheme was put into practice weaknesses were revealed which caused it to fail. Firstly zebra, more persistent than wildebeest, found a way round the fence up the steep rocky stopes, which the wildebeest then followed. Secondly the fence, whilst capable of turning back grazing herds, proved ineffective against animals determined to migrate. Those in the rear literally pushed the vanguard through the fence, till, in the eyes of one observer, it looked like a barbed-wire entanglement on the Western Front in World War I, after heavy bombardment. It is possible to make game-proof fences – if they are sited on top of a high embankment, with a ditch in front; this breaks the impetus of a migrating or stampeding herd, but it is much too costly to apply on the Serengeti, even if desirable – which it is not.

The Masai have been clever enough to evolve a *modus vivendi* which enables them to live with the wildebeest, and there is no apparent reason why they should not continue their age-old practices. They might argue that if the wildebeest were not using the grazing they themselves would be able to build up bigger herds: but the wisdom of this is doubtful till the present herds are put into full economic use for the benefit of the national economy. The Park authorities can argue with some force that ecologically the boundary is a bad one, and that 'their' wildebeest spend more time out of the Park than in it. The reply to this is 'So what?' The animals are as safe from poachers in the Conservation Area as they are in the Park – safer in fact than in the western boundary areas. This is largely due to the tolerant Masai attitude to wildlife and to the fact that their presence discourages the intrusion of others; they do in effect provide an unpaid corps of park rangers. But if the Masai were forcibly removed their present goodwill would be forfeited, with incalculable results.

The zebra are the next most important inhabitants of the Crater, at least in terms of biomass. They form 26 % of the total. Their social life is in complete contrast to that of the wildebeest. They have been studied in detail by Dr Hans Klingel who was able to observe the movements of individual animals without having to mark them. For nature has endowed the zebra with an identification as individual as a human's fingerprint. By photographic record Dr Klingel had a certain identification and by following the movements of his subjects for nearly three years he found that they stuck together in very close family groups:

> Family groups consist of one stallion, one to six mares and their foals, and may contain up to 15 animals. They are extremely stable with regard to the adults, and changes are exceptional. Over 2½ years nine adult mares disappeared from their families; two of them were later recorded with other families. Three single adult mares joined the marked groups. In five cases the stallion disappeared from his group, which was subsequently taken over *as a whole* by another stallion. This demonstrates that the family members are not held together by force by the stallion, but form a stable group even without him.
>
> The only regular changes that take place in the family groups concern the subadults. The young mares are abducted by other stallions at the age of one or two years, obviously at the time of heat. The young stallions leave their families at one to three years, possibly even later, and join up with other stallions.
>
> Surplus stallions stay single or form bachelor groups of variable numbers, up to 15 animals. Small groups of two, three

The first wildebeest calf of the year—interested mothers-to-be come to inspect

Four rhinos in the Crater. These are not 'white' rhino, but black rhino recently emerged from bathing in white alkaline mud

Mother and baby; about the time this was taken the mother was seen killing a lion in defence of her offspring

or four have been found to be extremely stable for the whole period of observation.

Zebra are perhaps one of the most pleasing features of the Crater. They, like the wildebeest, are getting tamer and tamer year by year. They let people approach them closely and frequently indulge in the game of 'last across', kicking up their heels as they jump across the track just ahead of one's vehicle. They always seem to be in first class condition, which is rightly or wrongly attributed to the fact that their teeth allow closer grazing than is possible for other species. Zebra calves spend much more time lying down than the young of other species. One frequently thinks that a calf on the ground is evidence of another tragedy of the wild, when on close approach up it jumps and runs off to its mother. If detached from the group the calf will approach a vehicle very closely, as the one illustrated facing page 129.

Like the wildebeest a proportion of the zebra wander out of the Crater at certain times of the year. Considerable numbers are frequently seen in the Malanja depression on the road to the Serengeti, whilst in dry periods they are found on the rim of the Crater and penetrate into the forest glades. The well-kept grass round the Lodge is an attraction to them at such times. It is a pleasant sight to see them grazing in between the cabins, but once conditions return to normal they drift back to the Crater and no inducements in the way of salt licks have persuaded them to remain around the Lodge.

The eland is the heaviest and one of the most magnificent antelopes to be found in Africa. A big bull weighs up to 1,500 lbs. They are not fussy about climatic conditions and are great wanderers. They can be found at considerable altitudes, 10,000 feet and over. In fact the highest block in the Conservation Area takes its name from this species, Sirua, meaning eland in Masai. Of all the antelope the eland resembles most closely the domestic cow in the flavour of its meat and in its milk yield. It is also most easily domesticated and it is somewhat remarkable that man has in fact never made it one of his domestic animals. I recall a Masai laibon who had a tame eland running with his cattle. Numerous experiments in domestication have been undertaken in Africa. Once at a wildlife conference the subject was under discussion and the delegates stressed the point that eland were more suitable for African conditions than cattle. They urged that more funds and endeavour should be put

6

into experimentation along such lines. Those enthusiasts were somewhat squashed when the Russian delegate drew the attention of the
meeting to the herd of domestic eland which had been established in
Russia in 1910, and now numbered 700!

One noticeable characteristic of the eland is the fact that it is more
difficult to approach than other antelopes. Whether on foot or in a
Land Rover it is certainly difficult to get good close-up photographs of a
herd of eland. No sooner do you feel you are approaching reasonable
photographic range than the herd breaks into a steady trot and maintains its distance. Dr Grzimek has attributed this to the fact that the
eland is one of the few animals whose flesh the Masai will eat. The fact
that they will eat it does not in fact mean that they are consistently
hunting and harrying the eland. I cannot myself recall a single case of
finding either a dead eland, eland meat, or eland hide in a Masai boma.
A curious point about this wildness of eland is the fact that solitary
bulls do not seem to be affected in this way: a solitary bull, or even a
group of two or three, can frequently be approached very closely.
Another feature is the variation of horn patterns. For some time a beast
with remarkable lyre-shaped horns inhabited the plain to the east of
the Lerai forest, and at another time a solitary single-horned eland
bull was frequently seen near Kitati Hill.

The gazelles, Grant's and Thomson's, are conspicuous among the
fauna both in the Crater and on the plains. It is very difficult to
distinguish between the two species from the air. In the latest census
(1966) the counters have not even tried to separate them but have
lumped the two species together at 2,100. In previous years they did try
to differentiate between them and in general it appears that there are
about twice as many Tommies as Grants in the Crater.

On the ground the visitor can easily distinguish between the two. The
buck Grant is about three times the size of the Tommy and the does at
least twice its size. Both male and female Grant have side stripes, but
less conspicuous and more variable than those of the Tommy. Both sexes
have horns, and those of the males are very impressive: there is a
separate sub-species of Grant called Robert's gazelle, with wider
branched horns. The Tommy is generally more rufous in colour and the
side stripes invariably well marked. Again the horns are more graceful
and conspicuous in the male than in the female. The Grant is more
graceful and sedate; the Tommy a more cheeky extrovert with his tail

constantly on the move. He is a bad subject for the photographer, keeping just out of range of anything but the more powerful telephoto lenses. A striking characteristic of both species is the stiff-legged gait known as stotting, whereby an animal moves along in a series of stiff-legged jumps, all four legs being fully extended. The movement is so similar to one phase of the Masai dance that one cannot help wondering whether the Masai copied this from the gazelle. A Grant's gazelle being chased by wild dog frequently breaks into a stotting gait just before the end of the chase: but this is not confined to a crisis. Young Thomson's gazelle particularly can be seen stotting along beside a trotting mother.

On the Serengeti plains the Grant exhibits his capacity for living without water for long periods: even in the dry season a few Grant may be found on the arid plains miles away from the nearest water supply. The Tommy on the other hand is one of the migrant species. At times the plains will be devoid of wildlife, at others tens of thousands of Tommies can be found stretching as far as the eye can see.

Waterbuck are called by the Masai 'the-one-with-the-white-bottom' for very obvious reasons. We only get one species of waterbuck in the Crater, called Defassa. In these the white on the rump occurs in a single patch. The common waterbuck to be found east of the Rift stretching from Kenya to Rhodesia has a target-type marking on its rump, a white ring with a dark centre.

The waterbuck is one of the few species at Ngorongoro which seems as happy in the forest and glades on the Crater rim as in the Crater itself. Although there are comparatively few waterbuck both on the rim and in the Crater, they provide enjoyment to visitors quite out of proportion to their numbers. The short necks and thick coats are reminiscent of the European red deer during winter. They are particularly tame and approachable both in and around the Lerai forest and in the neighbourhood of the Forest Resort. The buck, who is much darker than the doe, forms a striking picture with his forward-springing horns, whilst the fawns are one of the most attractive youngsters to be seen.

The hartebeest – Coke's – presents a most interesting problem. In the Crater their number remains down at about fifty. What is the factor that is keeping this species at such a low but steady level whilst wildebeest run up to 10,000 or more? Why wildebeest and not hartebeest?

Here is a problem for some future ecologist.

Outside the Crater a spot where hartebeest can invariably be seen is on the Dulen road where they are one of the few species of wildlife to be found, adding interest to a picturesque piece of the country.

The bushbuck is mostly seen on the Crater rim mornings and evenings. The valley immediately to the east of the Lodge is always worth a look as, in addition to the buffalo in it, bushbuck are usually seen.

The reedbuck is found in two species, the Bohor, a bright fawn and Chanler's mountain reedbuck, which is darker and greyer. The former is seen in the neighbourhood of the reedbeds on the Crater floor. Chanler's can sometimes be seen in considerable numbers on the dry rocky slopes in the Seneto corner of the Crater, also on the grasslands near the Forest Resort or to the west of the Lodge.

The klipspringer is one of the most striking of the small buck. His hooves are adapted for life on rocks. Instead of the hooves being at the usual angle they are in fact vertical, giving the appearance that the klipspringer spends his life standing on tiptoe. The hair is also unique in that each one resembles a thin, tiny porcupine quill, tapering at both ends. These are easily shed but quickly regrow. The klipspringer is infrequently encountered at Seneto in the Crater, but if the visitor wants to be certain of seeing klipspringer he should visit Nasera Rock on the west of Doinyoogol mountains, bordering on the Serengeti plains. in the course of several visits there I have never failed to see this species. Of the other small buck, steinbok and dik-dik are found within the Crater, and oribi on the western outer slopes.

The buffalo is not really a Crater animal, being more an inhabitant of the surrounding forest area. Occasionally, however, a few are seen on the Crater floor, particularly a group of old bulls which emerge from Layani forest and work their way through the damp area between Kitati Hill and the western rim. In the surrounding forest they are known to exist in large numbers though it has been impossible to undertake an accurate count. At certain times of the year they frequent the artificial salt lick maintained on the hillside opposite the Forest Resort. On a special track which has been opened up to make Buffalo Ridge accessible to the game viewer the animals, when in residence, become very tame and permit close approach. When disturbed they frequently gallop off into the thick undergrowth, turn round and push forward inquisitively with extended snouts.

The buffalo is a species very susceptible to rinderpest, the disease which played such havoc with the Masai herds prior to the introduction of immunisation by inoculation. It is of course impossible to immunise the wildlife, so in spite of all precautions, epidemics of the disease are liable to occur. When buffalo become infected they are liable to be dangerous, charging on sight. I can recall that in 1940 when aligning the Lemala Road I was chased by a sick buffalo: I ran straight through a thick bed of giant stinging nettles without feeling a thing! But afterwards, when the crisis was over, did I itch!

The classic newspaper story of 'man bites dog' was retold in a new setting in the *Tanganyika Post* of 12 February, 1964, under the headline 'Buffalo spears Man':

> The Medical Officers at the Arusha hospital were inclined to be incredulous when a wounded Masai brought in to the hospital recently was said to have been "speared by a buffalo."
>
> The unusual story was that, when two Masai were charged by a buffalo in the Ngorongoro area, one of them threw his spear which lodged in the animal's forehead. The spear stayed in place and the buffalo continued to charge with the six foot long spear sticking out of his head. Before the terrified Masai realised what was happening the haft of the spear was plunged into his chest, puncturing his lung!
>
> His friend finished off the animal and brought the injured man to hospital where he is reported to be progressing well.

Of the species found outside the Crater, but not inside, the most conspicuous is the giraffe. These are frequently encountered on the western rim as one drives down from the Crater to the plains. When seen on the plains they look very arresting and magnificent: they are of course always within range of their favourite acacia-tree diet.

The impala is another species not found in the Crater. The visitor wishing to see this graceful animal is advised to follow along the base of the outer wall of the Crater in the Balbal depression where the acacia woodlands provide typical impala habitat.

An antelope of the semi-desert country is the magnificent oryx. The type we get on the Sale plains is the beisa. It is characterised by long rapier-like horns as long in the female as in the male, but slightly more slender. The Masai name, 'the black-mouthed-one', is derived from its facial markings.

Of the two kudu the lesser has been very infrequently observed in the north-east of the Area straying up from Engaruka. The greater kudu does not appear on the check list, but I have reason to think that it ought to do so as when the boundaries of the Conservation Area were extended beyond the limits of the original National Park a large area of bush-clad hill country lying to the west of Lake Eyasi was taken in. It is from here that the local Masai say they obtain the kudu horns used as trumpets on ceremonial occasions.

A colourful visitor to the Area is the topi, an antelope about the same size as the hartebeest but characterised by large plum-coloured patches on its haunches. These are invariably seen in large numbers on the western Serengeti. During the rains a few penetrate to the eastern Serengeti and as far as the Doinyoogol mountains.

The primates are well represented in the Area: firstly the baboon is found not only in the Crater at Lerai forest, but also in the northern segment around Siedentopf's farm. The small white-faced vervet monkey is also found in the Crater, but not the blue (Sykes) monkey which is a pest to the Oldeani and Karatu farmers bordering on the lower edge of the northern highlands forest. The striking black-and-white colobus monkey is difficult to see. Portions of its skin are popular ceremonial adornments with the Masai and the neighbouring tribes who follow their fashions. A little to the north the Sonjo tribe tell me that the only way to secure the colobus is to light a fire in a glade in the forest. When the ash has cooled the colobus come down and have a dust bath, and can then be shot with bow and arrow.

The pigs, of which three species are found in the Area, are not frequently seen by visitors: in fact there is no record of any having been seen in the Crater; but as with the giraffe, local Masai say that wart-hog have been seen there in the past. However, if they were regular inhabitants they would have surely been seen over recent years with resident biologists keeping the Crater under close observation, day and night. There is nothing remarkable about the wart-hog or bush-pig in the Ngorongoro context: they occur in the habitats one would expect, but are not a feature as far as the visitor is concerned, though occasionally seen in the Dulen area.

What the visitor certainly will not see, but will be interested to know about, is the giant forest hog, the most interesting and rarest of the pig family. An animal about the size of a donkey would normally be difficult to miss, but it is of a secretive nature, sticking to its thick forest habitat. As a result it only became known to science when Colonel Meinertzhagen shot one in Kenya in 1904. Since then its existence has been established in Uganda and in Tanzania. The first – and I believe the only – scientifically reported record from Ngorongoro dates from 1921 when a specimen taken at 'Matjekgesberge' was given the status of a new sub-species *Hylochoerus meinertzhagani schultzi* Zekowsky. In the absence of further specimens from Oldeani it is not possible to determine whether this sub-specific distinction is justified.

The local Masai are well aware of the existence of the forest hog on Oldeani mountain. They have a specific name for it, *ol guya*, which is distinct from their names for the wart-hog and the bush-pig: if a hide can be obtained they say it makes the toughest possible shield. It is of interest to note that Colonel Meinertzhagen recorded these two points in his diary when he first saw the beast in 1904.

Another elusive forest animal might be mentioned in this connection, the bongo. This is an antelope, in form representing the bushbuck, but in size approaching that of a cow eland. It is well known in Kenya, its range extending right down to the Ndasegera forest on the Tanzania border. As this forest extends unbroken for 25 miles into Tanzania and then there is only a fifty mile gap till the Ngorongoro highlands are reached, I have always had a sneaking suspicion that the bongo may eventually be found on Oldeani mountain, where the bamboo and thick dank forest provides typical bongo habitat. This species is not yet established in Tanzania, though there is strong evidence that it exists on Mount Meru, where the local people are said to make ceremonial trumpets from its horns.

As so much of the Serengeti wildlife spills over into the Conservation Area at certain times of the year, it might be of interest to note the total number of animals in the Serengeti ecological unit. Two counts are shown in Table 2, Dr Grzimek's of 1958, and Watson's of 1965. The former shows a total of about 366,000. Dr Grzimek expressed disappointment at this number, when a count of about one million had been expected. But he need not have worried, as subsequent counts have

TABLE 2

Serengeti wildlife censuses 1958 & 1965

	1958 (1)	1965 (2)
Wildebeest	99,481	330,000
Zebra	57,199	150,000
Grant's gazelle	} 194,654 {	40,000
Thomson's gazelle		600,000
Topi	5,172	20,000
Buffalo	1,813	20,000
Giraffe	837	10,000
Impala	1,717	10,000
Eland	2,452	5,000
Hartebeest	1,285	5,000
	364,610	1,190,000

1 From B. & M. Grzimek – *Serengeti Shall Not Die*
2 From R. M. Watson – Game Utilization in the Serengeti: Preliminary Investigations, Part I.

indeed exceeded this number. This may have been due to an upsurge of the population in a series of good years, or to improved census techniques, or most probably to a combination of both these factors.

These figures help to put the Ngorongoro ecological unit into perspective – its animal population only amounts to *one seventieth* of the Serengeti numbers.

The early estimates of the Ngorongoro wildlife population must, unfortunately be disregarded as scientific data. They are, nonetheless, sufficiently interesting to be quoted. A little consideration proves their scientific unreliability. If, for instance, the figures of 100,000 or more wildebeest, quoted by German and British observers alike, had any validity, the stocking rate in the Crater would be quite impossible. For 100,000 wildebeest represents 45,000 thousand-pound stock-units. Recent censuses show that wildebeest form roughly 50 % of the total, which means that the total stocking rate would have been in the region of 90,000 units. The grazing area of the Crater, excluding salt lakes, forest and the like, is 97½ square miles. This means over 900 stock-units per square mile, or about 1½ beasts of 1,000 lb. weight per acre. Good pasture does well to carry one beast per five acres, so obviously the 100,000 figure for wildebeest is quite impossible. Such a number would eat themselves out of house and home in less than no time.

Dr Grzimek has unearthed several interesting early records, in particular he states: 'Dr Hans Poeschel, a former high German official in Arusha or Moshi told me in spring 1960, some weeks before his death, that he had been invited several times in the years until the beginning of the First World War by the farmer Siedentopf in the Ngorongoro Crater for hunting. One time they included, by a line of natives and ropes, etc., some 8,000 wildebeest in the corner between the hill and the northern inner escarpment of the Crater. Dr Poeschel told me that "Several experienced hunters and game specialists" at that time estimated – separately – the number of wildebeest in the Crater at more than 20,000.' These figures, whilst high, are not impossible, though I would be worried for the pasture if a modern aerial count revealed this number. Other figures which Dr Grzimek quotes are out-and-out exaggerations. Lindgen, for instance, writes of the Ngorongoro Crater: 'In the middle of the bottom of the Crater is situated a lake which contains water the whole year, the Soda Lake. Around the lake are green plains with *several hundred thousand* head of game.' (My italics).

The early British visitors were equally guilty of exaggeration. Major Dugmore's estimate in 1921 was 75,000 head of game whilst his companion T. A. Barns put the number of wildebeest alone at 50,000. Holmes in 1922 went one better with 100,000, which figure was capped by Captain Hurst at half a million.

Accurate figures only began to emerge when techniques of aerial counting or counts made from photographs taken from the rim of the Crater became available. Dr Grzimek's work in 1958 and that of staff members from the Game Department and National Parks, has been brought together in Table 3. These figures show a steep rise from 1958 to 1964, and then a slight tailing off. Part of the rise may have been due to improved counting techniques, but there is no doubt that there was a genuine increase in that period, when the stock was recovering from drought conditions. The drop over the last two years may be due in part to the wildebeest figure of 1964 including a large percentage of calves. It is of great value to have these figures recorded year by year so that if any serious downward trend were observed means might be sought for

TABLE 3

Crater wildlife censuses 1958–1966

	1958 (1)	1959 (2)	1962 (3)	1963 (4)	1964 (5)	1965 (6)	1966 (7)	Notes
Wildebeest	5360	7800	7600	7600	14000	11352	10438	
Zebra	1767	1500	2500	2500	5000	4145	4040	
Hartebeest	n/e	6	50	20	50	54	67	
Eland	112	155	200	300	350	267	320	
Waterbuck	n/e	n/e	n/e	100	35	85	85	
Gazelle	1130	700					2100	a
Grant	—	—	800	800	1500	1273	—	
Thomsons	—	—	1500	1500	3800	1229	—	
Rhino	19	42	20	20	27	100	109	b
Hippo	n/e	n/e	30	30	23	25	34	c
Elephant	46	2	n/e	n/e	n/e	n/e	n/e	d
Ostrich	n/e	25	n/e	n/e	37	n/e	n/e	
TOTALS	8,434	10,230	12,700	12,870	24,822	18,530	17,193	

n/e indicates 'not enumerated'

1 Grzimek, M. & B. *A Study of the Game of the Serengeti Plains* – aerial count.

2 Harvey & Molloy, quoted Grzimek (above): estimate.

3 Ngorongoro Annual Report 1962: estimate by A. C. Game.

4 Ngorongoro Annual Report 1963: estimate by A. C. Game.

5 Turner, M. & Watson, M. *A Census of Game in Ngorongoro Crater E. Afr. Wildl. J* 2:165 8 – aerial count.

6 Turner, M. & Watson, M. quoted Ngorongoro Annual Report 1966: aerial count.

7 Lamprey, H. & Turner, M. quoted Ngorongoro Annual Report 1966: aerial count.

a The two species of gazelle sometimes enumerated separately, sometimes together.

b The last two figures from detailed ground observations by John Goddard.

c 1966 figure from ground count.

d Too migrant to justify inclusion: up to 90 have been seen in one herd in Layanai Forest.

halting this. Recent work has proved that the hyaena is the most important predator in the Crater and control of its numbers would very quickly reflect on the number of its prey.

The optimum number of stock in the Crater naturally depends on the food available. As forest, scrub and swamp all contribute to the food supply, it is necessary to include these habitats, as well as the open grassland in the total 'grazing'. So only the $4\frac{1}{2}$ square miles of soda lake is deducted from the total of 102 square miles of Crater floor. This leaves $97\frac{1}{2}$ square miles or 62,400 acres available as grazing or browse. At the maximum wildlife count of 1964 (11,328 stock-units) the biomass, inclusive of domestic stock, amounted to 5.5 acres per stock-unit; at the 1966 level it was 6.7, whilst at the lowest year for which we have records, based on 7,610 wildlife and 1,179 domestic, i.e. 8,780 total stock-units, the biomass figure was 7.1.

These figures show a heavy, but not unbearably heavy, stocking rate. Some fall in numbers is indicated by the 1965 and 1966 censuses, which may be no bad thing, particularly as less fodder may be expected if the series of excellent rainfall years came to an end in 1965. The overall picture is a very healthy one and with more scientific knowledge becoming available it should be possible to maintain this good condition indefinitely.

Elephants are one of the major attractions of Ngorongoro; not every visitor sees them, but signs of their presence are always conspicuous. On the drive up from the lower gate-house the observant visitor will note impressions in the clay wall on the upper side of the road made by elephants' tusks. It is uncertain whether in this case they are just polishing their tusks or dislodging material to eat. This latter explanation certainly applies to the cavern excavated in loose rock just below the first (i.e. the highest) stream-crossing on the Lerai road. Here the elephant are obviously seeking some salt or chemical, perhaps a trace element, lacking from their normal diet.

This is also thought to be one of the causes of their ripping certain trees to pieces, notably the baobab, to chew the bark; a habit which has caused havoc in the Tsavo National Park in Kenya. Similar damage is caused by elephant to the vegetation in Ngorongoro, particularly the yellow-barked acacia in the Crater. This situation is being anxiously watched, for the Lerai forest is so valuable as habitat for rhino, waterbuck, baboons and monkeys, leopard, and the host of birds which inhabit it, that if it came to a showdown, the elephant would have to go. There are probably about a dozen more or less permanently resident there, though there is considerable coming and going. Lucky is the visitor who meets an elephant in the open, in transit so to speak, as did the writer when he took the photo facing page 128. It was in December, 1966 when I visited the Crater with my son Ian. We had often met up with good tuskers in the forest, we had at times seen elephant in the open on the floor of the Crater, but never before had we been so fortunate as to meet such a magnificent tusker right in the open. When meeting elephant on a forest track there is no room to manoeuvre, so it is unwise to approach too closely: if one comes up behind a herd moving along a road very often a cow is found acting as a rearguard, who turns round and makes token charges at intervals to ensure that no-one approaches too closely – and one is never sure when a token charge will turn into a real one! Out on the plains, however, one feels more confident in approaching the subject more closely, taking photos, and then moving on ahead to wait for the serenely undisturbed subject to catch up and have his photo taken once again. At certain times of the year the permanent residents of Lerai forest come out regularly of an evening to graze the attractive pastures of the surrounding plains, thus permitting close-up photography.

A more serious worry than the problems of the Lerai forest is the fact that the elephants of the Ngorongoro highlands are rapidly having their regular migration routes cut. Owing to the difficulties of aerial counts in thick forest we do not know how many there are in the forest areas, but up to 90 have been seen at a time, and a population numbering hundreds is not unlikely. There is evidence that this elephant population migrated regularly from the highlands to the lowlands at certain times of the year. One of the motivating factors is said to be the seasonal prevalence of the red safari ant in the forest; if an elephant gets these up his trunk the irritation is such that he will bash his trunk against a tree till it becomes badly lacerated. I have not seen this myself, but having from time to time had my camp-bed raided by these ants, I can well believe the story.

How Ngorongoro has been subject to a flanking movement is described above (p. 64) and illustrated by Fig. 4. The closure is almost complete, but the danger of the Ngorongoro elephant being isolated does not seem to be fully appreciated. The damage they might do, both to the tourist trade, by ruining the habitat, and to agriculture by interfering with water supplies, is incalculable. I hope that the selfish sectional interests which led to resistance to my proposals for migration routes will eventually be subordinated to the long term benefits of the nation as a whole.

The rhino were in a very bad way and very much in the news when I returned to Ngorongoro in early 1961 after five years absence from Tanzania. In July, 1959, the controversial excision from the Serengeti National Park and the creation of the Conservation Unit were legalised. In the ensuing six months eleven rhino had been speared by the Masai – of which two recovered. In the following year, 1960, twenty were killed or wounded by the Masai, eight of these in or near the Crater. This made headline news in the press and many heads nodded with an 'I told you so' expression. *Ngorongoro Doomed – Rhinos Exterminated – Ngorongoro's Last Rhino* – were typical headlines.

Dr Grzimek in *Rhinos Belong to Everyone* reveals how he fostered the agitation for stronger Government action by issuing all German tourist parties – which trade he has done so much to stimulate – with pre-drafted telegrams or letters of complaint about the situation in Ngorongoro. These were to be sent to the authorities and issued to the press of Tanzania by the tourists on arrival at Ngorongoro. If in fact these were issued in considerable numbers, very few were actually dispatched, though I can recall receiving one from Fritz Walther, who has so generously allowed me to reproduce some of his delightful antelope drawings in this volume – truly the *amende honorable*.

The Director of National Parks gave a factual broadcast which was subsequently published in *Wildlife* in December, 1959, in which he stated, amongst other things: 'To those who believed that the withdrawal of the National Parks from the Crater highlands would condemn the game of the Ngorongoro Crater to extermination, these spearings are indicative of the beginning of the end. To others, however, including the Park Trustees, they indicate as yet no more than the expected reaction of the more irresponsible Masai elements, who firmly believe that the 1st July marked the dawn of the golden age when all control over killing of game would lapse.'

In trying to ascertain the causes of this outbreak of rhino spearing, others went so far as to postulate that the Masai had launched on a policy of extermination of the rhino in the Area so that it would no longer be attractive to tourists and they would be left in peace.

I personally have come to the conclusion that neither of these theories was correct. It will be recalled that 1959–60 were years of severe drought which only broke at the onset of the short rains of 1961. Throughout all the pastoral and wildlife areas of East Africa grazing animals suffered severe hardships during this period. Certain areas of Masailand lost up to two-thirds of their bovine population. The Nairobi National Park was littered with dead wildlife. Famine relief was issued by Governments, both in Kenya and in Tanzania for the alleviation of human suffering.

Ngorongoro was, in fact, less severely hit than any other area of Masailand. This may have been in part due to the better water and grazing facilities in the area. It may also indicate that the stocking rate was not unduly high. But however that may be, the Masai were anxious to obtain money to purchase cereal foods. As explained elsewhere this is no new feature of Masai life. What was new was the fact that their cattle were so out of condition that they could not fetch a good price on the local market. How were they to raise money? The spearing of rhino provided the easy answer, particularly if the trader who provided the cereal was willing to take rhino horn in direct payment – and no questions asked.

The truth of this explanation is enhanced by the figures that I was given, but quote only from memory, in respect of Amboseli where the authorities estimated that during the famine period their rhino stock dropped from some 200 to about 60. This figure may be exaggerated, but there is a lesson to be drawn from this for the future: in case of famine, ensure that credit facilities are readily available for the Masai who are an honest people, and will meet their obligations when conditions return to normal.

At the time, however, when the situation was not so well understood it was obvious that speedy action had to be taken to bring the situation under control. In the case of burglary or housebreaking it is a well known police maxim that if you can get at the 'fences' you will soon control the situation. The same principle obviously applied to the rhino horn trade. Catch the dealers and exporters and the killers would cease to function. I was not alone in thinking that a nation-wide reward scheme might prove effective. At a meeting in Dar es Salaam in early 1961 representatives of the Ministry of Agriculture and Natural Resources, the Police, the Information Department and the Ngorongoro Authority decided on a nation-wide campaign offering a reward of Sh. 1,000/-, i.e. £50, for information leading to conviction for rhino offences.

A garish-coloured poster was plastered up at District Offices, local courts and schools throughout the country, in English and Swahili reading –

> Sh. 1,000/- reward will be paid to anyone providing information leading to convictions for killing rhino without permit or for selling rhino horn illicitly. Take such information to the office of the Local Government, Police, District Officer, or the Ngorongoro Conservation Area Authority, Box 3102, Arusha.

The response to this appeal was immediate and startling. A number of schoolboys thought they would receive the reward merely for submitting their ideas on how rhino poaching might be checked. One such idea which, if practicable, would doubtless have proved effective, was that convicted offenders should have both hands chopped off in public!

But apart from such verbal responses the practical results of this campaign were equally gratifying. One case, for instance, occurred near Tanga where 86 rhino horn were hidden in a deserted house. One of those concerned must have done a quick calculation and concluded that the Government reward of Sh. 1,000/- was greater than his share would have been when the horns came to be sold. In consequence he talked. The horns were recovered and convictions obtained. This was probably the most profitable of many cases which came to the courts and also led to the recovery of horn. The scheme was, in fact, more than paying for itself in recovered horn and fines.

But difficulties soon arose; it was obvious that we had interfered with an established market, well controlled by custom. This market was that of information. Police informers soon started complaining that the prices paid for information about rhino were quite out of proportion. If news of a dead rhino was worth Sh. 1,000/-, how much was news of a human corpse worth? Why were the police paying such paltry rewards in respect of murder, arson, burglary and the like? So the campaign was watered down by the insertion of two little words 'Up to' before the Sh. 1,000/-. However, in spite of this niggling attitude the campaign had served its purpose, not only in so far as Ngorongoro was concerned; it had doubtless been of assistance throughout the territory.

But the success of this scheme should not blind us to the effect of the local measures which were taken. In 1960/61 before I took over as

Conservator, the local officers, in particular the late Bill Moore-Gilbert of the Game Division, and Peter Doole of the Provincial Administration, were indefatigable in their efforts to cope with this trade. Their success is measured in the prosecutions instituted, and the convictions obtained – eighteen accused appeared before the Ngorongoro Magistrate's Court alone (in addition to others elsewhere), with imprisonment of a total of 48 months and fines totalling Sh. 7,050/-. At the Masai headquarters station ten cases led to 111 months imprisonment.

The rise and fall of the Ngorongoro rhino scare is best summarized as follows: during the years of the National Park regime when records were kept, 17 rhino were speared in $7\frac{1}{2}$ years. Then came an upsurge, 31 in 18 months. In 1961 the spearings were recorded as 12, and by 1962 killings were down to three at which level they remained over the next five years. The significance of these last figures is even greater when it is appreciated that they refer to the whole of the 3,000 square mile Conservation Area and not only to the Crater highlands, as was the case with the National Park figures.

In quoting these statistics I must be perfectly candid and state that I have rejected some of the wilder statements concerning the killing of rhino in and around Ngorongoro, particularly one by Elspeth Huxley in *Forks and Hope*, published 1963: 'The Olduvai Gorge used to be full of rhino. And then, in 1961, in the space of six months, the Leakeys counted over fifty rotting carcases in the Gorge, all speared by Masai. Whether or not their motive was political, they had taken the profit; every horn had been removed.

'Since then the Leakeys have not seen a single rhino at Olduvai.'

This demonstrably false account is unfortunately typical of the wildlife 'crusaders' and illustrates how a good case can be discredited by exaggeration. John Goddard's work has shown that the gorge was inhabited (1966) by over 70 rhino. With an animal of such static habits it is clearly impossible that the population built up from nil to 70 between 1963 when Elspeth Huxley was writing, and 1966.

The recent low figures of rhino spearing, as set out above, should not, however lead to any sense of complacency. Mr Guggisberg in his book *S.O.S. Rhino*, has shown with what rapidity the situation may change. In Nepal, for instance, there were till recently between 300–400 Indian one-horned rhino. By 1964 the encroachment of agriculturists and the action of poachers had reduced the number to 185. Again, Uganda was complacently reporting 300–350 white rhino

Zebra round a fresh water swamp, with the Crater wall in the background

Ngorongoro is famous for its black-maned lions. Here is an old warrior who disappeared when the crater was struck by a plague of biting flies

Following the fly plague the lion population rapidly increased. Many fine specimens, like this one photographed at dawn in front of the crater wall, can be seen by visitors

in the West Nile area in 1954–55–56. In 1966 this total was reduced to 71 and the only way of saving the white rhino in Uganda was considered to be the translocation of as many as possible to the Murchison Falls National Park.

The black rhino has also been greatly reduced in number throughout East Africa. As Guggisberg points out, the early explorers walked past them in their tens and twenties, day after day.

This scene has changed radically in 50 years. Some of the disappearance is due to shooting, for pleasure or profit, as witness the bags of the early sportsmen. Sir John Willoughby and three brother officers from the Indian army shot 66 rhino in the Taveta region near Kilimanjaro in the course of four months. Count Teleki and his party, the discoverers of Lake Rudolph, shot 99 rhino in the course of their safari. Another party was alleged to have shot 80 around Machakos in 1893 in less than three months. Further cases on the German side of the border are Dr Kolb, who killed 150 before one killed him; a Herr von Bastineller, a companion of Dr Kolb, killed 140; and Herr von Eltz, the first commandant of Moshi Fort, about 60 between Moshi and Kahe. These figures reveal not only the bloodlust of the so-called sportsmen, but also the extraordinary density of the rhino population.

There are, or were, folk who appeared to get a thrill out of rhino shooting. Joseph Thomson, in his *Through Masailand*, written after his journey of 1883–84, records his experiences thus:

> I was more successful in finishing a sleeping rhinoceros. I crept up to it with the customary precautions, and in the process I experienced the usual sensations as of crawling centipedes about my spine, a wildly pulsating heart, a feeling of sweating blood, staring eyes, and gasping for breath, till on getting into actual danger, my nerves became braced up, my muscles like iron. When within a few yards, I took swift and silent aim. As the report echoed with startling roar I dropped to the ground like a hare. The great black mass instantly became animate. Jumping up, it stared wildly around, and then with blood spouting out of its nostrils like water from a fountain, it ran a short distance, to topple over dead. It had been shot through the lungs.
>
> After this feat . . .

Perhaps this is actually what he felt, or perhaps he had his eye on his book sales and the impact this fanciful writing was likely to have in Victorian clubs and drawing rooms!

However, he and his ilk were shortly debunked by Dr Baumann, who, possibly with Thomson in mind, had severe things to say about rhino shooters. Granted he shot three in Ngorongoro himself, but this action at least had the merit of relieving the famine-struck Masai. Dr Baumann comments:

> Hunting [rhino] is not nearly so difficult or dangerous as it is claimed to be by professional Nimrods. The rhinoceros is not very shy, and if the wind is favourable, one can easily approach to within thirty paces, without disturbing them. To hit a rhinoceros at thirty paces, you do not have to be a spectacular shot and if the bullet hits the chest or (with a smaller calibre gun) the head, the animal usually collapses without further ado. If wounded anywhere else, it either runs away at such speed that there is little hope of catching it, or it attacks the hunter. This moment is usually the one described with vivid horror by the Nimrods. The companions flee and only the hunter bravely faces the charging colossus. This sounds terribly dangerous, but the 'charging colossus' is nearly blind and one step aside is sufficient to make it miss and it charges past. When it stops and looks around for its enemy the hunter has plenty of time to kill it with another bullet at close range.

Nevertheless rhino hunting continued, on licence as and when game laws were introduced into the East African territories. Some shooting was by genuine sportsmen, out for a good trophy, but much was by pioneer farmers, many short of cash, who sought to add to their income by taking out a licence to shoot elephant and rhino every year.

The horn-length of the Ngorongoro rhino compares favourably with the black rhino found anywhere in Africa. A cow rhino from the Oldeani forest had an anterior horn of 47¼ inches (world record 53½) whilst a bull from the Dulen area has produced the world record posterior horn at 32½ inches.

Another cause of reduction in numbers is, of course, the change in habitat caused when land was taken over for ranching or farming. For example, the establishment of the Oldeani coffee plantations must have cleared out literally hundreds of rhino. These were either shot – and I know that the farmers took a heavy toll of rhino – or moved out as the bush was cleared. A contemporary account recorded by A. R. Siedentopf – no relation to the Siedentopf brothers of Crater fame – in his book *The Last Stronghold of Big Game* refers to the clearing of the Oldeani coffee shambas: 'All the other game learns quickly that it is best to avoid any contact with man, and changes its trail accordingly. Only the rhino persists in the precedence of the right of way. So the stupid beast goes on stamping through the fields and flattening time and again the tender coffee seedlings which the farmer replaces meticulously day after day. Then comes the hour when the planter's cup of wrath overflows and the bully gets himself shot.'

The carrying capacity of country in respect of rhino can be extraordinarily heavy. Take for instance the Crater itself. Here John Goddard has recorded 110 rhino on the Crater floor in the three years 1964–66: this figure includes births during the period. Some, it is true, do not spend the whole time in the Crater, but there is reason to believe that their range is not very great and that they do not penetrate far into the surrounding forests.

It would have been possible to determine the range of these rhino had the proposal for fitting them with radio transmitters been carried through. Most conservationists are aware that this technique has been used successfully in other parts of the world, particularly on checking the range of grizzly bears in the Yellowstone National Park. When I saw it in practice there I considered whether to apply the same technique to rhino in Ngorongoro. There are many ways of fitting these transmitters to the subject of the research. The grizzlies carried theirs on a collar, which also acted as an aerial. In other cases where the subject pulls off an externally attached set these are inserted subcutaneously. As far as the rhino was concerned I suggested somewhat facetiously that the best method would be to drill a hole in the horn of the immobilised rhino and insert the transmitter. Carrying the fantasy further I pointed out that this could be a self-financing scheme as the horn drillings could then be sold on the black market to cover the purchase of the transmitters! When the biologists came to give serious consideration to the radio idea it did seem that the horn-drilling technique might indeed be the best way of fitting these transmitters. Unfortunately this idea has not yet been put into practice for lack of funds, but I record it here in the hope that it may be taken up later.

However, with our lack of knowledge of the depth of penetration into the forest let us suppose that the Ngorongoro rhino use an amount of forest equal to the Crater floor for grazing, which amounts to 97½ square miles. To double this area only requires a penetration of just over two miles, inclusive of the Crater wall. This area, 195 square miles, gives a stocking rate of one rhino to every 1.8 square miles.

This, however, is nothing compared to the situation in the Lerai forest. Here a total of 23 rhino are resident, of whom only six appear outside from time to time. The remaining 17 are permanently resident in the forest. To allow for the grazing consumed outside the forest, suppose we say the forest is carrying a permanent population of 21 rhino. Its total area is 750 acres. This means 35½ acres per rhino, or 19 rhino to the square mile. This appears to be an extraordinarily dense population, but looked at another way it is not unreasonable. Apply the concept of the stock unit, that is a 1,000 lb. beast. The rhino can be taken as representing about two stock units – the average male weighs around 2,150 lbs. and the female 1,950 lbs., but immatures must also be allowed for. This means 18 acres per unit. Granted the same bit of country is also carrying elephants, waterbuck, etc., so the total grazing rate must be something in the nature of 10 acres per stock unit. This is nothing remarkable as good pasture can carry cattle at twice that level of stocking. This criterion, of course, cannot be extended to the whole of the Crater which obviously could not carry 19 rhino to the square mile. The vegetation is less, the herbage is not so suitable, and it is grazed over by many other species.

The point arises, is the rhino population of Ngorongoro increasing or decreasing? The figures quoted earlier in this section show that over a 15 year period a total of 75 rhino were speared. This does not include the Huxley figures from Olduvai, but if we make some allowance for spearings there the average must have been something over five per annum. It can also be assumed that the population throughout this period has been roughly that which John Goddard found, namely 110 in Ngorongoro plus 70 at Olduvai. Add to these an allowance for the remaining portion of the Conservation Area – for the count of dead rhino applies to the whole Area. Here we are guessing, but a suitable figure might be 120, making a round figure of 300 rhino in the Area.

John Goddard, in a scientific paper, examines closely what is termed the recruitment rate, that is the rate of new individuals produced each year expressed as a percentage of the total population. The optimum recruitment rate would be obtained if each cow reproduced every 27 months and the calf survived till the next calf was born. This optimum would be 12.8 calves per year. From actual observations over the three years John Goddard estimated the recruitment rate in the Ngorongoro population to be 7.0 and at Olduvai 7.2. He concludes: 'The mortality rate deduced from skulls, reports, etc. is no greater than this, so there are good grounds for optimism concerning the rhino of the Area.'

In the same paper he has some interesting figures concerning the movements, or rather the lack of movement, of rhino. Hans Klingel published some figures in *Oryx* showing how static these beasts were. Guggisberg likewise mentions this feature, but uses the term stability rather than territoriality. Goddard went into the matter in much greater detail and worked out what he terms the average home range of these animals, that is the distance over which they wander. He finds that in Ngorongoro the males average 6.1 miles and the females 5.8. At Olduvai the range is greater, being 8.5 miles for the males and 13.7 for the females. These figures of course refer to undisturbed populations in a series of good years. One would like to know more about the movements in bad years, though here observation in the Tsavo Park during the drought years culminating in 1961 indicates that the rhino stay in their own territory and die rather than seek pastures new. Also, one would like to know more about the effect of disturbance in the case of country being taken over for settlement. Do the rhino move elsewhere, and if so, how do they fit in with the territorial claims of their fellow rhino in the country which they penetrate? Again, the observations quoted above indicate that they do not, but the sources I have quoted are chance records and not systematic scientific work. From this it can be seen that, although our biologists have greatly enhanced our knowledge of the rhino over the last few years, there are still a lot of questions to be answered. This can only be done by adequate expenditure of funds and manpower on research.

The widespread poaching of rhino throughout Africa, and the high price of horn both on the legitimate and the black market raises the question, why this sudden upsurge in rhino killing? The first point which is very clear is that it is due to external and not internal demand. As Guggisberg points out, no people or tribe in Africa believe in the medicinal properties of rhino horn. A few, such as the Chagga or the Masai, presented their leaders with carved rhino horn clubs as emblems of office, but natural deaths amongst the rhino would more than supply this demand.

The general assumption to account for the increased overseas demand is that as the Asiatic rhino was decimated to the point of extinction so the demand for the African product increased. But the trade in rhino horn from Africa is by no means a new feature. In fact, it was first mentioned in *The Periplus*, a traveller's guide to the East Coast of Africa written in the first century AD. Ivory and rhino horn are mentioned as exports from the Red Sea ports: then coming right down to Rapta – probably Pangani – it is recorded: 'There are exported from this place a great quantity of ivory, but inferior to that of Adalis and rhinoceros horn and tortoise shell (which is in best demand after that of India) and a little palm oil.'

When reviewing the trade in rhino horn, we find the uses to which it is put were and are numerous. The common concept is that it is used only as an aphrodisiac, particularly in India. This is only partially true; but even if the consumers could by education be persuaded that their belief in the efficacy of rhino horn has no scientific backing, nonetheless the trade would doubtless continue.

Many other uses for rhino horn have been recorded by authors both ancient and modern: buttons, belt-buckles, scabbards and knife handles. One of the most intriguing uses was as drinking cups, used especially by rulers, because of the belief that they protected the user from poison. Such cups were used in Asia up to recent times, but they also have been used by some British and European monarchs and Popes.

Describing the use of the horn as medicine, Dr Lee Talbot in *A Look at Threatened Species* says: 'Usually the horn is ground to a powder and mixed with water or coconut oil. Among the cures this mixture is supposed to effect are the following: to remove a thorn from the palm of the hand, apply the horn oil to the back and the thorn will work right out; to ease childbirth, the expectant mother should drink some of the mixture just before the baby is born; to shrink lumps, stop infections, close cuts, sooth irritations or cause broken bones to heal properly, just apply the mixture to the nearby skin surfaces and rub well.' In summing up he does write: 'Today the greatest demand for rhino horn is based on its supposed value as an aphrodisiac and this widespread belief accounts for the greater part of its market value.' But it is obvious from the information available that if this particular superstition were overcome a demand for rhino horn would continue to exist, probably in excess of the dwindling supply. So vigilant measures must be maintained to control the illegal killing of rhino and the illicit trade in horn.

But to return to the Ngorongoro rhino: whatever the external factors, whatever may be rightly or wrongly reported, here in the Conservation Area we have an opportunity second to none in the whole of Africa to preserve in perpetuity and to make accessible to the visiting public a healthy population of these unique survivals of past ages.

The strongest weapon which we in Tanzania have to maintain rhino stocks around Ngorongoro is the *co-operation of the Masai*. When I say that the excessive rhino spearing of the 1959/60 period was due to famine conditions, it must not be implied that if there is no famine there will be *no* rhino spearing. My own experience as a District Officer in the 1930's and 1940's confirms the figures of the National Park period: namely, that when man and rhino share the same environment there will always be *some* rhino spearing. This, however, is not an argument to say that the best way of ensuring the survival of the rhino is to move the Masai: *provided they are on our side*, they are better where they are, and more valuable to the cause of conservation than a whole army of paid game scouts.

What is the cause of this limited, occasional rhino spearing? Sometimes it is just plain juvenile delinquency; involving not particularly rhino, but any type of wildlife; like juvenile delinquency everywhere – Europe, America or Japan – it will always be with us. The issue is, to what degree? And to what extent can it be controlled? I recall the case of two young uninitiated Masai, aged about 14 and 12 respectively, who were out herding their cattle. When they arrived with their charges at the usual watering place, a deep gully, they found an elephant in possession. So they climbed the banks of the gully till they were above the elephant, and one of them planted a spear in his back, which penetrated the kidney and caused immediate death!

Also there occurred a case of a youth creeping up on a sleeping zebra foal and spearing it, but fortunately the more usual way of a Masai youth to show his prowess is to run down a buck and then take a nick out of its ear to prove his success, rather than killing it.

As far as rhino are concerned, I am convinced that many of the clashes are unpremeditated. A couple of Masai warriors will go wandering over the grasslands, spears in hand. A rhino is seen lying between them and their destination. Now the ordinary foot-traveller, be he black or white or whatever, on seeing a rhino in his way, will make a considerable circuit to avoid a head-on clash. But not so the Masai: with a devil-may-care attitude he steams straight ahead, just to prove to himself that he is not going to let a rhino deflect him off course. Then the rhino charges, the Masai stands and spears him, and if the case gets as far as the courts there is a genuine plea of self defence.

Sometimes one also gets the genuinely vicious rhino. The reason for such an attitude obviously varies: sometimes a rhino has been speared and retaliates by charging either the spearer, or perhaps sometime later, an innocent passer by. Others get worked up when another rhino intrudes on their territory and it may be, though this has not been proved, that if a human passer-by happens on a rhino in this state, he gets charged. Again it might happen that a human gets between a cow rhino and her calf: elsewhere I describe how a rhino gave a lion short shrift in these circumstances, and it is unlikely that a human would be treated otherwise.

But whatever the causes, these attacks do take place. I have myself seen one unfortunate young herdboy with the bone of his leg exposed from the calf to the thigh by one sweep of a rhino's horn. Again, during the famine period 1960–61 an old man, pretty emaciated himself, was driving his emaciated cattle across the Crater to market. A rhino for some reason resented his presence, he was not fit enough to take evasive action, and was gored to death.

So sometimes the boot is on one foot, sometimes on the other: but whatever the clashes – Masai/rhino or rhino/Masai – they are a small price to pay for preserving the *status quo*, and common sense, publicity and Masai co-operation can keep such clashes to a minimum. At one time the authorities were up against a blank wall of non-co-operation when investigating rhino killings, but I found that once the Masai leaders were led to understand that they were participating in the administration of the Conservation Area, and benefiting from it, their co-operation was assured. Of course, all the locals, men and women and children know when a rhino has been speared, and who the culprit is. If they inform the authorities the culprit is apprehended, and even if he produces a plea of self-defence, he can be punished for 'failing to report the wounding of a dangerous animal', if in fact it was only wounded, or 'failing to produce a Government trophy to the authorities' if the rhino was killed. For these very necessary and sensible provisions exist in the laws: if you, either as a licensed hunter or as an ordinary citizen acting in self-defence or defence of property, wound, but fail to kill, a dangerous animal, you must report the matter, so that the authorities may take action and warn the public. Many an innocent passer-by has been gored to death by a buffalo which some thoughtless hunter has wounded.

Equally, if under licence you shoot a rhino, elephant or whatever, you must produce the horns or tusks for registration: if on the other hand you have killed in self-defence, you must safeguard and hand over these valuable assets so that the nation does not lose their value.

Of course the Masai who spears a rhino and reports the matter is not punished, but the very fact that he has reported makes it highly probable that here is a case of genuine self-defence.

If the elders spontaneously come forward with information, as happily they have been doing in recent years, this keeps the number of spearings down. It makes the dare-devil moran think twice before approaching a rhino too closely, and discourages the genuine criminal: nothing is more discouraging to the would-be offender than a high ratio of convictions to offences committed.

This is one of the reasons – there are others, put forward elsewhere in this book – why I always resisted, and will continue to oppose, the removal of the Masai from the Crater. It would cause such resentment, not only amongst the Crater Masai, but throughout the Conservation Area and beyond, that the spirit of friendly co-operation which we have succeeded in building up over the years would be lost. Once again the investigator of a spearing would be up against a blank wall of 'don't know'. Offenders would get away unpunished, and further offences would inevitably follow. So let's leave the Masai where they are!

The hippo of Ngorongoro round off the picture, and complete the microcosm of East Africa which the Crater presents. People often wonder how the hippo got into the Crater – but it is really not remarkable as Hippo Pool in a direct line is only 18 miles from the nearest point on Lake Eyasi and 21 from Lake Manyara. Even allowing for a circuitous route, it is not more than could be covered by a hippo from early one evening to late the following morning. After all, they graze out from their watery homes for up to 5 miles, i.e. a ten mile return journey in a night, so there is no reason why a determined hippo should not double that distance without undue dehydration. A conservation officer once met a hippo on the eastern rim, but it is not certain in what direction it was making; the incident proves, however, that the Crater wall forms no obstacle to hippo movement.

At present there are about 35 hippo in the Crater. But for the resourcefulness of the late Bill Moore-Gilbert there might have been none – for when the drought was at its height in the latter months of 1961, all the pools were dry and the hippo, believed at that time to number about 18, were concentrated in Lerai forest in a swamp fed by the waters from the springs of Lerai. But 18 hippo in a small swamp soon turned the scanty water supply into thick mud. The hippo were so cramped that they were piled one on top of another, and it is believed that one, if not more submerged and never surfaced again. Then Bill had a brilliant idea. As anyone can observe from the Crater rim, the waters of the spring branch out in delta form, following four distinct water courses: this is most advantageous ecologically speaking, as the spread of water means a greater area of forest and more suitable habitat for its denizens. Bill argued that if all this water, currently being dispersed, were concentrated into one channel, it would make one good swamp instead of four bad ones. So he blocked the channels of the other streams so that all the water flowed down one, and thus the hippo were saved.

Readings taken at the time showed that the flow from the springs never dropped below a million gallons per day. So even if we get a recurrence of the 1961 conditions the same device can be applied to save our hippo stocks. There will always be enough water for this purpose, in spite of the relatively small quantities of water which is pumped up for use at the Lodges and houses on the rim.

6 The Carnivores

The lions of Ngorongoro have long been famous, but curiously enough were not mentioned by Dr Baumann, Ngorongoro's first European visitor. In the days of German rule, the Siedentopf brothers must have taken their toll, for ranching and lions obviously do not go well together. The only reference I can find to this period is one in Dr Grzimek's paper 'A Study of the Game of the Serengeti Plains', where in a footnote he says: 'Mrs Eva Wenkel, Berlin-Sehlendorf, who was living with the Siedentopfs . . . for more than one year, wrote me that one could hear lions roaring from a far distance during night time but that she never had seen some in the crater. Apparently lions behaved quite differently at those times when there was hunting in the Ngorongoro.' Dr Grzimek's view is confirmed by the early hunters of the 1920's whose accounts are quoted below.

The first hunting party of the British period of which we have a record is that of Sir Charles Ross, who, following his visit, purchased the Adolph Siedentopf farm on the Munge river from the Custodian of Enemy Property. Barns' book *Across the Great Craterland to the Congo* contains numerous references to lion hunting. Barns states:

> The lions of Ngorongoro were what we called 'daylight' lions, for, owing to their being unmolested, they were, more often than not, to be seen abroad in the day time. Although numerous everywhere they were located as being especially so on the opposite side of the crater, [i.e. opposite to Lerai where the party was then camped] which decided us to shift camp to the North-West corner of the Magad Lake.
>
> The crater wall on this side is cut into at frequent intervals by deeply wooded ravines or *kloofs*, which had become the

permanent homes of these beasts. Like all other animals within the Great Crater of Ngorongoro, they were especially tame and especially large and fat, and with fine manes. Preying on the abundant game around them, they had become numerous and bold, offering such sport as is seldom obtained in these days. This was the chance of a lifetime for D. L. and Sir Charles Ross. Several days, therefore, were spent in lion-hunting, seven very fine specimens being eventually bagged as well as two cheetahs. The Masai helped in driving out two of the lions, which gave everybody an exciting time, for they would only come out at the last moment, and when hard pressed. One of them, a big lioness, roaring fiercely, charged Ross, and came within an ace of getting him, no doubt giving him a thrill which he will remember to his dying day. . . .

Lions were to be seen every morning on this side of the crater if one went out to look for them. Some of them apparently made their lairs – the lionesses most probably – like the hyenas, in sandstone caves or abandoned burrows. Ross, one day, ran into what he described as 'a small troop of lions' near some such underground lairs. He shot one of the lions and wounded three others, but as the latter disappeared into some burrows he was unable to retrieve them.

Dugmore's reference to the same incident is terse and critical. 'An attempt was made while in this neighbourhood to have a lion drive with the help of some Masai. Several lion were found in the deep scrub covered ravines, but all attempts to photograph them were rendered futile owing to the amount of shooting that was done by members of the party; and though I had recovered to some extent from the fever I had to acknowledge myself beaten.'

Other early visitors describe lion hunting in Ngorongoro and on the Serengeti as practised in those early days. Some such as Livermore and Newbery conducted their hunting strictly in accordance with the best traditions of sportsmanship. Others, who shall be nameless, were even in these early days bringing motors across the border from Kenya to the Serengeti, and approaching their unsuspecting quarry, to whom motor cars were something new, to point blank range. Livermore's guide, J. A. Hunter, describes yet another method of lion hunting:

Back at Ngorongoro Crater, I stayed at Captain Hurst's cottage for a few days preparing for the long trip to Arusha. The kangaroo hounds were now in excellent shape, and I could not resist spending a few days hunting with them. In lion hunting the hounds made all the difference. As soon as the pack sighted a lion, on the plains, they would take off after him and bring him to bay, forming a circle round him. The lion was kept so busy snapping at the dogs that the hunter could walk up to within a few yards of him and place his shots. The dogs were smart enough never to close with a lion and kept well away from his great paws. If the lion charged, the hounds would open to let him through and then chase him again, snapping at his flanks until they turned him. I collected five good lions, knowing that their hides would bring a good price in Nairobi. It never occurred to me that the day would come when lions would be carefully protected as a valuable game animal. In those days we regarded them simply as a dangerous animal.

This was in early 1924; from then on for some years the Ngorongoro lions lived unrecorded, and as far as is known, uneventful lives. But not so their neighbours around Lake Manyara and on the Serengeti, areas which were becoming more and more accessible to motor vehicles.

This is only one example of large scale shooting of lion for commercial purposes or as trophies. The process went on till 1929 when the first control was established, and Monty Moore, V.C., was posted at Banagi to enforce these controls. But his jurisdiction was very limited: lion shooting was only prohibited within the immediate vicinity of Banagi. Beyond that they were still officially classified as vermin – as indeed they were throughout Tanganyika – and could be shot in unlimited numbers without licence. Audrey Moore, Monty's wife, tells in her book *Serengeti* how many of her favourite lions wandered beyond the prescribed limit and fell victims to visiting 'sportsmen' sitting in their motor cars.

Now what relevance has all this to Ngorongoro and its survival? This hunting at both Manyara and Serengeti directly affected Ngorongoro, as it may well be that stocks of certain species, depleted by this blood bath, were made up by immigrant individuals from Ngorongoro, since Ngorongoro did not suffer during this period as did neighbouring areas. This was due largely to lack of roads; if anyone wanted to go there, they had to do so on foot, and having got there, then hunt on foot.

On the other side of the medal, during the early 1930's two pioneers rendered great service to wildlife by encouraging the swing from shooting to photography. The first was the late R. R. (Ray) Ulyate, proprietor of the New Arusha Hotel who organised trips on a commercial basis from Arusha to the Serengeti for the purpose of lion photography. The second was the late F. J. (Frank) Anderson, an enterprising Australian who developed a first-class farm producing coffee, seed beans and flower seeds at Monduli and was for many years active in politics as a Member of Legislative Council. Whilst the farm was being built up, Frank Anderson, ably assisted by his daughter Patsy (now Mrs Wright – still living on the farm at Monduli) took up wildlife – and particularly lion – photography as an interesting and profitable sideline. I remember sending a striking portrait of a lion to my parents as a Christmas present in 1934, and now that they are both dead, I have this photograph in my possession. It says much for the technical excellence of the processing that even now this sepia print shows no signs of fading or staining.

Contrary to a widely held belief, the Oldeani coffee plantations, although largely German in origin, were not opened up in German times. They started about 1926 and led to the construction of the road from Mto-wa-Mbu, and a subsequent branch road to Mbulu which was previously approached from Mbugwe, or from the South via Dabil. The opening up of Oldeani also permitted the D.C. Masailand, named Murrels, to put the very first road up to the Crater rim from Kampi Nyoka, on an alignment very close to the present. This was around 1932, but of course only gave access to the rim. It was impossible to take cars into the Crater till the early 1940's and as late as 1955 the guide books were recommending visits not to the Crater, but to the Crater rim to see the game in the Crater 2,000 feet below. In fact traffic into the Crater was not regular or significant till 1959 when the Lerai road was completed.

This isolation had two effects on the wildlife of the Crater. In the first place they did not suffer a reduction in numbers such as occurred to the east and to the west. Secondly, their first acquaintance with the motor car was a friendly one; they were not chased and shot at by vehicles and so did not have to unlearn their early experiences before they began to accept the cars in the amazingly unconcerned manner that is apparent today.

So the lions of the Crater remained unmolested, except for the odd brush with the local Masai which doubtlessly occurred. Certainly on the several occasions on which I walked across the Crater in the 1930's the lions were not conspicuous, nor can I recall reports of their causing undue damage to livestock.

This brings us to World War II when hunting and tourism came to a halt and the lions were undisturbed. After the war the Lemala road gave access by car to the Crater and the flow of tourists started in a small way. Good photographs of lions were obtained by visitors, and these when published encouraged more visitors to come. A striking example of such is Dr Grzimek's photo of a lion in the Crater, in *Rhinos Belong to Everyone*, captioned 'The last rays of the sun, stormclouds drawing away. Soon it will be night in the Ngorongoro Crater.' Dr Grzimek, when describing his interesting and well illustrated study of lions' behaviour towards a dummy zebra in the above-quoted book, mentions three groups of lions, one numbering one male and eleven females which gives an idea of numbers before they were struck by the pest, *Stomoxys* described below. He also states that: 'the car could easily drive up to within five yards of the lion, even to one yard', which indicates their approachability. The position at that time is best summed up in the words of the Annual Report for 1959: 'At least three large black-maned lions, and a number of lionesses, two of whom had cubs. As many as 30 lions were seen in a single visit.' If 30 were seen in one day, the total number could well have been 60 which was indeed the estimate of the Assistant Conservator (Game).

It was most unfortunate that no sooner had Ngorongoro gained a name for itself than tragedy struck. The whole of the Crater became infested with a plague of flies called *Stomoxys calcitrans* in early 1962 and lion numbers were reduced from an estimated 60 to 15. These are the figures of the Assistant Conservator (Game) – I personally think the numbers dropped lower.

The cause and course of this infestation was as follows. It appears that this small biting fly, modelled on but smaller than the common house fly, is always with us in small numbers, but that it does not cause much trouble. In certain favourable circumstances in East Africa it can breed until it becomes a menace. It likes to breed in wet mud impregnated with urine and dung. Thus dunghills on dairy farms are ideal breeding places, especially during the rains, and dairy farmers throughout East Africa have to keep their eyes on this, otherwise the irritation of these biting flies can cause a heavy drop in milk yields. Although it is a blood-sucking insect like the tsetse or mosquito, *Stomoxys* has not been found guilty of carrying any disease, either human or bovine, other than by mechanical transmission.

What happened at Ngorongoro was that the years 1959 to 1961 were exceptionally dry, then the short rains of 1961 broke with a vengeance with 5.2 inches falling before the end of October, which is exceptionally early. The rainfall continued unabated so that the short rains up to the end of December amounted to 24 inches as against an average of 9 inches. Thereafter there was no distinct short dry season such as is usually experienced, the 1962 figures reading: January 4.58 inches, February 3.32 inches, March 7.73 inches, April 6.65 inches and May 9.56 inches. This heavy and consistent rainfall completely upset the normal factors which control the number of flies successfully hatched. At the onset of the rains, water levels rise and the majority of the pupae in the mud at the swamp edge are drowned out. Thereafter the short dry season results in a drop in swamp level and further pupae are dried out. The drowning process is repeated with the onset of the long rains and finally the drying out in the long dry season depresses the numbers still further. The heavy and consistent rainfall recorded above, however, meant that the swamp levels rose and then stayed up steadily without fluctuation. The entomologist who was finally called in to advise on the problem stated that a pair of *Stomoxys* could under ideal conditions successfully produce 100 offspring in 25 days. A little simple arithmetic shows that in the period November to May, 180 days, a single pair of flies could produce *one hundred million million* descendants.

This is very much what happened. Although we have no exact figure on the fly density, their numbers had to be seen to be believed. They followed one's Land Rover and when it stopped they covered the bodywork till it was black and impossible to touch with a finger without touching a fly. I saw an eland on the ground which was literally black with flies. Returning an hour or two later it had been bled to death. Mr Hocking, the entomologist, said that the situation was not dissimilar to that experienced in northern Canada with the blackfly. Here scientists had exposed small areas of their skin, captured all the flies that fed thereon and measured the blood they had extracted. By multiplying the area of skin exposed by the total area of the body it was calculated that a naked body would be bled to death in a matter of hours.

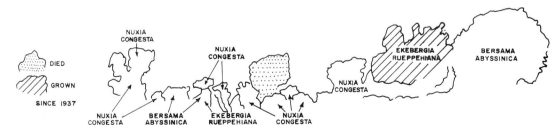

The clump of trees in front of Crater Lodge photographed *c.* 1939 (above),
with the Crater in the background, and today (below) showing how little they
have changed in thirty years; the overhanging tree on the left is unchanged, as
also the large trees on the extreme left and right of the group. One large tree in
the centre has gone, but another large tree, second from the right, has appeared.

Massed wildebeest in Ngorongoro: their numbers vary from ten to fourteen thousand in the 100 square-mile Crater.

Wildebeest with calves, showing the latters' half-shed coats. The Masai herdsmen regard the complete shedding of the coats as the end of the period of catarrhal infectivity.

In Ngorongoro not only were the breeding conditions particularly favourable during this period, there was also a tremendous food supply available to the emerging flies in the heavy wildlife population. But not all were equally effected. Those more energetic in brushing off the flies escaped serious ill effects. One noticed all the animals, wildebeest, zebra, and others, constantly switching their tails and throwing their heads back over their shoulders. This meant that the flies, whilst getting a quick suck of blood, never stayed in any number on the beast long enough to have any serious effect. This phenomenon was very noticeable in a herd of cattle. One beast wounded by a lion survived with a nasty gash on its shoulder. It was conspicuous in the herd, being covered with flies, whilst its companions were relatively fly-free. It had not the energy like the rest of the beasts to keep driving off its tormentors. As a result it was dead within eight days and the Masai owners observed when cutting up the meat that it was practically bloodless.

It was unfortunately the lions which seemed to be most severely affected by this plague. They completely altered their hunting habits. As debilitated lions frequently do, they turned to cattle instead of hunting the more unapproachable wildlife. They were observed climbing acacia trees at Seneto to a height of 40 feet. Alternatively others sought refuge by squeezing themselves into hyaena holes. Two were speared by the Masai while raiding their cattle and two were shot by Conservation staff as being too emaciated to live. The large sores which formed on the hides of the lions can be seen in the pictures I have published, as also the emaciated condition of the beasts. It is uncertain how many of the lions we lost actually died and how many fled from the Crater, but certainly in the period immediately subsequent to the plague only about half a dozen lions could be seen. The plague vanished more abruptly than it began. As forecast by Mr Hocking, as soon as the lakes and marshes dried up, the plague abated. To reduce the number of living flies we arranged to spray all vehicles entering the crater with residual insecticide, so that the large number of flies which settled on these vehicles flew off and died. Nature ensured that a further generation would not arise to take their place.

Luckily the recovery of the lion population was not long delayed. By October of that same year, 1962, 16 lions were seen in the Crater in one day and a small pride consisting of one male and four females shortly afterwards produced the first crop of cubs, in April 1963. It is certain that the increase in the population was not only due to

8

reproduction, but also to immigration. We have the case of the four tawny-maned lions who were observed for several months on the rim of the Crater, preying largely on immature buffalo. They were reported in November, 1964 as being seen on the roadside about once a week. The rest of the time they were doubtless hunting or lying up in the forest glades. By February, 1965 they were settled in the Crater. Since then one or more have been lost through death, but the remnants of the group could still be seen around Manduusi Swamp in December, 1966.

A great fillip to the lion population was given by the group of four females, with two attendant males, who in January, 1965 produced sixteen cubs. It is uncertain whether this is the group that produced the first crop of cubs, but it most probably is. The pride remained intact for many months and afforded great enjoyment to visitors. The cubs were frequently seen in playful mood, whilst the mothers suckled their young in public. An interesting thing about lions is that the mothers will accept the cubs of others and suckle them. The phenomenon is not unique in Ngorongoro as it has been observed and recorded by others, notably George Adamson. By the end of 1966 the cubs were well grown and the pride was dispersing. Eight cubs, however, were seen in a group in December, 1966. Some had fallen by the wayside, notably one which was killed by a rhino. Thus the lion population was back again to at least 40 by the end of 1966 ; a very satisfactory recovery in a matter of four years.

The *Stomoxys* story brings up the whole lion-in-trees problem. It has always been thought unnatural that lions should climb trees: I well remember from my childhood in a 'What is wrong with this picture?' series a lion up a tree. Mankind has been in contact with lions for the whole of his spell on earth, so how did the now patently false assumption that lions do not climb trees remain in being for so long? There is no real answer to this or to the question, *why* do lions climb trees? One's inclination is to seek a simple, single answer whereas this is probably a case of multiple determinants, as in so many behavioural problems.

The two most quoted reasons are to get away from flies, and to keep cool. Certainly as regards flies, we had an example of tree-climbing in Ngorongoro during the *Stomoxys* infestation, and since this abated little tree climbing is to be seen. Manyara, most famous spot for tree-climbing lions, is heavily infested with tsetse-fly, which are also found at Seronera where lions in trees are a familiar sight. So flies may be accepted as one of the causes.

It is also significant that Manyara is a park of long grass and thicket – excluding the lake shore, whilst Seronera is a long-grass area, with scrubby thicketed riverbeds, so that in both areas vegetation inhibits the free passage of air at ground level. Altitude and its associated temperature may also enter into the picture, Manyara being just over 3,000 feet and Seronera around 4,000. In contrast Ngorongoro is largely a short-grass area, at an elevation of around 5,600 feet, so the Crater floor is generally cooler than both Manyara and Seronera, with air in freer circulation. If this theory is sound then where the grass is long in the Crater, one would expect to see lions climb trees: this indeed occurs, as most of the tree climbings are observed at Kopon in the broad-leafed Kaffir-boom trees. It may be argued that the lions do not climb trees in most parts of the Crater for the simple reason that the trees just are not there to climb. But if the lions had a real propensity for tree climbing, then they would betake themselves to those parts of the Crater where there are trees. And so the argument goes round and round, and there we must leave the issue till research gives us the answer.

Apart from such disasters as the *Stomoxys* infestation any population naturally suffers a constant attrition. The lions of the Crater are no exception and the notes in the Annual Reports, Bulletins, etc., whilst not complete, form a useful record. In 1959 there is no record of lions killed or dying in the Crater, though the District Officer in charge of the Conservation Unit shot two cattle raiders at Mokalal, some 10 miles out on the Dulen road. In 1960 two lions were killed in the Conservation Area by Masai – one in the Crater: in both cases enquiry proved that these were genuine defence-of-property cases. In 1962 we had the *Stomoxys* losses, two speared and two officially shot with a further five, three adults and two cubs, killed by Masai in the Balbal. On the credit side the Bulletin records the darting of a wounded lion with a dose of penicillin and the feeding of another with meat shot for it till it recovered; this lion also drank water out of a *debi* (4 gallon petrol tin) placed nearby until it was strong enough to go to water.

In 1963 two lions were killed by Mangati tribesmen near Lake Eyasi – probably not self-defence but deliberate hunting for prestige purposes, as explained in Chapter IX. In 1964 one lion was speared near Lemuta Hill, and a Masai moran mauled in the incident: in 1965 there were no spearings in the Crater, though one lion was killed by another in a fight. In 1966 no spearings were reported, though the

Conservator found a dead lion, possibly killed by an eland; another was killed by a rhino, with a party of tourists as witnesses, whilst a further two were reported as dying of wounds as a result of fights.

And so the tale of life and death unfolds, amongst the predators just as amongst the prey. With their strong inclination to territoriality no doubt the stronger lions keep the population in balance with the food-supply with the surplus lions either killed or driven off in fights over territory. There is no evidence in Ngorongoro conditions that the steady but small toll taken by the Masai has a serious effect on the population – but this must be taken as an unscientific observation until the results of current research on population dynamics are available.

It is natural that the relationship between the Masai – a pastoral people – and the local lions should have always been close, and competitive. It is both the duty and privilege of the moran – the warrior set – to defend the flocks and herds from predators, of which the lion is the most important. As a result lion hunting is a well developed occupation amongst the Masai, and the killer gains great prestige. As is the custom with European sportsmen – it is the man whose weapon first wounds the quarry who is regarded as the owner of the dead beast. In the case of the Masai this entitles him to the mane, which he subsequently makes into a headdress; the others in at the death are rewarded with lesser trophies – the tail, the paws, and bits of skin subsequently used on the grip of the shield. The possession of a lion-skin headdress entitles one to a prominent position in a parade of warriors. The position is so coveted that in one case I know of, where a moran had obtained a lion mane but lost it (by decay or hyaenas) before he could make a headdress of it, he went out and killed a baboon, and made a very effective faked headdress from its skin. This specimen is now in the Museum of Archaeology and Ethnology at Cambridge.

There is, however, little evidence that parties set out on a lion hunt just to obtain trophies – though this doubtless happened in the past. Today it is more probable that a cattle-killer appears and the local moran organise a hunt to rid the district of the menace. But in the course of scouring the area any lion which they come across is attacked – they do not confine their attentions to the proven cattle-killer – and any lion and any number of lion, including cubs, are killed as met.

A further point which constantly crops up in discussions about Masai and lions, is the belief that lions recognise Masai as their hereditary enemy, and take flight as soon as a moran appears. Some hunters even

believe that the smell of a Masai is enough and that you should not even
have a Masai in your vehicle if you wish to approach lions closely.
Dr Grzimek perpetuates the myth in these words: 'Plains lions still
[1959] show a distinctive flight reaction when approached by a tall
Masai carrying a spear.' As a scientific observation this statement is
faultless, but it does not go far enough. These same lions would show a
similar flight reaction if approached by Dr Grzimek carrying an
umbrella, or a Klu Klux Klansman carrying a fiery cross, or even a
couple of Mbulu tribesmen carrying spears.

I can personally vouch for this last circumstance from an incident
which John Goddard and I observed in 1964. At that time the group
of tawny-maned lions – the survivors of which now live in the Crater
near Manduusi swamp – numbered four, and spent several months on
the Crater rim, living largely on young buffalo. One evening we came
across the group on the main road, just west of the Forest Resort. We
approached, by Land Rover of course, to within a few feet of one lying
by the roadside; a little further on another lion was relieving himself.
Suddenly the whole group was alert, and sprang off into the bush.
The cause? – a couple of Mbulu men who appeared over the horizon,
walking along the road. They were something under a quarter of a
mile distant – probably about 300 yards away, when they hove into
sight; even at that distance their appearance was sufficient to cause
'a distinctive flight reaction' amongst the lions.

If anyone doubts the thesis that this flight reaction applies to mankind in general and not just the Masai, let them try for themselves with
a stop watch and a tape-measure. First select a Masai, who should be
tall, according to Grzimek – other experts say he should be carrying a
spear, or again smell strongly of mutton fat or red ochre. Whatever
recipe you decide to follow, you should locate a pride of lions and
send the Masai walking towards them; you then measure the distance
at which the lions decide to run away and record the time the Masai
was in sight before the lions fled. Then when the lions have settled
down, this time, leaving the Masai in the vehicle, *you* walk towards the
lions – carrying umbrella, walking stick or whatever you choose. Again,
time and distance should be carefully noted and compared. But please
do not conduct this experiment in the Crater, just in case the lions on
that occasion might display 'aggressive visitor resistance' rather than
'flight reaction'.

The above digression turns one's thoughts to man-eating lions. Much has been written on the subject, and Major Patterson's *Man Eaters of Tsavo* describes how lion virtually halted the construction of the Mombasa–Nairobi railway line in 1898.

In all my years of contact with Ngorongoro, 1934–1968, I have not heard of a single case of man-eating lion – though of course such may have occurred but remained unrecorded. Numerous Masai have certainly been wounded, and several killed when hunting lion, but here it is man who is the aggressor.

Much has been said about the Masai method of hunting lion and one author, a young Belgian Jean Pierre Hallet in his book *Congo Kitabu*, claims to have joined in a hunt, armed only with a spear, and to have killed his lion single handed. Ideally, the Masai hunting technique is to surround the lion with a ring of armed warriors, who close in till the lion finally charges. The warrior who is charged receives the lion on his shield, whilst those on either side impale it with their spears. But I doubt if it ever works like that in practice – the variations in terrain and vegetation, and in human and lion behaviour, doubtless lead to each killing being different. In one filmed by Mr E. M. Queeney, the lion is first chased across a plain, with warriors throwing spears at it as opportunity occurs – though all miss. Finally the lion lies up under a bush and is speared whilst crouching – the whole performance has no relation to the romanticised hunt.

Whilst it is doubtful whether the lions co-operated in ensuring that these hunts followed a set pattern, certainly the Masai on their side had a ritualistic approach to the hunting. They decked themselves out in their full panoply – lion-mane headdress if available, otherwise a colobus-monkey plume or an ostrich-feather face-mask. Then very frequently a vulture-feather cape over the shoulders. I had missed the point of this until a Masai recently pointed out that this represented the mane of a lion. Weapons consist of a long-bladed spear and a double-edged sword (*simi*), and a knob-kerrie in the belt. Very often the group has come straight from an *ol pul*, that is, a meat-eating camp to which the warriors retire from time to time. Here they live on a diet consisting entirely of meat, and numerous herbs and barks are included in the soups; and these certainly have an exciting effect. Thus, at dances before setting out on a lion hunt, and again at its successful conclusion, the warriors often go off into hysterical fits not unlike epilepsy.

An interesting old photo, or rather a series of photos, are produced in

Beard's *The End of the Game,* the caption to which reads 'From out of the past, a Masai lion kill, photographed by Charles Cottar, the first American "white hunter". He hunted with Theodore Rooseveld in 1909, and was eventually killed by a rhino'. These three photographs depict 11 or 12 Masai warriors out on the open, flat, treeless plain. All, or nearly all, have lion-mane headdresses, two at least have vulture-feather capes. The lion is lying on the ground with at least four spears in it and a number of the warriors dancing around have bent spears in their hands. The significance of these photos lies in the fact that the lion had been killed out on the open, short-grassed plain with not a tree in sight, and therefore the hunting must have been conducted in a skilled and organised manner: from the fact that most of the warriors were wearing lion-mane headdresses one can deduce that they were experienced lion hunters.

Whatever the precise methods followed by this group, I have reason to believe that the Masai actually practise the technique of shoving their left arm – usually wrapped in cloth – down the lion's throat whilst attacking it with their short double-edged swords, the *simi*. I recall one case when I was D.O. i/c Loliondo, prior to World War II. A Masai was reported wounded by a lion in an out of the way spot inaccessible to motor transport. I sent out a Scotchcart, drawn by oxen, to fetch him in. When he arrived, two or three days after the wounding, his left forearm was in an advanced state of gangrene. But the wound substantiated the story that he had shoved his left hand in the lion's mouth: then his companion had taken a swipe at the lion with his *simi* and struck it a glancing blow. The sword was deflected and almost amputated the arm of his friend, above the wrist. One bone, the ulna, was completely severed, but luckily I was able to send the patient by lorry to Narok hospital in Kenya; he not only survived but his arm was saved, thanks to the sulpha drugs just then coming into use.

Many misconceptions appear in the popular press concerning lions' hunting and killing methods. Observations in the Crater have proved that they are in fact rather poor hunters. Something over half of their stalks end in failure. As for killing, the 'one swipe of the mighty paw and the animal fell dead with its neck broken' idea is quite wrong. Norman Carr in his *Return to the Wild,* when observing the two lions that he reared, Big Boy and Little Boy, making one of their early kills, records: 'The gruesome struggle went on for perhaps fifteen minutes before the buffalo finally succumbed. I felt nauseated by the cruelty of it.' The same scene is repeated in a series of photos frequently reproduced showing three lions killing a wildebeest in Kenya. The animal stands for what is obviously a considerable period while these full-grown, but obviously young lions, tackle it from varying angles and seize it in a differing series of grips, before it is finally brought to the ground. Again the picture is repeated in observations from the Crater which Moore-Gilbert reported in his Annual Report for 1961.

> A very clear sight of a lioness killing a wildebeest was obtained by myself and three scouts from a distance of less than 20 yards. The incident occurred at 14.15 hours on November 22nd in the Ngorongoro Crater.
>
> The wildebeest was cantering along when suddenly from head-on a lioness sprang out of some long grass. The wildebeest barely had time to swerve before the lioness grasped her around the neck from underneath and bore her to the ground by her weight. She bit her once midway between the ears and shoulder, but relinquished this hold immediately for one from under the neck. In fact she bit twice very quickly before closing on in a vice-like grip the third time. It appeared that she strangled her prey as it took several minutes for it to die, whilst it heaved and struggled. She remained with her teeth fastened into the neck for some time after the animal had finished moving.
>
> The other members of the pride made their appearance mean-while and had actually begun eating the udder and stomach before the wildebeest had finished struggling and whilst the original lioness still had her teeth in it.
>
> The pride consisted of the senior female who did the killing, three other females, one young, but fully-grown male, two one-year-old males and one three-year-old male. They had to all intents and purposes finished the wildebeest by 16.30 hours. All the pride fed together, and the younger members were the first to satiate themselves leaving the female who did the kill to finish by herself. When she left the kill there was a great show of affection for her, the others rubbing and pushing against her.

One final story about lions, concerning the frequently-recorded but false observation that the dutiful wives make the kill, and then according to the fixed rules of lion etiquette – father eats first. On one occasion I was showing round a group of Tourist Board members. We climbed to the top of Silalei Hill and through binoculars picked up a brown blob which on closer observation proved to be a group of lions with their heads down on a kill. We drove over and watched the feast: in the course of this a most interesting incident occurred. Of the four lionesses on the kill one walked off to a neighbouring gully and came back leading her cubs. As they lagged behind and got tired she flopped down half way and gave them refreshment, then she led them to the kill. After the party had photographed to their hearts' content we drove off and within 200 yards met the male of the group sleeping in the grass. None of the lionesses had thought to go and wake up father, even though one had gone off and brought back her cubs to the kill! Which only goes to show that lion behaviour, in common with human, is unpredictable and does not always follow its conceptualised pattern.

It was really John Goddard who introduced my son, Ian, and me to wild dog at Christmas time, 1966.

The three of us were staying in the National Geographic Chalet in the Crater. John took us out early one morning and at 6.15 a.m. we found his pets – a pack of nine – still asleep. Even before they had started hunting, a hyaena was trying to ingratiate himself into wild dog society. He made tentative approaches but withdrew without actually being chased off.

At about 6.55 a.m. the pack began to wake up and spread out, stretching, yawning, scratching and attending to calls of nature. After a few minutes they moved off in a spread-out formation and having selected their prey, a Grant's gazelle, they set off at a loping run – but they did not go far. Apart from the leading dog, the pack dropped further and further back, and did not seem at all determined. Finally, the leading dog looked over his shoulder, saw that he was not being supported and gave up with the remark clearly written in his attitude: 'Oh well, if you're not going to back me up . . .' John explained that, from the records of over 100 hunts which he and Dick Estes had witnessed, hunts were usually, but not necessarily, initiated by the recognised leader of the pack. It appeared that at times a dog which felt hungry first initiated the hunt and that the pack's concensus of opinion would be expressed by following this lead or rejecting it, as the case might be.

On this occasion they rejected the lead, and settled down to pass the day lolling around. Dogs normally hunt morning and evening, but John said that rain could easily stimulate them into hunting at any time of day. As December is the time of the short rains and there were in fact rainclouds about, we kept our eyes open all day and in between photography of other subjects returned to the dogs from time to time, especially when rain threatened.

We were in two cars and at times went our separate ways, but John said we should meet not later than 4.30 p.m. at the dogs. We were punctual, and so was John. His timing was magnificent as within a matter of minutes the dogs bestirred themselves. One went off, the others following, in a much more determined manner than in the morning. Soon the pack was in typical hunting formation strung out in a long line, with each beast in typical hunting posture – head forward, ears back, tail curved down and back. Then the leading dog selected his prey, a magnificent adult male Grant's gazelle, and the hunt was on.

Unfortunately I have no photographs or notes of the next few minutes, as with Ian driving, we followed the chase in the jeep, over the rolling downland, dodging hyaena holes, circling out to avoid water courses, cutting corners where possible. One could do nothing but hold on tight, but thanks to magnificent driving and a bit of luck we caught up with the quarry as soon as the leading dog did. The rest of the pack – and John, who got trapped on the wrong side of a gully and had to double back a bit – were some distance behind.

When we came to retrace the route it turned out to be 2½ miles; from the time the run started till the first dog caught the buck was 6½ minutes. This made an average speed over the whole run of nearly 24 m.p.h., but the speed definitely increased near the end. At times the jeep was doing 35 m.p.h. but this was possibly when we were closing the gap. (Colonel Meinertzhagen records African wild dog in Uganda as travelling at 38 m.p.h. when chased by car on road.) Luckily the finish was on the open plain, and curiously the hunt ended within half a mile of our camp.

The first dog closed up on the tiring buck, and brought it to a halt with a snap at the buttocks. As the second dog arrived the buck moved off again, only to be brought to a halt when the second dog grabbed its flank. The first dog circled round, and between the two of them they toppled the buck over. See photographs facing page 144.

Thereafter there followed a gruesome period during which the two dogs proceeded to disembowel the buck as he sat on the ground. It seemed, however, as though the buck was in a state of complete shock, and permitted the process to continue as though under an anaesthetic. It did not wince or writhe as the dogs gouged deeper and deeper into its guts, taking breathers at intervals, and with their muzzles becoming bloodier and bloodier. In the course of this process the strength of the buck ebbed – he started with the head held high, but finally collapsed. Then the rest of the pack arrived – it was noticeable how far in advance the two leaders were – and set upon the prey, speedily putting paid to its life and then to its body. The guts and hindquarters were eaten first, and before the dogs had completed their meal the scavengers appeared, jackal first, and then hyaena, but they remained at a safe distance till the dogs departed: they were not permitted to share the meal.

The process was very similar in another hunt witnessed during the course of our visit, this time of a female Grant, pregnant and nearly full term. She was run down over a much shorter distance, in $2\frac{1}{2}$ minutes. Again the leading dogs had their prey on the ground long before the tail end of the pack arrived on the scene; they even had the almost full-term foetus out when only five dogs had arrived. One dog made off with this still in its membrane, but it must have hidden this delicacy and joined in the general feast. For when the feast was nearly over and John went up to the kill to collect specimens, the foetus was still intact. Though the dog carrying it had already a full belly, he quickly demolished this tit-bit. Although identification is not 100 % certain, it seems as though it was the same dog – the white end of his tail was unusually long, broken by a chevron-shaped dark mark – which carried off the foetus in the first place and which later picked it up to finish off his meal when driven from the main carcase.

So much for the hunts we witnessed. Other accounts differ and this is natural, as the prey and environment inevitably mean adaptation of method. Other writers describe how in long grass, the dogs perform a characteristic movement of standing on their hind legs and looking around. In swamp, when hunting lechwe there is understandably no long chase. Colonel Critchley records:

> I watched one group [of dogs] select a large ram [lechwe] and pursue it towards deeper water. This ram was closely followed by one dog in the lead, followed at about 50 yards distance by another dog, with a further few dogs trailing well behind. The

ram was brought to a standstill in about 500 yards and after a few vain attempts to defend itself with sweeps of its horns, was knocked over by the first two dogs.

The characteristic, so often reported, of the prey being eviscerated when still on its feet must apply to the bigger animals, fully-grown wildebeest, roan, hartebeest, etc. which are reported as falling prey to wild dog elsewhere. The smaller gazelle and the young of larger animals cannot stand up to this treatment and are obviously floored before they reach the stage of evisceration. The selection of prey is of interest. Goddard and Estes from the results of 39 hunts have produced the following figures for the wild dog of Ngorongoro: Thompson's gazelle 60% of kills, young wildebeest 18%, Grant's gazelle 10%, and hartebeest 1 kill.

Many other prey species have been recorded elsewhere, ranging from hippo to oryx. The latter saw off the wild dog effectively, as the following account from Colonel Meinertzhagen's *Kenya Diary* shows:

> I was most interested to see the tactics of a small herd of oryx when attacked by a pack of 9 wild dog. I first saw the dogs galloping towards the oryx: as they approached they separated and went into the attack from three sides. The oryx closed ranks, faced outwards and kept their heads down. The dogs kept on charging up to them but kept out of range of their sharp horns. I think the dogs were after two calves which sheltered more or less in the centre of the group. After much charging almost up to the oryx in the hope of stampeding them, the dogs drew off. The oryx maintained their close formation for about a quarter of an hour after the dogs left them. I was glad to see that these wild dogs do not always have it their own way.

Not so successful were the wildebeest, who tried similar tactics when observed by Dr Grzimek:

> . . . we saw to our amazement that the wildebeest had formed four small groups. The adults stood with their heads pointing outwards, protecting the yearlings in the centre. The dogs had also split up, but all their attempts to break the ring of wilde-

beest failed. They were met by lowered heads and pointed horns. We waited. Suddenly an excited wildebeest calf broke out of the protecting circle. In a flash the calf was torn to bits.

It is remarkable how the wild dog of Ngorongoro give way when approached by man. John was making a collection of mandibles from all wild dog victims, so that when satisfactory methods of ageing have been evolved, the precise age of all kills will be known. As he was anxious to collect his specimens before they were damaged by the dogs, he always walked up to the kill long before the feast was complete. The dogs politely withdrew at his approach. It is indeed doubtful if wild dog attack man. I have only traced one alleged record. Von Lettow-Vorbeck, the German Commander-in-Chief in Tanganyika in World War I, as quoted by Dr Grzimek, records a story, admittedly hearsay, of a European who was attacked and killed by wild dog. 'All that was found of the settler was five empty shells (all the ammunition he had with him), five dead dogs and a few remnants of his corpse.' Most unlikely, particularly as wild dog are known to turn on and eat their wounded companions: in this case would they not have done so, rather than kill the man who was shooting at them?

The African wild dog is very uniform in appearance in the whole of its range throughout Africa, and zoologists have made no attempt to differentiate sub-species or races. A text-book description records that the dogs weigh up to 70 lbs., with a shoulder height of 30 inches and a length of five feet, the last 15 inches being tail. These dimensions – give or take 5 % – correspond to my Labrador Retriever/Great Dane cross and are very similar to a large Alsatian. The Ngorongoro dogs are however smaller than this southern variety and probably do not exceed 40 lb. in weight. The ears are large, upright and remarkably rounded. In colour the dogs show tremendous variation, the only constant features being a black muzzle and a white tip to the tail; this latter earns them their Masai name *Oloibor Kidongoi*, the white-tailed one. Between the two extremities the body is made up of black, white, brown and yellow blotches in no fixed pattern.

The history of the wild dog pack in the Crater is of interest. In the 30 years during which I had acquaintance on and off with Ngorongoro I only met wild dog once, and that was in 1961 at the entrance gate to the Conservation Area above Karatu. This was a solitary dog and it was very remarkable to meet it in temperate evergreen forest. It may have been a member of a pack which was hidden in the undergrowth, but such environment is very atypical. In early September, 1964 a large pack entered the Crater, consisting of eight dogs, four bitches, and nine juveniles. They disappeared for a short time in December, 1964, but were again seen in January, 1965. At one time the group was reinforced by some visitors, numbering 29 at its maximum, then the bulk of the animals disappeared and left a small group of seven, later reduced to six, viz five males and one female. They were down to this number when Prince Bernhard of the Netherlands visited the Crater at the end of August, 1965. Then the bitch produced nine pups in late February, 1966: eight male and one female. Unfortunately the mother died on 3 April, 1966. Her bloated body was pulled out of the hole by the males and deposited some distance away. All nine pups were alive at this time and survived for three months on regurgitated food brought to them by the males. Only four pups still survived when we visited the Crater at Christmas, 1966, but John tells me that the five that died did not perish from malnutrition as they were all past the weaning stage when they died.

This feeding of young by regurgitation is apparently common. Myles Turner, the Senior Park Warden of the Serengeti National Park, as recorded by Grzimek ' . . . observed that afterwards four of the dogs regurgitated some of the gazelle's flesh, which was promptly devoured by their children.' It is not clear whether this was a case of males rearing orphan pups, or of a mother giving a supplementary feed to her own young. But the fact that males do feed the young in this way has been recorded by the Director of the Moscow Zoo. He told Dr Grzimek that: 'one of his keepers did not follow the tradition of separating the dog from the bitch before the birth of the pups. The Russians were astounded to see a father take the whole head of each puppy into his huge mouth and regurgitate meat directly into the mouth of each youngster.'

The Crater pack is certainly to be congratulated on the way it brought up the motherless pups, but the continuation of the pack by natural increase is far from assured for the four youngsters now surviving are all males. The possibility of introducing a bitch has been considered. In fact, enquiries were made concerning the purchase of some stock. It was found, however, that the current price of wild dog was in the nature of £140, a large sum to gamble as the dogs might well set upon the stranger when released. On the other hand all reports show these animals as being singularly friendly to their own kind, as when two packs meet up, so the gamble might well be worthwhile if no immigrant females come to join the Crater pack. This problem lost its urgency, at least temporarily, when the pack moved out of the Crater in early 1967 and by the end of the year only two males were reported as having returned. If later the full pack returns it is hoped that the dogs will have recruited some bitches into the pack, and thereby increase the chances of prolonged residence in the Crater.

What is the effect of the wild dogs' hunting on the rest of the wildlife in the area concerned? In Ngorongoro singularly little. Wildebeest can be observed placidly grazing within a very short distance of a wild dog kill. Similarly when the pack is actually on the hunt it can go through a herd of wildebeest, intent on its prey, with the minimum of disturbance to the grazers.

Dr Grzimek has also noted this. He says: 'We saw four or five hundred gazelle peacefully grazing. They seemed unafraid although they could see some wild dogs a quarter of a mile away.'

These observations are in singular contrast to those of other observers. Ansell in his *Mammals of Northern Rhodesia* has this to say: 'In game areas, contrary to traditional belief, it [the presence of wild dog] is almost certainly beneficial to inducing game movements, thus conserving pasture as well as eliminating the unfit.' As to eliminating the unfit, it was significant that of the two hunts which I witnessed, in one the victim was a pregnant female Grant and in the other a robust male. Concerning Ansell's earlier remark that the presence of a pack of wild dog is sufficient to clear an area of the remaining wildlife, this belief is also recorded by Audrey Moore in her book *Serengeti*. It was doubtless on this belief that official policy was based. When reserves were established on the Serengeti and Ngorongoro in the early 1930's, protection was given to all types of animal except hyaena and hunting dogs. It was only in 1937 that they too received full protection.

The hyaena is an unpopular beast: 'A murderer and a coward, rivalling the crocodile in public detestation, unequalled in offensiveness of odour, as bloodthirsty as a hunting dog, as ugly as a warthog, the hyaena has also the most abominable voice in the African wild . . .' This denigration from *The Nature of the Beast* by T. Murray-Smith is typical. Audrey Moore, from whom you would expect a more balanced description, writes:

It was a grievous pity that God ever went on working that night. He had been hard at it all day for the past four days making cows and iguanas and gentle things like blackbirds and reed buck . . .

So God, having been busy amongst His birds and four legged beasts all day, pushed His hair back out of His eyes, looked out at all the herds of just finished animals, and, in a fit of despondency, made the Hyaena.

But whatever Mr Murray-Smith or Audrey Moore, or for that matter the Deity, thinks about hyaena, I like them. I like them both for what they are and for what they do.

Usually regarded as a nocturnal animal, in Ngorongoro they are, to a considerable extent, diurnal. So many are visible by day that they greatly enhance the interest of a drive round the Crater. One cannot go far without seeing a hyaena popping his head out of the mouth of a den or lolloping over the open plain, or wallowing in a mud pool – a particularly popular pastime. To meet up with their cubs is an even more interesting experience. They are attractive black, fluffy blobs which pop in and out of their dens like playful puppies. Or you may meet one half grown with the black head of the pup and the spotted body of the adult.

But in addition to their 'tourist attraction' hyaena play a key role in the ecology of Ngorongoro. They are in fact our family planning agency. I remember once reading of a biologist who had calculated that if every herring egg created was fertilised and produced a fish which lived to maturity, the North Sea would be solid herring in x number of years. A similar equation could be worked out to show that the Crater would be solid wildebeest in y years; that is, unless the numbers were controlled.

As far as Ngorongoro is concerned, Dr Hans Kruuk's researches throw much light on the role of the hyaena in the ecology of the Crater. He summarised the position of his work up to the end of 1965 thus:

Fifty Spotted Hyaenas have been marked in the Crater, by putting a chain collar around their necks and clipping notches out of their ears. From the returns of these marked animals, it appears that they live in clans with many males and females together, each clan having its own territory in which there is

Giraffe and calves on the Eastern Serengeti, with the Crater rim in the background. The calves are not twins; there is a second mother on the left, not shown in the photograph.

Two old buffalo bulls in the Crater: the animal on the right has a nostril split from fighting.

A zebra foal in the Crater: when detached from their family, very young zebra show little fear and approach vehicles closely.

Zebra live in family groups of great stability; note the eland (straight horns) and the waterbuck (forward curving horns) in the background.

a set of dens. The litters of the females of a clan are all put together in one or two dens. The members of each clan, which usually number 20–40 hyaenas, go hunting together at night; they specialise on large animals like wildebeest and zebra, which they always kill at night. Thus, hyaenas in the Ngorongoro Crater are not scavengers as is so commonly assumed; in fact, the lions in that area more often live on hyaena-kill remains rather than the other way round. From the recoveries of marked animals, there appear to be about 370 spotted hyaenas in the Crater; they are, therefore, the most important predator, and occupy a key position in the whole ecological system. The exact quantity of game consumed by the hyaenas is being measured, partly aided by microscopical analysis of their faeces.

Dr Kruuk's work in 1966 enlarges our knowledge of the species. It appears that the Crater is divided into eight clan ranges, each populated by a clan of hyaena. The point previously made that the hyaena of Ngorongoro are predators rather than scavengers has been amply borne out by further observations, as recorded in the 1966 Ngorongoro Annual Report:

> Dr Kruuk has been able to study the hyaenas' hunting methods extensively and, through many observations, he had been able to establish that the hunting methods for obtaining wildebeest are different from the hunting methods for obtaining zebra and again different for Thomson's gazelle. Zebras are hunted in large packs which are usually led by a female hyaena whereas wildebeest are usually run down by only one or two hyaenas with other hyaenas joining during and after the chase. The wildebeest is killed collectively, just like zebra. Thomson's gazelle, Thomson's gazelle fawns and also young wildebeest are killed by one or two hyaenas only. The spotted hyaenas have a very intricate social system with many different means of communication between the individual hyaenas. This social system is perfectly well adapted to the hunting life of this species.

One of the Ngorongoro hyaena's chief articles of diet is young wildebeest, but this is of course only obtainable seasonally as the wildebeest all calve at one time. Dick Estes has studied this subject in

9

detail and will be publishing his results in due course. I cannot quote statistics from memory, but from what he told me I recall that during the first weeks of the calving season hyaena took a very large percentage of the young. Then, when calving was at its peak, the survival rate reached a maximum – the hyaena just could not keep pace with the rate of production. Then towards the end of the season the hyaenas again got the upper hand and took a large proportion of the calves.

As with other species hyaena populations can experience 'explosions' and 'crashes', and as these can have a tremendous effect on the other wildlife we must know more about them. Thus, valuable though Dr Kruuk's work to date is it must be supplemented by continuing observations in other areas in the future.

The hard years of 1959/60/61, followed by the years of plenty had a considerable effect on hyaena populations. The amount of dead meat available during this period led to a large increase in the hyaena population. I know of no study which reveals whether this was caused by an actual increase in the birth rate or merely by ensuring that a larger proportion of those born reached maturity. But certainly the population did increase to such an extent that when the restoration of normal weather conditions stopped the high rate of mortality amongst domestic stock and wildlife, the hyaena population was far in excess of the normal food supply. As a result, the hyaenas were compelled to seek alternative food supplies, and turned both to man and his domestic stock.

In the Crater the situation was not acute, but in the surrounding areas the Conservation Authority had to take action similar to that of the Kenya Game Department, for the increase in the hyaena population had been due to bovine rather than wildlife deaths, and so the increase was greatest in the areas where cattle predominated over wildlife, e.g. Nainokonoka. Here particularly hyaena had turned on both living domestic stock and on humans and their numbers had to be reduced by shooting.

It is of interest to note that the hyaena is the only predator, indeed the only animal, that has turned against and injured one of our tourists at Ngorongoro. In view of the unique and dramatic circumstances it is worth reporting the incident at length. On 22 December, 1961 a party turned up at Ngorongoro consisting of a German schoolteacher and his twelve-year-old son who were travelling through Africa on a holiday in a pick-up. They had been joined by a German, Mr Hans

Kluver, a photo engraver from Hamburg, who was hitch-hiking through Africa. On arrival at Ngorongoro the party, who did not wish to use the Lodge, were offered tent accommodation by a Conservation official, but the schoolteacher said they had slept under the stars throughout their journey and proposed to continue to do so. They got their sleeping bags out and slept under a tree, the large spreading evergreen within a few yards of the Conservation Office. Hans Kluver reported:

> I was sleeping in a quilted sleeping bag under a tree within 50 yards of the Conservation Office at Ngorongoro. My bag was about two yards away from my two companions, who were also in sleeping bags.
>
> I was awakened by a roaring close to my ear and something pulled at my sleeping bag close to my head. My head was covered by the bag with only my face exposed. I saw over my head the open mouth of a big animal. I thought it was a lion. It was a little dark as the moon was behind a dark cloud. I curled up in my sleeping bag, calling out to my companions first.
>
> I appreciated that there were two animals involved as one was pulling at the head of the sleeping bag and the other at the feet. I felt myself being dragged away: I could move a little in the bag and so avoided being bitten. I heard Mr Smith getting up and thought he would come to my rescue.
>
> Meanwhile the hyaenas had dragged me across the road and then my sleeping bag was torn – one hyaena caught me by the foot and dragged me further away into the bushes. Then they stopped for a moment and the one at my feet started licking the blood off my wounded foot. The other hyaena was behind my head.
>
> I jumped up and cried out and both ran back a bit – only a foot or two. I grabbed one round the throat with both my hands to try and throttle it. I could not throw him down. The other was standing about two yards away. It did not come to the help of its companion. I again cried out and ran, but I could not run fast because of my wounded foot – I was still in the bush. They wanted to attack me again and again. I can't remember whether it was three or four times. I cried out each time and

waved my arms as if to attack them and this held them off:
I had now got back to the road and Mr Smith passed me
in his car but did not notice me. I fell down. The hyaenas
were about 20 yards away and coming slowly up. I again cried
out and Mr Smith heard me, for a few seconds later he came back
in his car to pick me up. He shot with his pistol at the hyaenas
which were about 20 yards away. He put me in the car and
took me to Mr Fourie's house. Mr Fourie dressed my wounded
foot and we left Ngorongoro about 3.30 a.m., getting to Arusha
in the early morning where I was admitted to hospital.

As a result of prompt medical attention he was discharged from the
hospital a week or two later with no permanent damage to his legs.
The only real loss was his passport and money which must have slipped
out from under his pillow whilst he was being dragged around. A
thorough search by a gang of 12 or more throughout the whole bush
area failed to reveal the missing articles. This is doubtless because they
were in a leather wallet, a particular delicacy to hyaenas. So the
German Embassy in Nairobi had to equip Mr Kluver with a new
passport and further funds to enable him to continue his journey.

The leopard is an animal of the bush and forest rather than the
plains, and hence is not conspicuous in the Crater. But nonetheless it
is there, both in the Lerai forest and at times on the Munge river,
where Dick Estes was able to take observations of a leopard's diet.
Over a month it was found to have killed two Grant's gazelle, and
eleven jackals. Thus the widely observed preference of leopard for
domestic dogs apparently applies also to wild canines.

When living at Ngorongoro we personally had experience of this diet
preference, as we had a small mongrel dog – a 'Tanganyika terrier',
named Spats. One evening about 8 o'clock we heard a yelp outside the
kitchen door, and rushed out with lamps. The light frightened off a
leopard, but we were too late to save Spats, who had been bitten by
the leopard in the small of the back, so that the tissue of liver and
kidney was protruding. It was obvious that the dog felt no pain.
He was in a state of deep shock, and pathetically wagged his tail and
licked our hands as we patted him. This must be much the same
condition as with other species taken by predators; the Grant's gazelle
that I have observed seem to sit in a state of equanimity whilst the

wild dog proceed to disembowel them. We quickly dispatched poor Spats and put his body in the charcoal store to await burial in the morning. This had a small gap between the top of the wall and the roof and through this the leopard entered later that night. However, the store was so small that he could not get room for a jump sufficiently powerful to lift the dog, and he was obviously afraid to stay and eat his victim in what he obviously suspected was a trap. So he scrambled up the wall as best he could – the charcoal footmarks on the whitewash revealed his difficulties – and made off.

Next afternoon my wife was trying to record some bird calls through the open bedroom window when she heard a thump below her, and right under her nose, within four or five feet, she saw the leopard, which had pounced on one of our cats and made off with it across the grass. A third incident occurred the following evening when I was sitting reading by lamp light: I saw a movement outside the french window and for a moment wondered whose dog had come to visit us. But then I realised it was the leopard again, checking on what livestock still remained in the Fosbrooke household!

Although we permitted staff to keep pets in the Conservation Area – and Masai to have dogs in the Crater – it is understood that this is entirely at the owners' risk. In consequence I instructed the game scout staff, seconded from the Game Department, not to take any action against the leopard. But what we assume was the same leopard appeared a few days later outside the shops three miles to the west, and in direct defiance of orders, a game scout shot it, unfortunately not a clean kill, so we lost not only the leopard, but also its valuable skin.

The policy, common throughout East Africa, is to try and trap leopards when they make a nuisance of themselves, and then release them in uninhabited areas, a process rather ponderously known as translocation. John Goddard and the game staff had tried for some time to do this, but our first success was by coincidence on the day we were honoured by a visit from the President of the World Wildlife Fund, Prince Bernhard. The leopard released that day was never seen again. A further two were trapped in 1966 and one was safely released: another unfortunately broke a leg in the trap and had to be destroyed.

The cheetah is one of our most attractive predators, and if accounts are to be believed, one of the few which make what we humans regard as a 'clean kill'. But accounts, unless substantiated by prolonged scientific investigations, are not always reliable. Take for instance the oft-quoted story that cheetah are the fastest living animals, whose speed can exceed 60 m.p.h. Of this I can find no record. Colonel Meinertz-hagen records a speed of 44 m.p.h. taken from three counts when chasing an electric hare in London: he also states that 51 m.p.h. was recorded 'when pressed by car on road in Kenya'. From another source the cheetah on the greyhound track reached 45 m.p.h. whilst the dogs running at the same time reached only 37.5 m.p.h. Similarly Dr R. Bigalke in *African Wildlife* refutes the 60 to 70 m.p.h. theory and puts the record cheetah speeds at 45 m.p.h. So until the protagonists of the cheetah prove otherwise this speed – fast but not phenomenal – must be accepted.

Cheetah live and breed regularly in the Crater, but in small numbers: in consequence the visitor is lucky to see one. But on the eastern Serengeti to the south of Olduvai, and up by Lemuta hill a little perseverance is usually rewarded by a sight of these delightful animals.

The smaller predators, apart from the 'big cats', add interest to a visit to Ngorongoro. All three species of jackal found in East Africa occur in the Crater. The black-backed is an elegant fox-like animal who always appears to be well groomed, in contrast to the golden or Indian jackal, whose coat looks untidy, not to say mangy: his de-meanour is also more furtive. The side-striped jackal, larger than his two cousins, is seldom seen, but in 1966 a pair raised a litter on the top of Kitati hill. The smallest of the dog-like predators is the bat-eared fox. This attractive little animal, though mainly nocturnal, can be seen at times outside his burrow, but usually goes underground before a photo can be taken.

The smaller cats are equally attractive: the one most frequently seen is the serval, resembling a miniature leopard, or cheetah, but with a conspicuously short tail. The caracal or African lynx shares with the lion the feature of a uniformly coloured coat – its distinguishing feature is the tufts of hair at the tips of the ears. Finally we have the humble Taita wild cat, of the same size and with the same markings as a domestic tabby, with which it frequently interbreeds.

7 The Birds

I must, in all honesty, start this chapter by confessing that I am not a bird photographer. I can cope with the ostrich, the bustard and such water birds as can conveniently be handled with a 200 mm lens, but not for me the (only just) portable telescopes, the hides, and the patience which are necessary for good bird photography. I did make one attempt on the smaller species – the Cape rooks which are nesting in the trees on Keshei Hill. I went out one morning by myself to photograph the damage which elephants had caused to these trees. A rook was cawing loudly on top of one tree, so I fitted a 200 mm lens, glued my eye to the viewfinder and slowly approached to get the closest possible shot. Just as I had taken my picture and was turning away feeling satisfied that my mission was accomplished, there was a 'Grrrrrrh!' from the leafy top of the tree, and a large lioness jumped down from branch to branch. I watched spellbound as I had a very personal interest in what she intended to do when she reached the ground. There was a pool in the reeds a few yards behind me, and it flashed across my mind that if she came my way, it might discourage her if I were to jump into the water. However, this was not necessary as, much to my relief, she bounded off in the opposite direction.

This incident served as a reminder to me, as I hope it will to my readers who visit Ngorongoro, that in spite of appearances the Crater is still wild Africa, full of wild animals, and one's conduct must be adapted accordingly. This particular spot is both attractive as a shady picnic spot and interesting as a prehistoric site, but my experience shows that it must be approached with caution.

There are over 300 species of birds to be found in the checklist published in the booklet *Ngorongoro's Bird Life*: of these 182 species have been recorded in the Crater itself. There are also checklists

published for Manyara National Park to the east and Serengeti
National Park to the west. When editing John Goddard's bird booklet
I discovered that 125 species which appear in the Serengeti list, do
not appear in the Ngorongoro, and that Ngorongoro has 100 species
not found in the Serengeti list.

Within a 100 mile radius of the Crater there occur over five hundred
species of birds. Although many of the species are not likely to be seen
by the visitor, it is of interest to know that the Conservation Area
contains ground high enough for the giant lobelia to grow, with a
result that the rare Johnson's sunbird, normally thought of in connection with the heights of Kilimanjaro or Mount Meru, is also found
here. Other rarities are the red-headed parrot, found at Empakaai, the
Teita falcon, and the lammergeyer.

But whether the visitor, bird-book in hand, wishes to linger over the
identification of the species he sees, or whether he is on a whirlwind
'package' tour, there are certain aspects of the bird life which cannot
fail to strike him. All the conspicuous plains birds of East Africa are to
be seen in the Crater. The ostrich breeds here, and whilst visitors are
not encouraged to disturb nesting birds those who accidentally stumble
across a nest may witness some interesting behaviour patterns. Sometimes up to three hens may share the same nest, and have been observed
competing for position to lay their eggs. The cock and hen take turns
at sitting to incubate the eggs, and may be found 'changing guard'.
If disturbed the hen may decide to make a stand, fluffing up her
feathers and advancing on the intruder with aggressive hisses, or she
may decide on deception, flopping away in simulation of a broken
wing. But in spite of all these efforts to safeguard the eggs, large
numbers of eggs and chicks are lost to predators, so the ostrich
population of the Crater is not a large one.

Other conspicuous birds of the plains are the kori bustard, the
secretary bird, and the crowned crane. Near the Lerai forest one
frequently sees the ground hornbill, a bird about the size of a turkey
with a heavy laboured flight, and flocks of the common helmeted
guinea fowl; another species of guinea fowl with a tuft of black feathers
on top of its head, instead of the bony crest, is to be found in the forest
on the rim of the Crater.

The storks are also a feature of the Crater; the European stork, the
period of whose visits corresponds exactly with the peak months for
overseas tourists, December to April; the saddle-bill, the largest of them

all, being five and a half feet tall, as compared with the marabou at five feet: the latter is often seen around Masai encampments waiting for offal. Then there is the yellow-billed stork, previously called the wood ibis, and the small black-backed Abdim's or white-bellied stork.

The hammerkop is an attractive, medium-sized, brown bird with a crest which gives its head a resemblance to a hammer; the nest is a remarkably large structure of sticks, lined with mud and said to be so strongly built that it will bear the weight of a man standing on it; examples are to be seen at the time of writing, which will probably last for several years, at the base of Kitati Hill and in the fig tree above the research cabin.

Flamingos, both greater and lesser, are to be seen from time to time in the soda lake in the Crater, sometimes accompanied by their grey-feathered youngsters, bred in the lakes to the north. The flamingos of Ngorongoro cannot vie in numbers with those on the Kenya lakes, Nakuru, Elmenteita, and others but if one is lucky enough to visit the Empakaai crater lake at the right moment one may see a concentration of flamingos as impressive as anywhere in East Africa, the shore thickly lined with wading birds, and the surface dotted with swimming birds like the confection 'hundreds and thousands' sprinkled on a cake.

The pelicans form a feature on the waters of the Crater, though their presence does not, as was at one time thought, indicate the presence of fish. So far no species of fish has been found in the Crater, and the same absence of fish applies, according to Elliott and Fuggles Couchman, to Empakaai lake. At times pelicans may be seen in large numbers wheeling and circling at a tremendous height – so high that it is difficult to distinguish individual birds with the naked eye. The flock seems to disappear when the birds present their shaded side to the observer, and then to spring into sparkling white life as they wheel into the sun. Pelicans rising higher and higher in a convenient thermal are a regular and striking sight at Mbulu, a little to the south, where huge numbers pass daily between Lake Manyara and Lake Eyasi at certain times; as far as I have been able to observe it this phenomenon is only a chance, not a regular occurrence in the Crater.

Other birds of the waterside are the egrets and the ibises: in particular the sacred ibis, especially in flight, provides excellent material for photography as the black tips to the wing feathers emphasise the outline.

The ducks and geese provide constant but varying interest, as many species come and go according to season: the great spur-winged goose, the knob-billed goose and the white-faced tree duck are migrants to the Crater, but the Egyptian goose, always to be seen in considerable numbers, breeds locally, often nesting in tall trees. On one occasion I observed crows raiding an Egyptian goose's nest at the top of a eucalyptus tree on Siedentopf's farm on the Munge: the eggs dropped 50 feet or more with a squelchy 'plop'. It made one wonder how the goslings would have got to earth if they had hatched out.

There is no end to the catalogue of attractive water birds; avocets, herons, spoonbills, coots, lilytrotters, darters and kingfishers all are to be seen, in greater or lesser numbers according to season, in the Crater.

The birds of prey present an equally attractive range, from the fish eagle with its proud carriage and its haunting cry, the bateleur with its almost non-existent tail, the augur buzzard, the martial eagle, down to the rare Taita falcon, thinly scattered throughout eastern Africa down to the Victoria Falls.

Vultures are denigrated by most writers, even ornithologists allowing themselves to lose their objectivity and talk of their 'disgusting habits' – disgusting to a human perhaps, but not to a fellow vulture! In Ngorongoro, vultures not only fill their accepted role of scavengers; they also add great interest to the visitor's day in the Crater. For it is seldom that one fails to spot a group of vultures on a carcass, and the fact that all six varieties common in East Africa may be found at one time gives added interest to the scene. Particularly conspicuous is the white Egyptian vulture and the lappet-faced, the largest of the lot, bigger even than the bearded vulture, mentioned below. A pair of lappet-faced, conspicuous by their size and purple wattles, will often be observed standing aloof from the seething mass of lesser fry squabbling over a carcass.

Vultures spend much of their time soaring in the heavens, almost beyond the reach of human eyes. It is said that the remarkably quick assembly that they achieve on a kill is due to the fact that they are thinly scattered over a wide area; then when one vulture sights some food and plummets down, the remainder follow, without necessarily having seen the food for themselves. But they come to ground to rest as well as to feed, and a considerable group can frequently be seen near the Munge ford, with their wings spread out for all the world like cormorants drying themselves in the sun. The reason for adopting this posture is uncertain: John Goddard thinks it may be for heat dispersal.

Some vultures nest in Lerai forest in the Crater, but there are two cliff faces on the periphery of the Conservation Area greatly favoured as nesting places. The first is the Sanjan gorge, where Michael Grzimek met his death on 10 January, 1959, when his plane collided with a vulture and crashed. This accident was not due to a failure to appreciate the risk for Michael and his father had already recorded details of birds' reactions to their plane in a joint paper in the *Journal of Wildlife Management*: 'Birds in flight (predators as well as storks) moved out of the way of the plane only at the last minute . . . We are aware that even very small birds when hitting an aircraft sometimes cause serious disasters, so we kept away from all birds as much as possible.' Tragically, avoidance did not always prove possible, the worst occurred and the wildlife of Africa lost a brilliant friend and advocate.

The second cliff face occurs in the stupendous Engare Sero gorge, which cuts into the Sale plains to a tremendous depth of some 1,500 feet. It is a terrifying experience to stand on the edge of this gorge and watch the vultures wheeling below, looking no bigger than pigeons or starlings. I do not know of any ornithologist who has compiled lists of the species of vultures which breed here, or recorded details of their nesting habits.

A very rare bird, the bearded vulture or lammergeyer, is found in the Crater highlands. It is remarkable for its sporadic distribution in very small numbers throughout Africa, occurring in Lesotho and in the Drakensberg Mountains in the south, then in the Crater highlands, and on Kilimanjaro, and to the north on Mount Kenya and in the Ethiopian highlands. One of the characteristics of this bird is its habit of carrying a bone to a great height, and then dropping it on a rock so that it breaks and the marrow can be extracted. By an extraordinary stroke of luck a lammergeyer was actually observed doing this by a group of conservationists, including Sir Julian Huxley, when they visited the Crater at the time of the Arusha Conference in September, 1961.

For those who have no opportunity to descend into the Crater or to explore the northern highlands, even the drive from the Conservation Area entrance gate on the east to the Serengeti on the west can provide an interesting cross section of bird life. A conspicuous and beautiful bird which nests in the side-cut of the road as it climbs through the temperate evergreen forest to the Crater rim is the carmine bee-eater.

The turaco, also called laurie or plantain-eater, can frequently be spotted running along the branch of a tree in the characteristic manner of a clockwork mouse – you cannot see its legs moving; then when it takes to the wing, its rich crimson flight-feathers are revealed. A stop at the Forest Resort will probably produce the sight of a brilliant sun-bird sucking honey out of the fuchsias planted there, whilst further on, a look around the Lodge will probably reveal a shrike or a woodpecker.

On the Loirobi grasslands to the west of the Lodge one can often see little black birds with long tails, bobbing up and down out of the grass, like ping-pong balls on a jet of water in the shooting gallery at a fair. These are Jackson's widow-bird, and Machworth-Praed and Grant describe the display thus: 'The cocks make rings in the grass as playgrounds from which they dance up and down in the air most of the day. These rings have a tuft of grass in the centre, in which are usually two recesses. The bird springs about two feet with head thrown back, feet hanging, and tail curved up to touch the nape except for two feathers which point outwards and downwards. The playground ring is worn almost bare of grass and a female often sits on the tuft of grass in the centre.'

As one descends into the lower thorn country the bird life changes, but is equally attractive and colourful. The lilac-breasted roller will be seen, as also the brilliantly coloured superb starling. Fischer's love-bird, an attractive miniature parrot is found in the acacias on the plains, and sometimes a congregation of the Sudan dioch or red-billed quelea may be met. These sparrow-sized birds can become a most destructive pest, assembling in such numbers that they can completely devastate a wheat or millet harvest. The weight of a flock sometimes breaks branches off large trees. Drastic but effective control measures have therefore to be applied in agricultural areas, such as the use of dynamite or flame throwers on their roosting places.

An interesting bird of the plains is the sand-grouse, which may be met with in large flocks right out on the open plains, near the Shifting Sands, for instance. Two species are found, the yellow-throated with male and female presenting very contrasting plumage, and the chestnut-bellied, with again the female recognised by her speckles.

So wherever you go in the Conservation Area there is a rich birdlife to be seen, whether in the Crater itself, in the alpine heathlands, the evergreen forest or the semi-desert plains. In a book on survival the question should be considered: 'Just how safe is this wonderful heritage?'

The answer is simple: 'Just as safe as its habitat!' Our birds are not poached for food, there is luckily no fashionable demand for their plumage, and if only their habitat remains unchanged, the birds may be considered safe. Just how the habitat may be safeguarded is considered in the concluding chapter of this book.

8 Ancient Man

It can be said without exaggeration that no place in Africa, indeed no place in the world, offers such a complete spectrum of man's development as the country in and around the Ngorongoro Conservation Area. The brightest star of the galaxy is of course Olduvai Gorge, where the work of Dr and Mrs Leakey has over the years unfolded the story of man's development from 1,750,000 years ago to relatively recent times. A very brief outline of the Olduvai site is given below. Then the Crater itself provides one of the earliest archaeological discoveries of Tanzania – early graves, which the visitors can see today, whilst the rich prehistoric site of Engaruka lies immediately below the Rift, just outside the Area.

But the story of man's development does not cease with the dead. There are living examples of man the hunter to be found in the click-speaking Hadza of the Eyasi trough, and the Masai-speaking Dorobo of the northern Serengeti. Man the pastoralist is typified by the Masai, whilst the Iraqw or Mbulu people, through whose country the road to the Crater passes, typify man the farmer, developing from the careful terrace-cultivators of Kainam to the tractor-using wheat grower of Karatu. It has long been my ambition to see a museum set up in Arusha and a visitor centre at Ngorongoro with displays to illustrate this fascinating story of man's development; the deeper understanding of the area would make a trip to Ngorongoro much more meaningful to the visitor.

The Olduvai gorge is a deep erosion scar cutting into the vast Serengeti Plain, running from Lake Ndutu on the National Park boundary to the Balbal depression just west of the Crater. Over its 30 mile course it gets progressively deeper till it is about 200 feet deep at the main archaeological sites, and then gets shallower as it cuts through a series of steps (faults) till it debouches into the Balbal depression. The first hint of its archaeological potential came from a Professor Kattwinkel who tells how in 1911 he was chasing a butterfly on the Serengeti when he stumbled across the gorge and appreciated its palaeontological significance. When he reported his finds to Germany, Professor Reck's 1913 Olduvai expedition was organised, in the course of which Professor Reck examined the Engaruka site and the already known graves on the Siedentopf farm in the Crater. There was much controversy about the age of a human skull found by Dr Reck, as its low position in the beds (at the top of Bed II) suggested that modern type man was on the earth much earlier than was previously suspected. It is now apparent that this skull had found its way into the lower bed in comparatively recent times by intrusive burial or some other means, at a spot where Beds III and IV had been eroded away.

It was not till 1931 that Dr Leakey, on an expedition to Olduvai, recognised the first stone tools. The more recent startling discovery of early hominids has tended to obscure the fact that Olduvai had already yielded tools covering a long span of time from the beginning of the Lower Pleistocene to the end of the Middle Pleistocene and also some sites of the Upper Pleistocene. Over and above these lay the evidence of more recent stone-age hunting cultures – typified by carefully fashioned lunates of chert and a few of obsidian, used as barbs when set in wooden arrow heads.

It was in 1959 that the Leakeys' first find of ancient man raised Olduvai from an interesting to a world famous archaeological site. All the work since that date has been financed by the National Geographic Society, and in the last phase of development no less than 17 human finds have been recorded. Some of these are single teeth or fragments of bone, others, although incomplete, have permitted skull reconstruction, particularly '*Zinjanthropus*', more properly called *Australopithecus boisei*, and *Homo habilis*. It is arguable whether either or both of these are direct ancestors of man: it is sufficient for our purpose if we call them near-man.

The story of the finding of '*Zinjanthropus*,' 'Nutcracker man', is a great tribute to the persistence of Dr and Mrs Leakey, who had been working the site, at intervals, since 1931 in the belief that it would ultimately reveal evidence of early man himself. This persistence was not only rewarded from 1959 onwards, but was given a 'freak' bonus when a '*Zinjanthropus* type' mandible (missing from the Olduvai find) was found to the west of Lake Natron. It was exposed on an erosion area perched on a plinth of soil as though mounted in a museum. If the area had been visited a few years earlier, the mandible would not have been exposed; a few years later and its supporting plinth would have eroded away and the jaw tumbled down and probably been covered again by hill-wash. Just what were the odds of this 1¾ million year old relic being seen by someone who could recognise it, when it was exposed for what in the time scale concerned represents no more than a few minutes in the life of a man? This mandible when placed against the reconstructed '*Zinjanthropus*' skull corresponded closely.

The other hominid found at Olduvai, *Homo habilis*, was '*Zinjanthropus's*' contemporary, as some remains have been found above and some below the Zinj level. This was a very different type of proto-man, smaller, delicate, with a larger brain and indications that he was capable of making and using primitive tools.

But the value of Olduvai lies not only in its contribution to the history of man, but equally to the tremendous light which it throws on the previous topography and fauna of the region. The beds of Olduvai reveal a picture of alternate dry and wet periods. In the latter, what is now the Serengeti Plain was largely covered by lake, with a lacustrine fauna. In the age of gigantism, there were sheep-like beasts, with a horn spread of over six feet; pigs the size of hippo, with three foot long tusks; and rhinos about twice the size of the present black rhino. There are many popular reconstructions of the country, the fauna and of man himself, particularly in the articles which have appeared at intervals in the *National Geographic Magazine* and in *Early Man* in the *Life* Nature Library series.

Whilst the above in no way gives a full and balanced picture of Olduvai and its treasures, enough has been said to show that here we have something of world wide significance and interest. Now, what about the survival issue? It may appear paradoxical that the extinct species of man and other animals of the past can help to preserve the present day fauna for the edification and pleasure of men of the future, but this is indeed so. Tourism can play an important part in the present day economy of emergent African nations. East Africa's greatest attraction for tourists is its rich and varied wildlife, and by a combination of chance and foresight all three countries, Kenya, Tanzania and Uganda, have preserved wildlife, and the wild places, to about the same degree. It would be foolish to disguise the fact that there is an element

Wild dogs are transient animals, here today and gone tomorrow. They are relentless and efficient hunters who, once they have selected their quarry, seldom fail to bring it to bay and effect a rapid kill. Here the prey is a Grant's gazelle

Elephant inhabit the thick forest all round Ngorongoro, and some live in Lerai forest within the Crater. Here a very fine tusker is changing his home from the rim to Lerai

of competition involved, and that Kenya, by virtue of its position as a centre of communication, and by its lead in the race, is attracting the bulk of the East African tourist trade. Ngorongoro is of course a tremendous asset to Tanzania, but many of the features to be seen here can equally well be seen in the Kenya or Uganda Parks. But no other has an Olduvai within its borders, and this, if fully exploited, can 'give an edge' to the Manyara-Ngorongoro-Serengeti circuit.

A good proportion of tourists on the trip between Ngorongoro and Seronera now turn in to Olduvai. It is only since 1962 that Dr Leakey and his organisation, with help from the Conservation Unit and the Department of Antiquities, have catered for and tried to attract tourists. The following figures show how successful these efforts have been: 1962, 2–300 visitors; 1963, 600; 1964, 1,240; 1965, 3,333; and 1966, 5,499. This means that one in four visitors to Ngorongoro now visit Olduvai. It appears that the Ngorongoro growth rate is 30%; if Olduvai, currently doubling its numbers every year, settles down to the same rate as Ngorongoro it can expect 57,000 visitors by 1975. Fantastic? Not so fantastic when one considers the development of supersonic aircraft, giant helicopters, hovercraft, jumbo jets, and all the modern developments in transport. Are the people of the world sufficiently interested to enable this growth rate to be maintained? Here are some figures to consider. When the TV show 'Dr Leakey and the Dawn of Man' was screened in the United States in November, 1966, according to one system of rating, 26.2 million people viewed the show. Another rating gave the figure as 27.2 million.

In the United States one park alone, Yellowstone, attracted 2,200,000 visitors in 1967 whilst the total for all parks in 1966 reached 112,000,000, a growth from 2,054,000 in 1925. This represents a growth rate of just over 10% per annum. So it is not so fantastic to consider 50,000 visitors to Olduvai in the foreseeable future.

The necessity from the scientific angle for continuing and expanding the research work at Olduvai is irrefutable. The figures quoted show that it is also economically advantageous to preserve, to develop research, and to provide visitors' facilities on an ever expanding basis; and of these the basic requirement is *preservation*.

Here there arises the problems of trampling of sites by herds of Masai cattle, and to a lesser degree by game. Great damage has already been caused: in one case a human skull was broken into fragments little larger than grains of rice. After considerable negotiation between

10

Dr Leakey, the local Masai and the Government Ministries concerned, it was agreed in 1965 that Dr Leakey should build a series of dams in the parts of the gorge which were not important, to divert the cattle from trekking down to water and trampling the deposits in the places that did matter.

The goodwill of the Masai Rain-God was also apparent as early storms quickly filled the dams; the co-operation of the Masai herdsmen was, alas, less forthcoming. Whilst not neglecting the convenience that the dams provided for cattle watering the young Masai herdsmen were not only failing to keep cattle out of the enclosed areas, but were deliberately opening gaps in the fences to drive their cattle in. But the height of vandalism was reached when a group of moran (warriors) looking for a sheltered site in which to hold a meat feast – they frequently use caves for this – broke into the enclosed museum-on-the-spot which preserves man's first known dwelling; nearly two million years old. They lit a fire and considerably disturbed part of the ancient hut circle. Fortunately the Leakeys' work is so meticulous that the position of each individual stone is plotted on a plan, so that the relic can be restored, but that does not lessen the seriousness of the offence. Tanzania cannot permit the wanton destruction of her treasures any more than Greece can permit its building contractors to demolish the temples on the Acropolis for building stone, or France to allow its beatniks to throw stones through its cathedral windows, or America to grant concessions to lumbermen to fell the last of its giant redwoods. It is a sad reflection on western civilization that these things have been happening; either greed, or lack of appreciation, or worst of all, the folly of war, have played such havoc with man's heritage. But that is no excuse; rather it is all the more reason why the world's treasures, of which Olduvai is indisputably one, should be meticulously safeguarded.

The archaeological interest of the Conservation Area is not, however, confined to Olduvai. An interesting site exists on the western end of the Doinyoogol Hills. Named in the textbooks Apis Rock, its correct name is Nasera, derived from the Masai root meaning to mark or write; this originated in the streaks of weathering down the side of the rock.

The rock is a magnificent boulder more than 100 feet high. One feature is a rock shelter the roof of which is nearly 50 feet above the ground and the overhang large enough to cover a Masai encampment: the inhabitants have left their signatures in the visitor's book in the

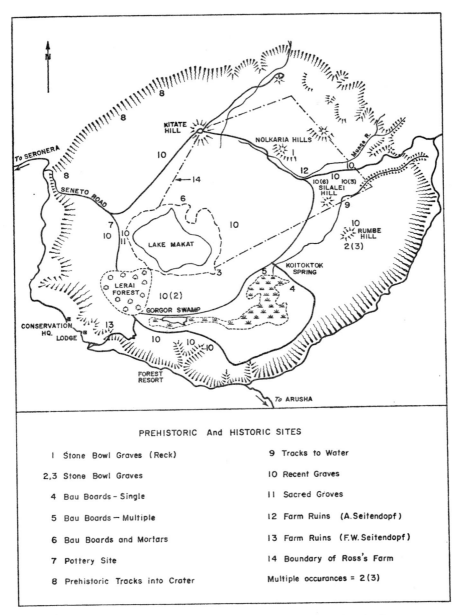

PREHISTORIC And HISTORIC SITES

1	Stone Bowl Graves (Reck)	9	Tracks to Water
2,3	Stone Bowl Graves	10	Recent Graves
4	Bau Boards – Single	11	Sacred Groves
5	Bau Boards — Multiple	12	Farm Ruins (A. Seitendopf)
6	Bau Boards and Mortars	13	Farm Ruins (F.W. Seitendopf)
7	Pottery Site	14	Boundary of Ross's Farm
8	Prehistoric Tracks into Crater		Multiple occurances = 2 (3)

Fig. 5 Ngorongoro Crater showing prehistoric and historic sites

form of Masai shield patterns painted on the rock face. To one side of the shelter is a much lower overhang area used by Masai warriors for their meat feasts, but the main archaeological interest lies in the excavations conducted here by Dr Leakey in 1932. Specimens of middle and late stone-age cultures have been found here, the earliest dating from possibly 30,000 to 10,000 BC – when Europe was in the throes of the last ice age – up to quite recent late stone-age finds, fashioned when man had already discovered how to make pottery.

Considering that its area is only 100 square miles, the Crater floor is extraordinarily rich in proto-historic remains. It is not only in recent years that Ngorongoro has been considered attractive by man. There are numerous graves of varying origin, grinding mortars formed out of the living rock, stone *bau* boards, used for a game analogous to chess or drafts, obsidian blades and barbs, various types of pottery, and ancient cattle tracks, see Fig. 5.

The first find, one of the earliest archaeological sites recognised in Tanzania, was the graves in the neighbourhood of Siedentopf's farm. When this pioneer was seeking building material for his house and barns, the ruins of which can still be seen, his assistants and labourers picked up loose stones from the neighbouring hills some of which proved to have come from cairns: as early as 1908 human remains, and 'vessels' (doubtless stone bowls) were noted, but it was not till 1912 that the cairns were recognised as burial mounds. Thereupon an assistant of Siedentopf's named Rothe excavated a mound, unearthing human remains, stone bowls and obsidian flakes. Later in 1915 Dr Arning, a geologist, undertook a more careful excavation, and then in March 1916 Professor Reck excavated yet another.

It was later in the same year that the Germans retreated from northern Tanzania and unfortunately most of the excavated material from Ngorongoro was lost in the retreat.

In 1941 Mrs Leakey and the late Dr Trevor conducted further excavations, the results of which have been published recently by Mrs Leakey in *Tanzania Notes and Records*, No. 66. Dr Trevor, a physical anthropologist, did not publish his findings, but the material is carefully preserved at Cambridge.

Briefly, the Ngorongoro graves have revealed multiple burials: these have been thought by some to indicate the burial of a chief whose wives and/or slaves were buried with him. Mrs Leakey, in the light of her own work, considers them to be family or clan burial grounds, the grave being reopened from time to time, whereby the earlier burials were disturbed. The finds in the graves included stone bowls, beads and pendants, and obsidian flakes. No pottery was unearthed.

Further excavations were undertaken in 1967 by Mr Hamo Sassoon, Tanzania's Conservator of Antiquities. Although the results have not yet been published it is understood that they confirm and amplify, but in no way contradict, the conclusions drawn from earlier research.

Although the human remains have not been scientifically described, it can certainly be stated that they represent a long-headed, long-faced people, representatives of an earlier race of people who lived in eastern Africa prior to the advent of the present inhabitants.

Dr and Mrs Leakey have conducted excavations in Kenya at Nakuru and Njoro River which revealed several features comparable with Ngorongoro. Particularly in relation to the latter Mrs Leakey records: 'The occurrence of stone beads and pendants, of which two other isolated examples are known from East African sites, together with the similarity in material culture and in the disposition of the burials, cannot be purely matters of coincidence, and it must be accepted that the two sites are closely connected.'

This association helps to provide an answer to the question everyone asks; 'How old are these graves?' The Njoro river cave material has been dated by the Carbon 14 method as around 900 BC. So it is at least safe to say that Ngorongoro graves can be dated in millennia rather than centuries.

These early graves are different in construction from the later cairns erected by subsequent inhabitants. The early graves consist of large stones now frequently covered with humus so that only the tops of the stones emerge above ground: if in a position where silting is impossible, as on a rocky hillside, they form impressive structures. The later cairns (it is premature to call them graves till further excavation has been done – though they most probably are) consist of much smaller stones, heaped up on the flats. They have not been in existence long enough to be held together by accumulations of silt, and so have become widely dispersed through the trampling of wildlife and cattle. Both the Tatog, neighbouring Nilo-Hamitic pastoralists believed at one time to have inhabited the Crater, and the Masai, mark the graves of important elders, but insufficient evidence exists to ascribe these cairns to any particular tribe.

Pottery, significantly absent from the early graves, is also found at certain spots in the Crater in circumstances which indicate that it is of considerable antiquity. But here again insufficient evidence exists to give a date to the pottery and a name to its makers. Other surface finds occurring in the Crater are blades and flakes of obsidian and chert. These minerals are not found in the Crater, so their presence indicates considerable mobility on the part of their users: which is of course only to be expected of hunters.

At Keshei Hill (Fig Tree Kopje) grinding and pounding mortars have been hollowed out of the rock (lava). Their existence does not necessarily indicate the presence of agriculturists in the Crater at some past period. Hunters and food gatherers equally require grindstones to treat the roots, bark and seeds which they use as food. Even today Masai use these very mortars for crushing the red ochre which some still use for adorning their persons and clothing on ceremonial occasions.

At the same spot and in the same rocky outcrop is to be found an example of a *bau* board, fashioned in stone. These 'boards', consisting of rows of holes used for a game common throughout Africa are more frequently made of wood, hence the English 'board' – c.f. chess or draft board – and the Swahili *bau*, meaning board. The existence of this relic accounts for the Masai name for this spot *En doinyo en Keshei*, 'the hillock of the *bau* board'.

Other examples can be seen in the neighbourhood of Koitoktok, both at the spring and out on the open plain. On the plain there are a remarkable number of boards in a very confined area – no similar occurrence is known in Africa. Although I thought, in common with others whose work has taken them in and around Ngorongoro, that I was well acquainted with the Crater floor, it was only a year or two ago that a Masai led me to this unique proto-historic feature.

The Masai are enthusiastic devotees of this game and it is said that keen gamblers can win or lose a considerable herd of cattle at this play. The game appears in many forms – sometimes a board of 8 holes long by 4 broad is used, as amongst the Sukuma. The Masai use a board of 8 by 2. Wins and losses are recorded by the passage of the wooden counters, called and shaped like tusks. Other tribes use a board 9 by 2, whilst Dr Leakey has found two row boards up to 13 holes long, which appear to be associated with the pre-historic Gumban graves in Kenya. From this it might be thought that the existence of a particular type of board in a particular area would be conclusive evidence that people of the tribes using that type of board once inhabited the area. But such conclusions might well be erroneous, as Masai herdboys have been observed pecking out additional holes with their spear butts, thereby elongating existing boards. No valid reason exists for this practice, as the boards are thereby lengthened beyond the requirements of the game as played by the Masai. The answer appears to be that they do it 'for kicks' to alleviate the boredom of herding.

Another type of evidence as to the previous inhabitants of the Crater is cattle tracks, like those so conspicuous on the west wall of the Crater. Similar tracks are to be found throughout the highlands, some in forested areas where large trees are found to be growing in the bottom of deep-cut tracks. This is evidence not only of age, but also of the fact that the tracks have not been cut any deeper during the life of the trees. These tracks take another form in the northern and eastern corners of the Crater, where a number of depressions lead down from the surrounding grassland to the valley of the Lonyokie stream. These have obviously been eroded in the past, but are at too frequent intervals to represent water erosion caused by rainfall run-off: furthermore the erosion has ceased and they are now grass covered. A feasible explanation is that at some time in the past there existed settled villages in the vicinity, and that cattle trekked to water down regular tracks, which in the course of time wore down and formed these gullies. This and other evidence indicates that the land of the Crater highlands was in the past subject to greater pressure than it is today under the Masai.

In this connection an interesting series of 'dams' can be seen on the Loirobi grasslands: the road to the Serengeti in fact passes along the crest of one such dam. These features are rightly called 'dams', if by this we mean a barrier in a streambed which holds back water. But it is a matter of opinion whether such dams were deliberately constructed by human effort, or are the accidental bi-product of soil-wash down cattle tracks. I myself favour the latter view, but the supporting evidence is too long and detailed to be recorded here, and will I hope be published elsewhere.

Several archaeological features of national significance occur in northern Tanzania outside, but close to, the Conservation Area. It is appropriate that they should be mentioned here, as a visit to these sites could well fit in with specially organised 'archaeological' tours – also including Olduvai and Ngorongoro – and so contribute to the cause of survival.

The first site is at Engaruka at the foot of the Rift Wall adjacent to the Conservation Area boundary, about 35 miles north of Mto-wa-mbu. The site is about five miles long and consists of massive stone circles on the gentle slopes at the base of the Rift Wall, many hundreds of platforms cut and hut sites built into the steeper slopes of the foothills and numerous stone cairns. On the plains below are to be found two elaborate field systems, each covering about 500 acres, which were perhaps irrigated in the past from the Engaruka river, a delightful stream dependent on water conserved in the Ngorongoro highlands: after flowing a short distance into the plains it loses itself in the sands of the Engaruka depression.

Although Dr Leakey's preliminary work of 1935 has been followed by more detailed study by the Tanzania Department of Antiquities, it is as yet too early for the full story of Engaruka to be told. Although irrigation and the system of building house-site platforms at the foot of a steep scree slope is practised by the Sonjo tribe some fifty miles to the north of Engaruka, it would be rash to postulate any direct connection between the two: the similarities may merely indicate a common reaction to similar circumstances. The pottery so far found has a very distinct form of decoration which bears no resemblance to any known pottery from Kenya or Tanzania. Datings have been obtained by the Carbon 14 method on charcoal from one of the stone circles of 1460 AD $\pm$ 90 years, and from the hillside sites of 1445 to 1750 AD. When further work permits more definite statements, no doubt the site will be fully signposted and provided with guides and a handbook issued.

The Kondoa rock paintings, lying from 140 (nearest) to 180 (farthest) miles to the south of Ngorongoro, provide a larger and more developed gallery of rock art than any other site in East Africa, and rival in interest the rock paintings of South Africa and Rhodesia. They have already been the subject of considerable study and publications and guides are available to visitors at the sites.

The northern shores of Lake Eyasi are of interest archaeologically, as it was here on his 1934–6 expedition that Dr Kohl Larsen found skull fragments of ancient man. Portions of three skulls were discovered, but only one yielded sufficient material to permit an attempt at re-construction. From the meagre evidence available it appears that 'Eyasi Man' represents one of the branches of the human stock which reached a dead end, as did Neanderthal Man at a later date. The Eyasi remains come from upper Pleistocene beds and equate most closely to 'Rhodesian Man' from Broken Hill (now named Kabwe) in Zambia, some 900 miles to the south.

Back now from the past to the present – how can all these relics of the past be led to serve the cause of survival? The answer lies in multipurpose tourism: Ngorongoro is particularly richly endowed not only with its wildlife, but with scenic grandeur, geological interest and archaeological remains. If each aspect is preserved and developed it reinforces the status of the other features.

As long term policy I would like to see the road constructed which I envisaged in Chapter II, from Empakaai via Lengai to Engaruka. This would enable not only a most spectacular general tour but also a specialised archaeological tour to be offered to the public. This could in fact be inaugurated straight away, but with a bit of repetition, using the same road twice. It would run something like this: first day leave Arusha, visit Engaruka, sleep Manyara; second day to Ngorongoro, day in Crater visiting sites, sleep at rim accommodation; third day, Olduvai and thence Nasera Rock, where a small lodge might well be established. But even without this, Nasera can be visited from Olduvai and the party could sleep at Ngorongoro or Seronera as desired. To include the Kondoa rock paintings would be possible, but the visit would be less tiring if rest house facilities could be developed at one of the sites to make this a two day diversion.

This chapter should not be closed without reference to the fact that just as the flora and fauna of Tanzania is protected by National Parks, Game Reserves, Conservation Areas, etc., so are the nation's archaeological treasures protected by law.

Under an Act of Parliament passed in 1964 to replace previous legislation, Reserved Areas are declared in which it is illegal to ex-cavate or disturb material without permit, and from which the public are forbidden to pick up or remove any object of archaeological or historical significance. Within and adjacent to the boundaries of the Conservation Area the following areas have been declared: Olduvai – the whole length of the gorge, Engaruka, West Eyasi and East Eyasi – to cover areas where ancient skulls have been discovered;

Nasera Rock, and the whole of the floor of the Crater. The Conservator of Antiquities and the Conservator of Ngorongoro co-operate closely with Dr Leakey and other workers in the field to ensure that these very necessary rules are enforced.

9 Tribal Man

There is no doubt that the Ngorongoro area has been hunted over for millenia. The stone-age folk living at Nasera Rock several thousand years ago were most certainly hunters. In Chapter V, I have quoted several references to the trade in rhino horn along the East African coast, dating from the first century AD onwards. Every reference to rhino horn is coupled with the trade in ivory, which is also referred to by many additional authorities. The earliest missionary map, 1848, shows the area beyond Kilimanjaro as inhabited by Wandorobo (i.e. hunters), 'a very poor people despised and maltreated by all tribes around'; the next map, 1870, shows the area west of the Rift in the neighbourhood of Serengeti as 'country of the Wabilikimo or Pigmies', and also shows specific Dorobo villages. By 1882 the Serengeti is correctly placed and marked 'open pastoral', whilst immediately to the west, roughly around Banagi, is shown the country of the Wandorobo described on the map as 'a tribe of elephant hunters who neither cultivate nor keep cattle'.

Dorobo or Ndorobo, plural Wandorobo, is a name given in up-country Swahili to the hunting tribes, irrespective of their ethnic group; it may come from the Masai root meaning 'short'. Some confusion may arise as the word is also applied to tsetse fly. There are in fact many different types of 'Dorobo' or hunters, two of which are found in and around the Conservation Area.

First there are the Hadza (singular Hadzabi) centred mainly in the Eyasi trough. These folk resemble the Bushmen of southern Africa in several respects. They both speak a 'click' language, they live by hunting and food-gathering and they smoke a tubular stone pipe. The Hadza differ from the Bushmen physically; they are much larger, and dark-skinned, in contrast to the small delicately formed, light-skinned bushmen. They use an extraordinarily large bow about 6′ 6″ long – with arrows to match; this is a much bigger bow than that used by the Masai-speaking Dorobo, bigger than the bow of any of the adjacent Bantu tribes, and much bigger than the South African Bushman's small bow and reed arrow. Research has revealed that the major portion of their food comes from their food gathering activities rather than from hunting. They are few in number, only about 500, and their impact on the wildlife is no more than any other predator, well within the limit for the species concerned. There is no record of their having entered into the ivory or rhino horn trade; in fact the group I contacted several years ago had no use for money and were only persuaded to part with bows, arrows, and other items of their material culture required as museum specimens on a basis of barter for cloth, beads, etc.

The other hunters which concern us are the Masai-speaking Dorobo. They form in effect a lower caste of Masai, a social situation not uncommon amongst the pastoralists of Africa. It occurs for instance amongst the Somali, where the hunters and the smiths are regarded as low caste. Amongst the Masai the smiths are similarly placed; their wives are also potters, where suitable clay is found, and the caste provides the circumcisors for the tribe.

It is most probably this type of Dorobo to whom the early mission records refer; these are certainly the people whom Dr Baumann found in the Crater when he visited it in 1892. His description of 'a Wandorobo camp, the surrounding of which was littered by game refuse, over which ravens, marabus and vultures were fighting', tallies entirely with my own impressions of the Dorobo camp which I visited at Engare Nanyuki on the northern Serengeti in 1935. These folk sometimes acquire a few cattle, and some become rich enough to 'pass' as Masai. But as a Dorobo of another group explained to me: 'When we get cattle from marrying one of our girls to the Masai, we eat them, even heifers, so then we have no means of acquiring other girls to replace those who have left our group.' In this way social custom and food habits are leading the group to extinction.

From the records, e.g. the 1882 missionary map quoted above, it looks as though these people hunted for profit as well as for a livelihood. But there is no evidence that, with their poisoned arrows, they did more than crop the wildlife at a level of sustained yield, and the impact of these hunters was doubtless greater on the environment than on the stock of wildlife. For they were frequent users of fire, not only in connection with their hunting, but equally as an adjunct to their honey collecting activities. On the other hand, the traders themselves, with their muzzle-loading muskets, must have commenced the devastation of wildlife which the Europeans who followed them so effectively continued.

When one mentions pastoralists in association with Ngorongoro one naturally thinks of the Masai, the present occupants of the Area and the Crater, around whose presence there so much controversy has raged. But another Nilo-Hamitic tribe of pastoralists has also been associated with the Crater in the past, some of whom still live in the south of the Area. These are the Tatog, associated culturally and linguistically more with the Nandi and Kipsigis of Kenya than with the Masai. Divided into small sub-tribes, they moved down from Kenya many generations ago, some to settle to the west of the Serengeti, some to the south of the Wembere Steppe, and some to Mbulu District immediately to the south of Ngorongoro. The largest group, called Barabaig, live round Mount Hanang, a 12,000 foot extinct volcano whose peak is visible from the Crater rim. A small section lives in the Lake Eyasi trough, some families making their homes within the boundary of the Conservation Area.

There is no doubt that at some time in the past some of these folk lived in the Ngorongoro highlands, and in the Crater. The Masai deny this, for fear of weakening their claim to this country, but up till very recently members of the Tatog tribe used to come back to the Crater and perform religious ceremonies at certain sacred trees. This group *may* also be responsible for some of the grave cairns in the Crater, for the Tatog perform very elaborate funeral ceremonies: today, however, these rites are centred round pylons constructed with poles and mud, and not cairns of stones.

The impact of the Tatog on wildlife is made in the following some-what bizarre manner: for certain reasons the underprivileged in Tatog society can attain status, socially and sexually, by proving themselves as hunters. As proof of their prowess they must produce trophies before their elders or their girlfriends from certain acceptable animals – elephant, lion, buffalo, etc; human beings also fall into this category. Unfortunately, what was doubtless instituted as a test of bravery has degenerated into a custom of cold-blooded murder. Women and children of neighbouring tribes, out cutting firewood, are attacked in the bush, beaten to death and mutilated by the removal of an ear, a finger or a breast. In spite of constant Government vigilance and numerous convictions and hangings, sporadic outbursts of this degenerate barbarous custom still occur.

We have had no case of such murder in the Conservation Area, but there have been cases of the wanton killing of lion, and for this reason, pressure was exerted to get the few Tatog inhabitants moved back to the Mbulu District. I do not know how the matter now stands.

Turning now to the Masai it is impossible to appreciate their position in Ngorongoro both past and future, without some knowledge of their history, their social organisation and their mode of life. The Masai are a Nilo-hamitic tribe of pastoralists who have earned for themselves a place in history out of all proportion to their numerical strength. The same can of course be said of many people of an aggressive disposition and/or a strong belief in their culture. The Masai came down in the past from the north and, by the middle of the last century, their territory or raiding radius covered Kenya from Lake Victoria to Mombasa and extended south beyond the Central Railway of Tanzania.

It is however a mistake to imagine that they dominated the whole area. They had no genius or inclination for conquest and the governing of subject people. In general they occupied the plains and grasslands, whilst the agriculturists – mainly Bantu – inhabited the salubrious highlands and mountain slopes which stand up from the plains of Eastern Africa as islands of fertility and plentiful rainfall in a sea of semi-desert.

In the period immediately prior to the 1890 famine, of which more anon, the records of missionaries and explorers confirm that, whilst the Masai most certainly raided the agricultural tribes they also traded with them. Contrary to popular belief the Masai do not live on a diet of blood and milk. True, the warriors consume these foods extensively, plus the meat eaten at the meat feasts held in special camps. The elders, women and young folk eat considerable amounts of agricultural crops, cereals, beans, bananas, etc. In the past they obtained these from the hill dwellers at barter markets at numerous points on the foot hills where highlands and plains meet. Many such traditional markets still exist today, held at regular fixed intervals. The market cycle, four day, seven day, or eight day as the case might be, virtually establishes a local 'week', which varies from place to place – a system which has the advantage of ensuring that market days in adjacent areas do not clash with each other. From such markets the Masai carried the agricultural produce of the hills far out into the arid steppe land, whilst the hill folk took back with them the products of the plains, sour milk in large quantities, hides for grain bags, calf and sheep skins for garments.

Today the exchange of hill crops for the produce of the plains still goes on, with certain modern adaptations. The traditional means of transport to and from the markets, pack donkeys, whilst still used in large numbers, are supplemented by motor lorries: the four gallon kerosene tin is used side by side with the indigenous gourd. Urbanisation and close settlement in the hills has made firewood a scarce commodity, so it is now a valuable item of trade. Modern trade goods, colourful cloth and beads, cooking pots, both locally produced clay pots and imported metal – all these figure in the markets of today. The two most colourful and popular markets which can easily be seen by the visitor, are at Himo to the east of Moshi at the base of Kilimanjaro, and at Engare ol Motonyi on the Ngorongoro road to the west of Arusha.

This system was, and still is, of great dietary significance both for the hill folk and for the plains dwellers. From the point of view of the Chagga or the Arusha, the inevitable protein shortage of the agriculturist was met in the past by trade with the Masai. This is still largely so today, though as well as the surviving barter markets there are now stock markets organised by the Government, with veterinary control to prevent the spread of disease. Though this marketing system is currently under some strain, at its best it channelled some 42,000 head of cattle per annum from the Masai of Tanzania to the consumers – largely the coffee-producing Chagga and the workers on the sisal estates. This trade, at present day prices, involves the injection of a little under half a million pounds – something over a million dollars – into the Masai economy. The cereals which this system brings into the Masai economy – by barter in the old days, today by the sale of maize flour through the shops – supplements the heavy protein diet of the Masai. Apart from the milk consumed, a census reveals that the Ngorongoro Masai slaughter for home consumption some five to six thousand head per year, i.e. between 4 % and 5 % of their total herds.

This dietary system has a considerable impact on wildlife survival at both ends. The Masai, being protein sufficient, have no urge to kill the wildlife which surrounds them in such abundance. The Chagga, the

Arusha, and other hill tribes having available, and being able to pay for an adequate supply of protein, have no physiological urge to go out poaching. The wildlife both in the forests of Kilimanjaro and of Meru, and on the plains below, is relatively unmolested. It is certainly not subjected to the large-scale commercialised poaching which is such a regrettable feature of other parts of East Africa where protein-starved agricultural people abut on heavily stocked wildlife areas.

We have, however, digressed from the Masai, about whose social and political organisation and history we must know more before we can fully appreciate their position in the survival picture.

The state of equilibrium then existing between agriculturist and pastoralist and between man and wildlife was rudely disturbed when around 1890 the Masai were hit by a triple disaster, smallpox which decimated the human population, rinderpest, a virulent bovine disease which nearly annihilated the herds of cattle and many species of wildlife as well, and an invasion of locusts which by destroying the grazing made recovery more difficult. As a result the raiding potential of the Masai was reduced to vanishing point.

Some writers talk of the 'military power of the Masai', but that suggests an organised military machine under a single command implementing a national policy. No such 'nation wide' co-ordination existed, and to understand the reason for this it is necessary to look at the Masai social and political organisation. There is not, nor did there ever exist, a single 'chief' of the Masai, at the apex of a pyramid of subchiefs and headmen such as was found in certain African states. Instead the Masai were organised in a truly democratic fashion, by a system based on age-sets. Under this system all the youths, on attaining the age of 16 or thereabouts, are circumcised and accepted into a particular age-set, a unit possessing a single name and a sense of unity. The initiates over a period of some 7 years all enter one set and thereafter a new set with a new name is formed. It is rather like belonging to the 1953 army call-up, or the 1949 year at Oxford or Harvard. One essential difference is that such groups are exclusive, whereas the Masai age-sets are inclusive; anyone who claims to be a Masai must be initiated and enter an age-set.

As the years go by an individual climbs from grade to grade, but not by individual promotion; the whole set moves up after certain elaborate ceremonies have been performed, first from junior to senior warriorhood, and then to elderhood and marriage. The elders them-

An early safari in the Crater taken in 1923, this photograph shows Norman Livermore from San Francisco, second from left, with his companion A. Newbury and two professional hunters, A. J. Hunter, extreme left, and A.P. de K. Fourie, extreme right

A Masai village, note the complete lack of fencing, although a pride of lion is resident a mile or two away. Children are greeting an elder

The last drop!

A young married Masai woman, resident in the Crater

A Masai woman standing at the edge of the Crater wearing traditional bead necklaces and embroidered leather garments. The two garments indicate married status

selves are graded, with varying duties, being first junior elders, then senior elders and finally 'elder statesmen' without formal status.

The warriors are under the tutelage of the grade next-but-one above them, who are their teachers and mentors; by being in control of the warriors, these are the virtual rulers of the tribe. Each age-set appoints leaders, basically at local level – i.e. covering a group between whom association and contact is reasonably possible. In this connection it must be borne in mind that a pastoral people are naturally very thin on the ground, and that close contact between large numbers is impossible. But from time to time the local groups get together for ceremonial purposes and more occasionally the whole of a sub-tribe's warriors may assemble – as for promotion ceremonies.

A counterbalance to the power of the age-set leaders is the *laiboni*, the prophet or seer who must be consulted before any of the ceremonies mentioned above may be performed. There is no one *laibon* or paramount seer for the whole of Masai, each sub-tribe or group of sub-tribes recognising a different spiritual head. But by tradition certain rights in respect of the whole tribe are vested in the seer of certain sub-tribes. Thus the Kisongo *laibon* is responsible for choosing the name of the age-set for the whole of Masai when the junior and senior warriors amalgamate to form a single generation.

It is of course the warrior grades which provide the picturesque figure of the typical Masai 'moran' or warrior. Apart from the calf-skin, hip-length cloak, now frequently replaced by an ochre-dyed cotton cloth, the moran's panoply has shown little change over the years. Efforts by the Tanzanian Government to replace the short red cloth by modern clothing are described below (p. 163). The hairstyle consists of one major queue or pigtail down the back, two minor ones over each ear and a small one hanging over the forehead. The hair is heavily dressed with ochre and mutton fat and is allowed to grow to considerable length. On certain ceremonial occasions the pigtail may be undone to form tresses falling over the shoulders to the middle of the back.

Adornment consists of bead and brass ornaments in the ear lobes, which have normally been pierced and extended so that they form elongated loops reaching down almost to the shoulders. An armlet of buffalo horn, with two protruding antennae may be worn on the upper arm, brass rings on the fingers, and heavy iron bells, in the shape of bean pods, strapped around the thighs. The ankles are frequently adorned with black and white anklets made from the skin of colobus monkeys.

The headdress shows considerable variation. The most coveted status symbol is a lion-mane headdress, reserved for those who on a lion hunt have been awarded the mane. But other striking headdresses are made from colobus monkey skin, or from ostrich feathers in the form of a mask. The vulture feather cape worn over the shoulders is made to resemble a lion's mane, which makes the warrior appear more fearsome to his enemies.

The arms carried consist primarily of a long-bladed spear – in the past the blade was broad and shovel shaped, which shows that fashions even in the most basic piece of equipment can change amongst the most conservative people. The 'side arms' consist of a short, razor-sharp, double-bladed sword carried in a red leather sheath, and suspended from a belt, into which is tucked a short, heavy knobkerry. A large shield is carried, made of heavy hide, either buffalo or occasionally giant forest hog. The markings on the shield indicate the group to which the warrior belongs, whilst sometimes individual marks for bravery are carried.

The warrior grade had the duty of defending the cattle against predators or hostile neighbours and of attacking non-Masai cattle owners in the vicinity with a view to returning home with booty to increase the wealth of the group. This, incidentally, meant that new blood was constantly being introduced into the herds which thus became a mixture of many breeds and strains, not excluding the long-horned Ankole stock. The Masai cattle are larger than those of their Bantu neighbours, not because they are of a different breed or strain, but largely because of the better nutrition provided by skilled nomadic pastoralists, in contrast to static agriculturists: 'One part breeding, nine parts feeding', as the British farmer used to say.

The young uncircumcised boys, who have not attained warrior status, do most of the herding. They can be recognised by their short calf-skin cloak and short-bladed spear. They go through a long informal training in herdsmanship, beginning at an early age with the lambs and kids, then moving on to the calves which are herded separately near the homestead, then the sheep and goats which go further afield, and finally the adult cattle. By this time, in their early teens, these lads are steeped in bush-lore, and as tough as nails. In addition to the incident of the two herdboys spearing an elephant described above (p. 103), there are numerous cases of such boys tackling lion, leopard, etc., both single handed and in groups.

Immediately after circumcision, the boys go through a phase of not belonging: they are neither youths nor warriors. This status is symbolised by the wearing of the long (woman's) cloak; they paint their faces with designs in white and wear headdresses of ostrich feathers supplemented by the skins of small birds which they shoot with bows and blunt-headed arrows.

The elders have no formalised dress: the former status symbol of a cloak of blue-monkey skin is seldom seen nowadays. Sometimes leather cloaks can be seen, but the standard dress is an imported blanket – second-hand imported greatcoats are also in favour – frequently supplemented by a European-type hat, or even in cold areas a woollen 'Balaclava helmet'. The popularity of imported clothes indicates that the Masai are willing to adapt their culture and their customs when they can do so without undermining their basic social structure or economic organisation. The elders have accepted a change in dress as this is a culture trait which does not hamper their nomadic way of life; likewise they accept with alacrity western drugs, both for their women and children and for their cattle: but they take slowly to the establishment of schools and of cattle dips, as these hamper their traditional migratory moves.

The above was written before the current (early 1968) campaign by the Regional Administration to force the Masai to wear 'modern' clothing. As in every controversial question, from teetotalism to mini-skirts, there are two sides to the issue. I have had the privilege of hearing the views of Mr A. W. Mwakangata, M.P., the energetic Regional Commissioner of the Arusha Region, under whose jurisdiction the whole of Tanzania Masailand lies. He, and indeed the TANU Government behind him is dedicated to the cause of change and modernisation. Mr Mwakangata made the point that he is not insistent on any particular type of dress – shorts and shirts, or whatever – for the Masai. All he insists on is that the Masai's clothes should firstly be decent and secondly clean. He feels, with justification, that the short ochre-dyed cloth of the moran fulfills neither of these requirements. If the Masai see fit to adapt their present clothing so that it more adequately covers the person, and is easily washable, by all means let them do so.

This estimable attitude fails to take sufficient consideration of three basic points. Firstly, most of the Masai live in such unhygienic conditions and so far from water that it is unpractical for them constantly to appear in a clean, freshly laundered set of clothes, whether togas or khaki shirts and shorts. First things first, the critics of the policy contend: lay on more water for the Masai, educate them to improve the hygiene of their homes, and the problem of dress will solve itself. Secondly it is a common feature of such campaigns that the good intentions of the top leaders are distorted by the lower echelons of the ruling party. Such a tendency has been seen in Zambia in the anti-miniskirt campaign where gangs of youths, acting in the name of the party, but actually contrary to its instructions and contrary to the law, have publicly humiliated and ridiculed girls and young women whose dress lengths they found unsatisfactory. There is an element of jealousy in such a situation; a girl dressed in a miniskirt has probably reached a stage of economic and social advancement beyond that of the youths concerned. It gives them sadistic satisfaction to disturb the status and poise of those whom they secretly feel are superior to themselves.

The same phenomenon appears to have arisen in Arusha where, according to a report in the London *Times* (8 February, 1968): 'Many Masai have been forcibly bathed, and scrubbed to remove their paint, and their tribal costumes have been publicly burnt.' Children, it appears, are encouraged to ridicule Masai who wear tribal dress, and bus drivers were ordered not to carry Masai who do not wear western dress. If accurately reported, these incidents certainly do not reflect the policy of Government and can only be interpreted as spiteful indiscipline in the lower echelons of the ruling party and amongst junior local officials.

The third neglected basic consideration I referred to earlier is the trait which makes an indigenous people likely to reject something which they regard as a threat to their social cohesion and group solidarity. That is just how the Masai must inevitably regard this movement. In fact that is how it is interpreted by critics of the policy particularly those living north of the Kenya/Tanzania border. Their criticisms have appeared in the press under the headline 'Humiliation of Masai Tribe', with the treatment the Masai warriors are receiving described as 'psychological castration'. Because the present policy is regarded by its victims in this light – as any sociologist could have warned the Administration in advance that it would be – it seems unfortunate that it should be implemented in the manner reported just at the time when Government is anxious to improve the animal husbandry of the Masai, and to get more livestock onto the market. This can only be done if co-operation and goodwill exist between the Masai and the Government and it seems shortsighted to prejudice the existence of such harmony over a relatively minor problem, when such major issues are at stake.

Furthermore, if the pressure for change were to cause the age-set system to break down, a complete absence of discipline can be anticipated. It is often asserted that the moran system encourages cattle theft. Certainly this can happen at times, but when the leaders are prepared to co-operate with Government, there exists a machine to ensure that the whole age-set behaves itself. Without such a system a generation of unorganised, undisciplined youths will arise. In such circumstances it seems inevitable that they will 'gang up' into small groups intent on crime, a situation which will be much more difficult to deal with than the present one.

There exists, I appreciate, a natural resentment amongst many modern Tanzanians that some of their countrymen should be regarded as 'museum specimens' or 'tourist attractions'; there is even a misconception that the previous government deliberately refrained from developing the Masai for this reason. My personal view is that in an age of self-determination the individual should be offered the opportunity to change – schools, roads, markets, trade, goods, etc., rather than having the change imposed on him by force.

The Masai women do not have a formalised system of age-sets, but the unmarried girls, whose co-habitation with the warriors is socially accepted, can be recognised by their single leather garment and broad beaded belt. Married women wear two leather garments, a skirt and a cloak, together with a broad unbeaded leather belt. They are heavily adorned with bead necklaces and earrings, with extensive heavy armlets and anklets of iron wire. Whilst the dress and adornment of the Masai, particularly many items of the warriors' outfits, derives from the wildlife of the country, there are no 'fashions' or customs such as occur in other parts of the world (both primitive and advanced) which draw heavily on one particular species and so threaten its existence.

Another aspect of Masai life which minimises their impact on the environment is their mobility. They live in villages or encampments with the huts in a circle within the thorn-enclosed perimeter, with space for the cattle in the centre. These units are frequently referred to in error as *manyatta*, a term which should properly be confined to those villages inhabited only by a group of moran, together with their mothers, siblings and girl friends. The Swahili term *boma*, meaning enclosure, is locally used for a Masai dwelling unit, or encampment, and is used hereafter in that sense in anglicised form. A typical boma consists of a group of from two or three up to ten or a dozen families, each with a family head, his wives (each with her own hut) and children. It is frequently a fortuitous grouping, not always dependent on kinship: at times the nucleus of a boma is based on a group of age-mates who lived in a *manyatta* together and have continued to associate in elderhood. It is not an immutable group, as sometimes an elder moves off with his wives and his herds. Again a newcomer may join an existing boma: in which case his enclosure and huts can be seen as an excrescence breaking the circular symmetry of the original structure.

Ideally the Masai move at least twice a year – out to the plains during the rains, when normally dry gullies, depressions and rainponds fill with water and the arid countryside carries a flush of grass, then back as the dry season progresses to the permanent waters – rivers, springs, or wells, where the grazing has rested and accumulated during the rains. Frequently each move involves the construction of a new boma, as the old one may well have been burnt – though seldom deliberately. In some cases this constant cutting of brush for boma and house construction may put a strain on local vegetation, as out on the Serengeti Plains, where the only source of building material is around the rocky granite outcrops. But generally speaking there is so much brush about that this factor is negligible or even beneficial. Even where this attrition is damaging to the environment it is not a valid argument for the removal of the Masai (although it has been adduced as such), for the problem can these days be remedied very simply by carrying a few lorry loads of suitable material from an area where cutting can do no harm, to the area of the shortage. This is in fact what I did in the Crater, where thorn trees – which are of course popular for boma building – are scarce, and provide valuable habitat for animal and bird life. Bamboo, also useful in boma construction, was brought from Oldeani mountain, where cutting could not adversely effect the thousands of acres of solid bamboo growing there.

The disadvantages of this system of movement or transhumance are, ecologically speaking, minimal; the advantages are tremendous. In addition to the rotational benefits of grazing as outlined above, the scouring-out of cattle tracks to fixed dwellings is avoided. This track erosion is very marked amongst settled agricultural people who also possess cattle, especially in hilly country, as in the neighbouring districts of Mbulu and Kondoa.

The deserted boma is not often re-utilised and it is frequently burnt accidentally, which clears the site of fleas, bugs and ticks. Sometimes bomas are constructed of permanent materials – particularly cedar slats, a wood which is impervious to termite attack. Here again the site is moved from time to time, the stakes being pulled up and removed to the new site. But even if the permanent, dry-season boma remained constantly on one site, the system would still have the advantages of resting the grazing and curbing track erosion during the absence of the stock on the plains: only the loss of a new clean house site would be entailed.

I am not holding up this system as ideal – nothing is ideal in this world. It has several disadvantages, particularly on the social side, raising problems in the provision of education and other social services. Also the acquisition of what the economists call 'durable consumer goods' is inhibited: it is difficult to move sideboards or fridges by donkey! Not that the Masai feel any great urge for these manifestations of western culture, but if they could be stimulated to purchase them, they would sell more cattle to obtain the necessary cash – to the ecological benefit of the area they inhabit.

I do contend however, that where stock owners live in a country where large areas of grazing can only be utilised for part of the year, the system of transhumance is the only feasible way of using that country to the optimum benefit of the people concerned, and of the nation as a whole.

It is the solution which has been evolved by the Norwegians and the Swiss, whose upper pastures are snow-covered in the winter; by the inhabitants of Salonika and elsewhere where mosquitoes render low-lying swamplands unusable at certain seasons; by the Basuto and other tribes in temperate southern Africa, where a winter season renders the highlands untenable. There are those who think that the solution to the social and economic difficulties arising out of movement lies in getting the people concerned to 'settle down', to take up cultivation, and to live 'normal' sedentary lives. This idea is just too easy, an oversimplification which overlooks the damage which the tying-down of large herds of cattle will inevitably cause in the country. The grazing, unrested, will deteriorate and eventually be replaced by unpalatable grasses or inedible woody vegetation; erosion will occur down the cattle tracks. More subtle consequences will follow – a drop in the health and growth of the stock, due to the lack of minerals and trace elements which under the nomadic system, when lacking in one area were picked up in another.

It should, I feel, be the aim of those interested in the wellbeing both of the Masai and of the country they inhabit to encourage the growth of a modified system of transhumance such as is practised by, for instance, the Swiss or the Norwegians. They have their permanent homes, but in the summer the bulk of the stock moves to the alpine pastures herded by the young men. The family, however, remains at the permanent home, so schooling and medical services are uninter-rupted. Milch stock is also retained at base, so that the economies of milk, butter, and/or cheese production remain unhampered. In the case of the Masai certain difficulties arise over disease control amongst the stock, and particularly over East Coast fever, the effective control for which lies in dipping or spraying. This cannot be done out on the plains, so until veterinary science evolves more refined means of control a dual system must evolve. In spite of difficulties it should be possible for a portion of the herd, attached to the permanent home-stead, to be dipped regularly: it would still remain susceptible to East Coast fever and so incapable of going out onto the plains. The remaining portion of the herd would be dipped less frequently and allowed to develop its own natural immunity: it would thus be able to remain mobile and so take advantage of the temporary winter grazing on the plains.

There are unfortunately only a few areas in Tanzania's Masailand where such an ideal system can be practised; luckily Ngorongoro is one of them. To understand why this is so, it is necessary to go back into the history of the Masai, particularly since 1890. When the Germans and British occupied Tanzania and Kenya respectively, they found the Masai very weakened by the triple plagues of rinderpest, smallpox and locusts referred to above (p. 160). Both Governments adopted policies of restricting the reduced numbers of tribesmen and cattle to smaller areas, and making available the areas so freed of habitation as farms for alien immigrants. In Kenya, after declaring by formal treaty two reserves for the Masai to be valid 'as long as the Masai shall exist as a tribe', the Government bundled them all into the southern reserve and alienated the abandoned northern reserve to European settlers. This led to pressures in the south so that part of the sub-tribe called Purku penetrated as far south as Ngorongoro.

The Germans for their part pursued a similar policy and attempted to confine the Masai to the country south and east of the Great North Road. In furtherance of this policy they permitted the brothers Siedentopf to take up land in the Crater, set aside the Serengeti for sheep farming (though the idea was never implemented) and alienated numerous farms around Mounts Kilimanjaro, Meru and Monduli. By granting land and water rights over numerous small streams running from the mountains to the plains, they virtually 'picked the eyes' out of the country as far as the Masai were concerned. The latter were confined to the plains, and unable to practise their seasonal withdrawal to their erstwhile highland grazing and water reserves – now alienated.

The case for the two Governments, British and German, taking these steps was more valid at the time than appears in retrospect. For the Masai in both countries were in a very weakened condition. Their members were dispersed, many keeping themselves alive by agriculture, having been accepted into neighbouring tribes of cultivators; some lived by hunting; others again entered into virtual domestic slavery or concubinage in the households of the coastal people. The means by which the tribe succeeded in restoring its fortunes, in re-acquiring cattle and attaining considerable political influence is itself an epic of survival. It emphasises how the achievements of man derive from an inner fire which physical adversity is unable to quench. To tell the whole story is beyond the scope of this book, but one incident is worth recording.

In the early years of the century the Germans based at Moshi mounted punitive expeditions against the unsubdued tribes to the west: Iraqw, Tatog, Iramba etc. To reinforce their trained askari they enrolled Masai warriors as irregulars, who were paid by a share of the plundered cattle with which the expeditions returned from these forages. The cattle were brought to a spot between Arusha and Moshi which still bears the name acquired at that time 'Boma la Ngombe' – the enclosure of the cattle. Here the erstwhile Masai irregulars were employed as herdsmen, in which capacity they made the most of their opportunities by exchanging their (second rate) share of the plunder for the choicest heifers, which the Germans had retained for themselves. This, I am informed by several Masai, was the method whereby the family herds were restored.

By the time World War I broke out the Masai herds were considerable, but they could not re-establish their previous grazing pattern – with the highland waters and grazings taken up as farms. With the relaxation of administrative control during the war years, and with a build-up of people and stock, the Masai of the plains below Mount Meru, called Kissongo, felt the need for expansion. A number moved up with their cattle to the Ngorongoro area. Here the original sub-tribes had not achieved the same build-up, but the pressures from the Kenya side of the border had pushed down the Purku Masai as far as the Crater. The new mandate administration favoured their own people at the expense of the intruders from Kenya, and pushed the Purku back over the border. This then accounts for the fact that a considerable proportion of the Conservasion Area population originated in Kissongo.

The only German alienation in the Crater highlands had been the Siedentopf farms: of these the Lerai farm of W. F. Siedentopf, never legally alienated, was allowed to lapse whilst the Munge farm of Adolph Siedentopf was purchased after the war from the Custodian of Enemy Property by Sir Charles Ross, who undertook no development and did not enforce his rights. As a result the Masai were able to re-establish their pastoralism in and around Ngorongoro on the original basis of transhumance.

Presumably because most of the administrators and observers come from temperate climates, there has always been a tacit assumption that anyone, Masai included, prefers to live in the highlands rather than on the plains. It is true that the Masai have songs in praise of the highlands for which they have a specific term, *osobuko*, as distinct from *olpurkel*, the lowlands. Equally the Scots have many nostalgic lyrics about the Highlands and Islands, but that has not prevented these areas being virtually depopulated. In the same way the Masai, though sentimentally (and economically) attached to the highlands, prefers life on the plains. He considers that his cattle thrive better and fatten quicker there: his family are less liable to bronchial trouble than in the damp, misty, highlands and because the waters are temporary malaria usually presents no problem.

So there are many factors which will keep the Masai mobile if they are permitted by circumstance and encouraged by Government to remain so. There are also factors which tend to tie them down. Many elders like to see their wives take up a bit of maize cultivation, as this saves them from the necessity of selling cattle to purchase maize meal. But it is very poor landuse practice, since for the sake of a few sacks of maize, worth no more than one good ox, an elder may tie himself and his hundreds of cattle down in an area near a permanent water which should be rested during the rains.

Another factor inhibiting Masai mobility is the presence of the tsetse fly in large areas of his country, but as these pests are luckily non-existent in the Conservation Area, save around Lake Eyasi, it is not proposed to enlarge on the subject here.

By far the greatest factor which ties down the Masai, inhibits their movements, and leads to the distressing symptoms of erosion and vegetational change so apparent in other parts of Masailand is the loss of land which they have suffered. Their land and water resources have been subjected to this process of attrition by alienation to agriculturists since 1890. The unfortunate practice started in German days has been carried on right through the period of the British mandate and into the era of independence. For example, the 'Sanya corridor' comprised a series of German demarcated farms which the mandatory government held back from re-alienation so as to allow the Masai to the north and west of Kilimanjaro and Meru to cross over the saddle between the two mountains and utilise the grazing of the Sanya Plains and beyond. As part of the boundary readjustments which led to the notorious Meru land case the Masai lost this corridor and much of the Sanya Plains as well. To the west of Arusha hundreds of thousands of acres were alienated to form the Esimingor farms and ranches. Much of the area was infected by tsetse, but the existence of Masai watering troughs high up on Esimingor mountain testified to the fact that this area was used in emergency.

The same process is going on today. The new independent government of Tanzania has very rightly adopted a policy of non-tribalism. This has opened the door to non-Masai cultivators to go into Masai country, frequently with tractors and ploughs supplied by expatriates, and put large areas of grazing land under crops. Much of this is done under the guise of co-operating with the Masai to utilise their country to the full. Whether the share-cropping agreements are fair to the Masai is a matter for conjecture: what is certain is that they are unfair

172 Ngorongoro – The Eighth Wonder

to the land, which is literally 'mined' of its fertility, without thought to the application of fertilisers or anti-erosion measures.

The foregoing should not be taken to imply that there is no place for agriculture in Masailand, or indeed in the Conservation Area. There certainly should be both crop and fodder production, sited in suitable areas and conducted on lines to ensure the maintenance of and ultimate build-up of fertility. But, if the principles of optimum land use are to be applied there will always be room for, indeed a necessity for the pastoralist who is prepared to live a tough life out on the arid plains.

Following the hunters and pastoralists, who are the main inhabitants, the agriculturists must be described, but only briefly, as cultivators are not present in large numbers in the Conservation Area. Nonetheless the overall picture cannot be fully appreciated without these people, for even when they do not attempt to infiltrate the Area, their activities, even a hundred miles away, have repercussions on the wildlife whose distribution may be radically altered thereby.

The Iraqw or Mbulu, mentioned earlier (p. 23), are the Crater's closest agricultural neighbours. Their home country 40 miles south of the Crater is closely cultivated, with small gardens dug out of the hillside, carefully levelled and in some cases terraced. It may well be that the tradition of careful husbandry has enabled them to turn themselves into efficient modern wheat farmers. Their old production methods really proved too successful, as they did not suffer the periodic famines which kept down the numbers of their steppe-land neighbours. As a result of population pressure they had to spill out from their original homeland. This overspill began long ago, but was accelerated as modern conditions led to the cessation of tribal war, better hygiene and improved medical services. So the outward spread commenced, with the result today that the southern boundary of the Conservation Area abuts on fully developed farmland. In consequence the wildlife has been deprived of large areas which it previously occupied, and has even had its migration routes cut (see Fig. 4, p. 63).

Away to the north, some 40 miles distant, there exists an island of agriculture in the surrounding sea of pastoralism, the Sonjo. These are Bantu folk, practising irrigation on a few small streams emerging from the highlands to the west of Lake Natron. Their main agricultural tool is still the digging stick, and until recently they only herded sheep and goats – no cattle, owing to the presence of two constant enemies,

Masai and tsetse fly. Their population has not increased like the other agriculturists in the neighbourhood: as a result they have not been a threat to the wildlife and its habitat, save for sporadic rhino poaching which has been held in reasonable check.

In Chapter I the Arusha and Meru of the Mount Meru foothills have been mentioned. Their agricultural and indeed their demographic pattern is similar to the Chagga, who inhabit the slopes of Kilimanjaro. The general pattern is one of intensive agriculture based on a fertile soil and adequate rainfall, supplemented by irrigation from the numerous streams rising in the mountain forest. Population increases are, in these conditions, staggering. The Chagga were thought to number about 50,000 at the beginning of the British period, and now they number over a quarter of a million.

This human fecundity has brought about equally dramatic changes in the wildlife and its habitat in the surrounding areas. Today the plains all around Kilimanjaro are largely denuded of game and rapidly being taken over by agriculture and pastoralism. Luckily on the northern flanks a portion of the area falls within the boundaries of the Tsavo National Park in Kenya, whilst the Sanya Plains in Tanzania declared a Controlled Area, still carry some zebra and gazelle. The virtual loss of wildlife from the immediate vicinity of their homes makes it all the more important for the Chagga and the other agricultural folk of northern Tanzania that easily accessible game viewing areas like Ngurdoto, Manyara and Ngorongoro should remain inviolate for all time.

10 Modern Man

The period of modern man divides itself conveniently into three phases, beginning with that of German influence, dating from Baumann's visit in 1892 and ending with Siedentopf's departure in 1916. Then followed the period of British tutelage, first as a military occupancy, then as a mandate under the League of Nations, 1920–1944, and finally as a trusteeship, 1946–1961. Tanganyika became fully independent under a Governor-General on 12 December, 1961, and a Republic under President Nyerere one year later: shortly afterwards on 26 April, 1964, it amalgamated with Zanzibar and became the United Republic of Tanzania. For ease of reference, the main events of each phase as it affected Ngorongoro are reported in Table 4. Whilst these successive Governments had a tremendous influence on the shape of developments in Ngorongoro, each in turn imposing its own character on the country, it must be appreciated that certain influences were at work and would have existed whatever government were in power; the opening up of Africa to trade, and the introduction of a cash economy, the breakdown of barriers by modern means of transport, the introduction of western medicine with its profound demographic impact – all these factors have influenced Africa whether controlled by indigenous or colonial governments.

Following Baumann's visit in 1892 numerous expeditions visited the Crater highlands, which had such scientific and scenic attraction. But the Germans set up no administrative machinery in the region, the nearest stations being Arusha to the east, Mbulu to the south, and Ikoma to the west; the old fort at the last-named appears in Dr Grzimek's book and film *Serengeti Shall Not Die*. The one remaining relic of the German regime, and a very creditable one, is the northern Highland Forest Reserve, the boundaries of which were surveyed and

TABLE 4

A brief chronology

1892   Baumann visits Crater (March)
1899c. Siedentopf establishes himself in Crater
1908   Fourie visits Siedentopf
1913   Professor Reck's first visit
1916   Siedentopf departs (March)
1920   British mandate over Tanganyika
1921   Sir Charles Ross, Barns and Dugmore visit Crater: first Game
        Laws introduced
1922   Holmes' photographic expedition: Hurst living in Crater
1923   The Livermore safari
1926c. Veterinary camp established at Lerai
1928   Crater declared Complete Reserve
1930   All Ngorongoro and Serengeti declared Closed Reserve
1932   First motor road to crater rim
1934   Author's first visit to Ngorongoro
1935   Building of first Lodge commenced
1940   East rim road to northern highlands: first National Parks
        legislation: unimplemented
1948   First National Parks Ordinance receives assent
1951   National Parks Ordinance comes into operation: boundaries of
        Serengeti gazetted (1 June)
1952   Park administration moves in (August)
1954   D.O. posted to Ngorongoro: cultivation prohibited by law:
        'squatters' evicted
1956   Sessional Paper No. 1 publishes Government's proposals re
        Ngorongoro and the Serengeti
1957   Committee of Enquiry Report (October)
1958   Government Paper No. 5 announces Government's decision
1959   Conservation Area inaugurated (1 July)
1961   Arusha Conference and Arusha Manifesto: author takes over
        as Chairman of Authority (September)
1963   Authority disbanded and Conservator appointed
1963   Catering first started at Lodge
1965   First Tanzanian Conservator appointed (September)

demarcated by German foresters. It remained to the British to give legal protection to the area marked out on the ground by their predecessors.

The Siedentopf farms have been frequently referred to in this story of Ngorongoro. They were established by Adolph Siedentopf as the dominant character, with his brother Friedrich Wilhelm in a more subordinate role. Adolph entered the Crater in about 1899 as a squatter, but finally obtained legal title to his land before World War I broke out. The boundaries are shown in Fig. 5, covering about one third of the Crater floor. The ruins of the farmhouse on the Munge river are a well known landmark for visitors. The brother's farm at Lerai, marked by the conspicuous grove of eucalyptus trees, never received legal title. An application was pending when war broke out in 1914. If it had been approved the farm would have taken in a portion of the Crater floor and a large area of the Loirobi grasslands lying to the west of the Conservation Headquarters. If legal title had been granted, and after the war disposed of by the Custodian of Enemy Property, the farm might have fallen into much less sympathetic hands than those of Sir Charles Ross – who bought Adolph's farm – in which case the subsequent history of Ngorongoro might have been very different.

As things were, Siedentopf left the Crater in 1916, in the face of the advancing British. Professor Hans Reck gives an eye-witness account.

> For this man, the new times brought a very tragic end to his dream. When I last saw him, during the war, he had just received instructions to leave his farm in the face of the approaching enemy. I saw his wonderful cattle, fifteen hundred head of mixed breeds, being driven under a cloud of dust towards the South. They were approaching the slopes of the mountain in an almost endless train, and disappearing into the jungle on the slopes.

> A few years later, Siedentopf had lost everything, the change of climate and the strange food having killed the animals off in hundreds. Siedentopf returned to his defeated homeland, after being a prisoner of war, as poor as when he had first arrived twenty years before.

Such was the Siedentopf story as recorded by a reliable contemporary witness.

Olduvai gorge, home of ancient man 1,750,000 years ago, with Dr Leakey in the foreground: note how erosion has exposed the strata from a study of which man's history can be read.

The grave of Michael Grzimek on the rim of the Crater.

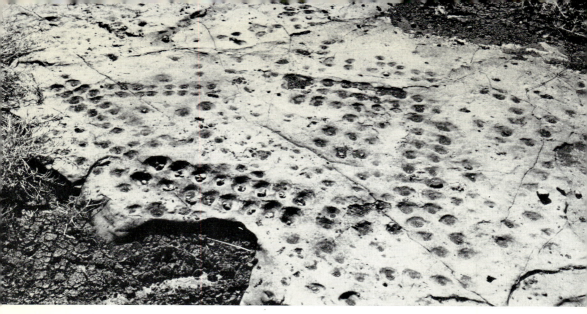

A unique occurrence in the Crater of an assemblage of prehistoric *bau*-boards; the holes carved out of rock are used for playing a game somewhat dissimilar from but no less complicated than chess or mahjong. Counters in the nearest 'board' show that it is still in use.

Masai elders playing *bau* with a wooden board. The counters are moved according to rule and the play is so fast that both parties may make their moves simultaneously. The tally of games won and lost is recorded by the passing of wooden chips called 'tusks'.

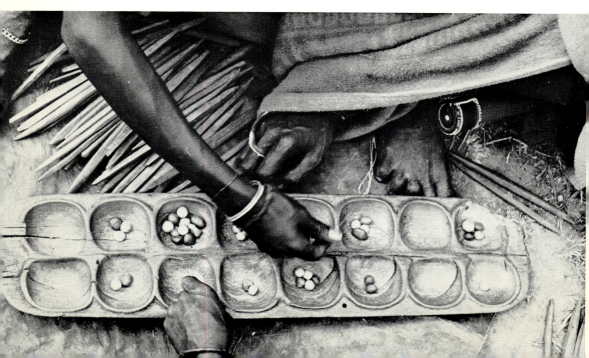

The first record I have of the British presence in Ngorongoro is of the visit of a military cattle-buying party. Mr H. C. Allison of the Mumbwa Copper Mine in Zambia tells me that he visited the Crater with Lieutenant Middleton in 1917 to purchase cattle for the British troops. He recalls shooting a hippo and extracting ten gallons of fat, which, removed in a milk-can lifted from the abandoned farm, provided a fat supply for himself and his friends for several months campaigning. Thereafter, with the establishment of a civil administration, visits by officials became more frequent.

Ray Ulyate, proprietor during the 1930's of the New Arusha Hotel, was the first to organise trips by road to Ngorongoro and the Serengeti. He established a tented camp at Ngorongoro on the site of the Dulen road turn-off, subsequently occupied by a mission school. This was the half-way house to Banagi, where the lions became a popular attraction, as described in Chapter VI.

Other early arrivals on the scene were veterinary officials, assigned to control the cattle diseases, particularly rinderpest. An old friend of mine, Neil Reid, started his distinguished career there by identifying rinderpest in wildebeest at a time when many people contended that this species could not carry the disease. Reid eventually became Director of Veterinary Services and only recently has retired from the post of Animal Health Officer in the Food and Agriculture Organisation in Rome. An early resident was John Hamman, who took over the camp at Lerai, originally established by F. W. Siedentopf as his farm and later occupied by Captain Hurst. Hamman was succeeded by Eric Howe, and it was he and his wife who acted as host to my wife and myself on our first visit to Ngorongoro in 1934.

Personal recollections enable me to describe what things were like at Ngorongoro a third of a century ago. There were no permanent buildings on the rim of the Crater; in fact the 'road' had only been completed a year or two previously. It was a narrow, ungravelled track on roughly the same alignment as the present road, but with the gradients much steeper and the corners much sharper (believe it or not): it was liable to turn into a sea of mud under the smallest shower, and back again to dust in a matter of hours.

The only building on the Crater rim was a temporary erection, a grass-roofed, mud-walled store situated on the open ground a few hundred yards east of Michael Grzimek's grave where, till recently,

the ugly corrugated-iron P.W.D. camp stood. This store was built by
Eric Howe, the Stock Inspector (Veterinary Department) who lived in
the Crater and who required a depot for dumping his stores or for
waiting for lorries at the point where the footpath for Lerai took off.

I remember the first time I passed there, 9 August, 1934. My wife
and I were driving to take up my posting as A.D.O. in charge Loliondo;
she was new to the country, and I had a two-and-a-half year tour of
Tanganyika behind me. We were in a 1½ ton lorry with all our goods
and chattels on the back, and were looking for somewhere to camp on
the first stage of our journey from Arusha. We came across this veterinary
department store: our driver advised us to camp in it as it was the
only shelter on the Crater rim, but Jane was doubtful about the wisdom
of this. Howe had evidently been having trouble from passing traders
and the early tourists who also were tempted to use it as a *pied-a-terre*.
So he had drafted a suitable warning notice. My wife looked at the
notice and said tremulously: 'I don't think we'd better go in there.'
She was fresh from a short medical course and had obviously put a
different interpretation on the notice than that which Howe intended
when he painted up 'V.D. KEEP OUT!'

On our second visit, in October, 1934, we were going to a cattle
auction due to be held on the north rim of the Crater, near the Munge
river. There was then no road along the east rim – I only constructed
this in 1940, though as the following record shows, I was looking for an
alignment to take a road to the northern highlands as early as 1934.
The drill was to collect porters from the settlement at Lerai, and walk
across the Crater floor; just how we did it is described in the following
letter which my wife wrote to her parents at the conclusion of the trip.

Approaching the Crater from the Loliondo side we arrived at
Malanja:

> At length we reached the Crater rim and look down into the
> Crater itself. It was looking even more beautiful than when we
> first saw it. The floor was golden, with purple shadows, caused
> by the clouds passing over it. We were seeing the Crater from a
> different angle. The 'lake' in the middle seemed further away.
> It looked like a lake, but, in actual fact, we found when we got
> down there, the next day, that it was quite dry and sparkling
> with soda.

We drove along the rim for 9 or 10 miles till we reached the veterinary camp. We were hoping the stock inspector, Eric Howe, who lives in the Crater, would have left us a message or some porters, but he hadn't. He had already departed himself for the auction. The only living creature was a young goatherd, who, when we asked him if there were porters for the morrow, said he didn't know if there were any, probably there weren't! We asked for water, but he said he couldn't get any as the elephants were drinking at the stream. We asked for firewood, but he gave us only a few sticks of bamboo, not very helpful. However, Shabani soon found some and got a fire going. Dick, the messenger, was meanwhile sent down into the Crater to collect as many porters as possible and send them up the next morning.

Next morning we rose with the first sign of light and had breakfast. It was bitterly cold. We then arranged all our belongings in head loads on the ground. There seemed to be an amazing number of things; our camp beds which folded into very small bundles with their thin corrugated mattresses; two very light folding chairs and a table which folds into a little roll; a more solid table and two camp chairs for the auction. There was one bath, with lid, full of blankets. This was a two man load and had to be tied to a pole; ditto box for Micky [the cocker spaniel] which was light but bulky. There was one cook's box, one box of stores, one medicine box, a basin with miscellaneous objects, petrol tins for water, guns and ammunition. Then each askari and each messenger had his own bundle, and so had Maliko, Shabani, Dick and Samuel, the clerk. None of these dignified persons carry loads, they each have their own porters. In addition there were the tents, ours and those of the porters, made up in large bundles; and finally those ghastly heavy cash boxes, and also the ledgers and office impedimenta.

The sun rose over the Crater and tinged the mist, which was enveloping the crater floor, with a soft pink. Henry inspected the loads. Micky inspected the loads, but still no Dick, still no porters. At length, when the sun was well up at about 9.30 we decided to go down to the house of Mr Howe, the Stock

Inspector, which was on the Crater floor below, to investigate. It was a wonderful walk. The path goes zigzag down the inner wall, which is practically sheer, and all the way magnificent views of the Crater floor from which the mist had lifted. As we climbed lower we could see landmarks more distinctly. First the forest just below us, then the flat golden floor, then the shining soda pans and beyond, the Crater wall on the other side. Our guide, a local, pointed out Howe's house at our feet between the Crater wall and the forest [the old F. W. Siedentopf farm, still marked by a grove of eucalyptus trees]. Then he pointed out our own route which was practically straight across the Crater from Howe's house. Although about ten miles distant we could actually see the trees on Ross's farm where we were to camp for the night, and the hills beyond above the Crater wall, where the auction to which we were going was to be held.

As we descended the slope, to our intense relief, we met the vanguard of porters coming up. Very tough they looked, like mountain goats leaping up the hillside. The rest followed behind, not quite so rapidly. The hillside seemed alive with them, and loose stones were rattling down behind them. You may wonder how porters in such numbers could appear from nowhere – there were at least 25 of them. It seems that they live down below, and are allowed to cultivate provided they act as official porters. As we climbed lower we could see the *shambas* [maize fields] laid out round Howe's house. Then we went through a nice little bit of forest, with a beautiful burbling brook rushing down from the rim of the Crater. This was the first sound of running water we had heard since we left Arusha in September. There was luscious green grass growing by the stream and wild banana trees and bright coloured flowers in the grass. [This is the Olgeju lol Mongi which provides an attractive feature of the Lerai Descent road, where wild bananas are still to be seen.]

We reached the house, a tumbledown affair with a roof of papyrus-type leaves. A similar building, the office, was even more tumbledown. There were also some old stone outhouses, now used as a kitchen. These we were told were the remains of another German farm owned by the first German's brother.

Behind the house flowed the stream making a lovely rushing noise, and round the house a little garden with tidy paths and beds, but not much in them. The site of the house is really on the hillwash from the Crater rim, and so it is a little above the true floor of the Crater. The result is that from the house there is the most beautiful view right across the Crater floor. From here it has a dreamlike appearance, with the shining soda lake and behind it the blue mountains which back the rim on the other side.

After a long wait for the porters at last we started, at about 11 o'clock, to cross the Crater. We took with us one of the Forest Guards as a guide, a pixie-like youth, very slender, with bright eyes and a lovely smile. He told us he was a Mbulu, and his name was Tlehema. First we crossed the shambas, where the hedges are made of wild tomatoes, most delicious to eat. Then through the forest, this was very thrilling. There were tall spreading acacia trees, with yellow trunks and tiny green leaves. It was refreshingly cool in the forest which is called Lerai by the Masai, their name for these acacia trees. We passed the edge of a swamp. The guide told me that hippo lived here but we didn't see any.

We had lunch in the cool at the edge of the forest, and then at 12 o'clock we set off to cross the arid centre of the Crater. At length we reached the *magadi*. The soda on the ground was sparkling like snow, and the surface was broken up into a series of slabs, like a jigsaw puzzle, and you could pick up these pieces like cardboard plates, they were solid soda. The glare from it was very trying, and as you walked on it it made a crunchy noise under your feet. As we walked over it we found we were making footmarks as though we were walking on snow.

At length we reached the other side of the *magadi*. It has shores like a real lake, in fact it is a real lake, only it is dry at this season. Beyond the *magadi* we began to see game in large quantities, big herds of 'Tommies' and Grant's gazelles, and zebra and gnu, hundreds and thousands everywhere. We came across the spoor of lion, where four had been walking abreast but as usual we did not see them. Further on we saw what looked like two men coming towards us in a mirage, but they turned out to be two ostrich. Ross's farm ahead looked so near, shimmering in a mirage, but we had to walk many more miles before we really reached it. Then it began to get green, evidently it had rained here; and the number of gazelle increased. The nearer to Ross's farm the greener it became. At last we were nearly there. It was getting cooler and just ahead was what looked like a beautiful stream. We all had visions of a lovely drink and a lay-down on the green grass. But it was not as easy as that. Shabani and Maliko put down the lamps they were carrying and ran to the stream. But it turned out to be a mud wallow. We had to cross it, but no one wanted to drink it. [This was the Munge river, almost dry after a succession of bad years.]

Then the tent arrived and was pitched under some tall eucalyptus trees. A glorious site for a tent on a green hillside, with the Crater below looking even more crater-like from this side, sheer sides like a cake tin and blue mountains behind, most beautiful in the afternoon sun. Behind us was the valley leading up to the hills where the auction was to be held next day.

After tea we followed the little stream till it became much clearer and we paddled in it refreshing our swollen feet. Then we inspected the ruins of the old German farm, and climbed the hills behind. Below us, grazing on the hillside, were herds of wildebeest streaming over the hills in long lines. Then, when one heard a sound, the whole lot would scamper first this way, then that.

After supper we went to bed in our little tent having first seen Micky was alright in his box. About one o'clock we were rudely awakened, even Henry woke this time. I have never heard anything like it in my life, not even at the zoo. All the hyaenas in the Crater seemed to have congregated for a pow-wow at the river just below our tent. They howled and they laughed and they shrieked and emitted every kind of diabolical sound all at once. It sounded like myriads of fiends let loose. Even Henry was shocked. It went on for quite a long time. Micky, fortunately safe in his box, was far too frightened to say anything.

Next morning we rose, had breakfast, broke camp, and then started climbing up the hillside to the site of the auction. It was really idyllic in the early morning, the fresh grass sparkling with dew and bright with small carpets of wild pink flowers like petunias. We followed the path up the hillside, over one hill and down the next, rising all the time. We passed zebra galloping over the hillsides and little gazelle looking so fresh in the early morning. Then we entered the valley proper. Here it was steeper and more stony. Higher up we entered the woods. Here it was like springtime, the trees were just beginning to burst into bud, and under the trees were patches of bright green grass. There were flowers here, too, mostly big lillies, white with pink markings; and higher up we saw bright scarlet ones like pom-poms three inches across.

After about two hours' walk we reached the top, in fact the rim on the other side . . .

Then follows a description of the auction, and the two small stores owned by Sikhs. I well remember that over 1,000 cattle went through the 'ring' – if a rough brushwood structure is worthy of the name – in the matter of five days. The average price was just over 15 shillings per beast, which was considered very satisfactory, as Sh.15/- was the current rate of tax. If the selling price fell below that – as it had at the previous auction at Malambo, where 1,700 head were sold at an average of about Sh.14/- it meant that many Masai, who had brought one beast in the hope of meeting their tax obligation, could not in fact pay their tax.

These figures disprove the myth that 'Masai never sell their cattle'; but the history of the cattle trade in Masailand is another story.

But to take up once more the story of our walks across Ngorongoro. My wife describes the return trip thus:

Mr Howe very kindly lent me his donkey so that his wife Margaret and I could ride back together across the Crater; whilst he and Henry explored on foot the possibilities of making a road round the western rim.

We reached the Howe's house at about 1.30 and the firs thing we did was to have a long drink of their lovely water. No cattle or humans are allowed near and it's absolutely pure and crystal clear; they don't even have to filter it. No sooner had we done this than the men arrived from their long tramp. They had walked over 20 miles along the western rim, scrambling up and down gullies. It was very rough and they decided that it would be too difficult to make a road along this side, it would be better to try the eastern side first. Henry's feet were a shocking sight, raw with blisters. We gave them liquid in every possible form – tea, water, whisky and fruit juice, and they lapped it all up and asked for more. Poor Henry had to set to then and there with *shauris* (cases) which kept him busy till after sundown.

Meanwhile I talked to Margaret. The house was built of mud like ours at Loliondo; the roof of reeds was very nice and cool but there was no ceiling. Margaret had to make a ceiling of americani cloth slung across to catch *dudus* (insects). The floor was of stone and very uneven; it was covered with skins – zebra, Tommy, leopard, etc. so it looked furnished. There was one easy chair; the other chair was not so easy, it was made of two petrol boxes. There was one kind of sofa structure covered with skins, and they had made little bookcases and tables from petrol boxes. Margaret had livened things up with nice little covers and vases of flowers. Considering the odds they had done very well, but the windows, like ours, were without glass and very small, and the house, especially the dining room, very dark. There were only three rooms in the house, so we slept in a tent, which is the customary procedure out here in the absence of a spare room.

Margaret produced a sumptuous dinner. All her most precious tins were opened; asparagus, grapefruit, salmon, and tins of fruit. After a short chat we all went to bed.

So that was Ngorongoro a third of a century ago! It might be well at this juncture to take up two or three themes which run right through the British period, and then on into Independence. One such theme is the cattle trade, another the development of legislative protection for wildlife, then the Serengeti controversy and finally the development of tourism.

The cattle trade was of considerable economic (and ecological) importance as early as 1934, as the figures of my first cattle auctions show. At that time sales were held even in areas unserved by motor transport. The auction 'rings' were rough structures of thorn, with few amenities for buyer or seller. But they did provide an outlet for surplus stock and a means for the Masai to obtain cash for the purchase of maize flour and trade goods. These were brought in by retail traders, who set up stalls in tents round the periphery of the auction. The figures quoted above of 1,000 head of cattle at one auction and 1,700 at another in the same month are above the normal for that period. The long drought of 1933–34 had led to a drop in price, a drop in sales, and a consequent drop in tax collection: a big drive to get the tax in before the end of the year resulted in the high figures recorded above.

At that time the auction system had only recently been introduced. Previously cattle traders had wandered through the length and breadth of Masailand, making individual deals with the sellers and taking their beasts to the consumer markets in Moshi, Arusha and Korogwe. This system had the disadvantage that the stock movement lacked veterinary supervision and control and so led to the spread of disease. Further, lacking the competition of the open market, the shrewd trader was frequently able to strike a bargain very satisfactory to himself but unfavourable to the backward, gullible Masai. From small beginnings the auction system built up till by the mid 1940's it was handling up to 42,000 head of Masai cattle per year. The trade of course covered all the cattle-producing areas, Mbulu, Sukuma, Gogo, etc., ensuring a steady supply of meat to the sisal and coffee areas.

During the war years local demand had greatly increased, in part owing to local troop movements, the expansion of the sisal industry and other war efforts, in part to the requirements of the army for corned beef – bully. Messrs Leibigs, of world-wide fame, had earlier been encouraged to set up a canning plant in Kenya in anticipation of large quantities of culled cattle from the Kamba districts, which failed to materialise. The firm was thus in a position to divert staff and plant to Arusha to turn out corned beef for the army. The problem was to ensure sufficient supplies of cattle, and the idea was put to the Masai that this could, and indeed should, be their major war effort. I had studied the history of the Masai during World War I and seen how conscription had served no useful purpose. The Masai so recruited were in general unamenable to military discipline whilst their conscription had caused such ill-will that at one time the Kenya Masai were in open revolt against the government. Seeking to avoid a repetition of this situation, of which one effect would have been to bring the cattle trade to a halt, I discussed with the Masai of Loliondo – where I was then posted – the possibility of their contributing stock rather than man-power to the war effort. The idea proved acceptable to them, but when I first mentioned it to my D.C. he thought it might be regarded as a device for the Masai to buy themselves out of army service. But the merits of the scheme were apparent and it was eventually accepted by the authorities.

The Masai fulfilled their obligations with a minimum of administrative supervision. Each of their own indigenous local divisions (about 10 or 12) was given its quota to make up, a total, as far as I can recollect, of 6,000 head per annum for the whole of Tanganyika Masailand. The indigenous leaders then decided who should contribute, and how many.

The individual Masai did not handle the proceeds – his beast was a free contribution to the war effort. The money was divided up on a formula by which one-third was contributed as a gift from the tribe to the local war fund, one-third was invested in war loan, earmarked for post-war development, and one-third devoted to current development works, to demonstrate some immediate benefit from the scheme. Something in the nature of 22,000 head of cattle were contributed during the duration of the scheme, but I have no access to the exact figures of numbers and the cash realised; at present-day prices the total would be about five million shillings. Auction sales, of course, continued meanwhile, the war effort stock being over and above the normal output.

On two grounds this story deserves a place in a Survival book. Firstly it shows how an indigenous political system, lying outside Government's orbit, and indeed based on a system – that of age-sets – alien to any known modern government, had continued to survive and can be made to function not only to fulfil its original purposes, but equally to carry a burden arising from a completely alien situation. It also illustrates that the Masai will part with their cattle even beyond their normal sales to meet cash requirements, *provided the motivation is strong enough*. The Masai knew about war, they even had their own special method of preserving meat as rations for raiding parties. They did not want to enter the European war, which was not theirs; but if they had to do something they would rather contribute cattle than manpower. So it was comparatively easy to 'put across' the merits of the 'gift stock' scheme and get Masai co-operation. On several occasions they have also contributed stock in considerable numbers for the improvement of water supplies. If only it was as easy to put across the necessity for stock reduction in the interests of land use, how simple our task would be!

The normal trade continued to expand till it reached a peak of about 42,000 head per year. But in recent years the numbers passing through the markets have decreased. This is largely due to the diversion of the trade through black-market channels, which has the advantage both for buyer and seller of avoiding the payment of market dues and cess. This is unfortunate, as not only is revenue lost but veterinary control rendered impossible. I had foretold this eventuality at meeting after meeting, when the authorities decided to levy a cess on cattle sold in markets. A fee to cover the cost of running the markets is reasonable, but when a cess is levied with the express intent of raising revenue, the burden falls on just the wrong man. It is paradoxical that so much is said about the necessity for stock reduction, for a greater turnover in the herds, for encouraging the Masai to sell more cattle and so modernise their lives; and then a tax is put on those who do just these things! Rather than penalise the 'good boys' the obvious answer is to remove the deterrents to selling, even to the extent of remitting *all* market fees and cesses, and collecting the same amount of revenue from the 'bad boys', those who do *not* sell. This could be in the form of a graduated cattle tax, mounting steeply so as to fall heavily on those who hold cattle in numbers in excess of their economic requirements. Such has been imposed in neighbouring districts and, whilst difficult to administer, it is not an impossibility. But as things stand, the black market will continue to flourish – but even then it is better for the land (and for the cattle owners and consumers) that cattle should be sold, albeit illicitly, rather than bottled up in Masailand.

A concomitant of a cattle trade is adequate stock routes, along which the purchased cattle are moved on the hoof to the consumer markets. One such route crossed the Crater floor, and climbed the rim at Baumann's Point. Here the veterinary authorities had erected a trade-stock camp, a very necessary amenity. But one wondered, must this ugly structure be immediately alongside one of the most scenic tourist routes in Tanzania? Luckily the present Conservator has devised alternative routes and authorised the demolition of this eye-sore. Another point about stock routes is that the drovers must be educated in conservation, so that they do not cut trees unnecessarily or allow their grazing stock to damage the countryside. I recollect in one period of drought, when normal water supplies were disrupted, a trade-stock safari camped on Koinonyi Island (Lake Makat being totally dry) and cut the few yellow-barked acacia trees growing there for their thorn encampment. In the event, these trees would doubtless have died in the recent flooding but if and when the lake level falls, it would be pleasant to see the clump of yellow-barked fever-trees re-established on the island.

Is Ngorongoro overstocked? In discussions on conservation, wildlife preservation, land use planning and so on one hears much talk about the carrying capacity of the land, and from this deductions are made concerning the degree of overstocking. But as experts in range management point out, there can be no absolute figure of carrying capacity; so much depends on *how* the land is ranched, over and above the numbers of cattle on the land. If cattle are introduced into high-standing grass, as much fodder will be trampled and destroyed as is eaten; equally if they are put onto newly sprouting grass, they will eat it off before the plants have a chance to establish themselves. But if the grass is grazed at the optimum time, and given periodic rests at scientifically determined intervals, the stocking rate can be increased beyond belief, without detriment to the land or to the beasts. On sown and fertilised pastures, it has been demonstrated that the stocking rate can be raised from around five acres per beast to less than one acre per beast by these methods.

It will, however, be a long time before the Masai adopt such advanced methods of animal husbandry, so to get some idea of the present picture it is necessary to think in terms of acres per beast, *ranched according to present methods*. In the analysis which follows it is assumed on the one hand that advanced methods are not practised, but on the other that the Masai are left with sufficient freedom of movement to practise their traditional system of migration. This means that the pastures round the permanent waters are rested whilst the cattle are out on the plains during the rainy season. Then when the Masai return to base they find a reserve of grazing sufficient to take them through the dry season, till the onset of the next rains. If, as has in fact happened in many places, the Masai are deprived of the best of their permanent waters, there will naturally be overcrowding and degradation of habitat round those that remain to them. Luckily this has not happened at Ngorongoro. Here the Masai have (except in the Forest Reserve) retained access to their traditional dry-season grazing and water; equally important they have retained the will and the ability to move with their stock out onto the plains in the rainy season.

Once the nomadic pastoralist settles down, but still attempts to retain the previous numbers of cattle, herded in the traditional manner, soil and habitat degradation soon sets in. In several cases, however, the Tanzanian husbandman has demonstrated his capacity to adapt to settled conditions in favourable habitat. The Chagga of Kilimanjaro or the Arusha or Meru of Mount Meru are examples; they practise stall feeding with chopped banana plants and with fodder carried for miles; pastures are fenced, weeded and even manured. But there are other examples where settled agriculturists have allowed their unadapted methods, together with their determination to maintain the largest herds possible, to ruin the country, as in Gogoland or certain parts of Sukumaland.

It must be repeated that this analysis is based on present pastoral practice. This is such that in good years much grazing is unused, and is destroyed either by trampling or by fire. In bad years cattle would have a hard time and lose condition, but would not, at the stocking rate suggested, die in large numbers.

Even in developed ranching countries the lean years present a very difficult problem. If one stocks down to the worst possible year, then in the majority of seasons one is understocked, grazing goes to waste and the ranch not used to its optimum productive capacity. This is not good either from the personal angle or for the national economy. What is the answer to the dilemma? It is all very well for the critics speaking in the knowledge of hindsight to say: 'If only the Masai had sold their stock before the drought hit them, they would have had lots of money in reserve to help them weather the famine, whilst much suffering and loss of protein would have been avoided.' But this argument neglects two points; firstly, one cannot know in advance just how severe a drought is going to be. Secondly, if a flood of beef comes on the market, the trade may not be able physically to handle the beasts, and in any case prices will drop.

This shows that the problems of ranching are by no means

susceptible to simple solutions; we must for a long time be content with small scale measures of alleviation which are capable of immediate application and *acceptable to the people concerned*. In so many fields the natural scientists, or the economist, or the planner says: 'Yes, we have the solution to this, that or the other problem.' But to this the social scientist must answer: 'Your solution is not a solution so long as it remains in the laboratory or on the drawing board. *It is only a solution when accepted and applied by the people concerned.*'

Two immediate measures at Ngorongoro are the encouraging of more marketing of cattle, firstly by lightening the taxes on the seller and increasing the taxes on the hoarder, and secondly by meeting and even stimulating Masai wants, which may be in the form of consumer goods, or in the form of social services. Just one small example; if there were better roads and more buses, the Masai would travel more and so require more ready cash.

The second step is to ensure that the cattle are distributed according to the capacity of the grazing. A scheme, with legal backing to ensure enforcement, is already in being, but has never been applied, by which the Area could be divided into blocks, each containing dry weather and wet season grazing, within which cattle movements would be regulated and numbers controlled. This is not the place to go into details, but the gradual application of some such scheme is essential. The days of free-for-all land use, letting nature take its course, went out when disease control and the introduction of a money economy came in.

What is the Masai of Ngorongoro currently getting out of his herds, and what is his potential income – without the injection of a large amount of capital and without radical change in ranching methods? In the analysis which follows, we are speaking in terms of carrying capacity when open range migratory pastoralism is practised.

Noel Simon in his book *Between the Sunlight and the Thunder* estimates that before the severe famine of 1960–61 the total usable acreage of Kenya Masailand, 9,789,000 acres, was carrying 973,000 cattle. After allowing for small stock and donkeys he calculated that one beast was grazing 7 acres, whereas the country, apart from a few selected areas, had an average carrying capacity of nearer 15 to 20 acres per unit of stock. Simon does not make it clear whether he means a 1,000 lb. stock unit, or whether his unit represents an average Masai beast, weighing about 650 lbs., but whichever way it is looked at it means that Kenya Masailand was carrying either just under or just over twice the stock that the country could bear. Indeed the heavy mortality of the famine years bore this out, as something like 300,000 cattle died i.e. about one third of the total. The mortality was equally or even more severe in parts of Tanzania Masailand, particularly at Longido.

It is evident that the Conservation Unit was not so heavily over-stocked as these other areas at that time, as the recorded figures show the deaths to amount to 26,000 out of a total cattle population of 161,000, i.e. about 16%. In a normal year up to 10% loss can be expected from deaths from natural causes, so the Conservation Unit's increased mortality due to the 1960–61 drought was not unduly severe.

TABLE 5

Stocking capacity of Area

Type of grazing as on Fig. 3 (p. 45)	Total of area sq. ml.	Forest Reserve sq. ml.	Balance Available sq. ml.	acres	Carrying Capacity (a)	Optimum stock units
1. Heath	55	32	23	—	Nil	—
2. Bamboo	15	15	—	—	Nil	—
3. Temperate evergreen forest	240	240	—	—	Nil	—
4. Highland scrub and woodland	330	27	303	193,920	20	9,700
5. Highland grass	400	33	367	234,880	10	23,500
6. Sand-dune grass	280	—	280	179,200	50	3,600
7. Short low grass	650	—	650	416,000	20	20,800
8. Medium low grass	410	—	410	262,400	15	17,500
9. Lowland bush and woodland	790	—	790	501,000	15	33,400
	3,170					108,500

(a) in acres per 1,000 lb. stock unit.

Looking at the stocking problem in another way, the carrying capacity of the various types of grazing can be estimated, the ideal stock numbers calculated and these can then be compared with the actual numbers. Earlier on, in Fig. 3 (p. 45), I have given an estimate of the area of each of the main types of habitat. Now, in Table 5 an estimate of the carrying capacity of each type of grazing is given, and from this the total stock carrying capacity is obtained. The weakness in this appraisal is that it fails to take into account the wildlife population. In considering this factor the following points deserve consideration: firstly, the elephant population, the buffalo, and many of the rhino are in the Forest Reserve, which has been excluded from the calculation: and secondly, if the figures are adjusted to exclude the Crater floor, which carries a very large proportion of the Area's wildlife, a truer picture of the carrying capacity of the Area is obtained, and so the Table 5 figure is reduced from 108,500 to 102,100 stock units. Incidentally, in giving up the Crater floor grazing to wildlife the Masai deny themselves some 10,000 stock units capacity. This represents about 12,000 head of cattle, with immatures, small stock and donkeys *pro rata*. At the present rate of usage, 10 %, this can be valued at £12,000 per annum. It is not perhaps realised by the casual visitor how thinly the wildlife is spread over the Area other than in the Crater, whilst on the plains the heavy stocking is confined to the comparatively short period of the migration. For this reason a figure of 102,000 units of domestic stock is considered to be reasonably close to the optimum.

TABLE 6

Stock units in Area

	1960			Optimum		
	Number	*Factor*	*Stock Units*	*Number*	*Factor*	*Stock Units*
Mature bovines	128,000	2/3	85,300	120,000	2/3	80,000
Immature bovines	34,000	1/3	11,300	30,000	1/3	10,000
Small stock	100,700	1/10	10,100	80,000	1/10	8,000
Donkeys	7,700	2/3	5,100	6,000	2/3	4,000
TOTALS			111,800			102,000

How near to this optimum does the actual stocking rate come? Table 6 shows the total stock units in the Area in the peak period before

An elephant family crossing the road on the Crater rim near the Lodge. Note the breasts of the cow on the left showing between the front legs. All around is temperate evergreen forest.

Both cock and hen ostrich take turns at incubating the eggs: here they are seen changing guard at a nest on the Crater floor. The cock is on the right.

Sacred Ibis at Hippo Pool in the Crater: the bird's most distinctive features are its black-tipped wing feathers and naked black head.

the famine led to a reduction in stock numbers; it reveals that the stocking capacity was well above the optimum, hence the deaths in the famine period. Table 6 also shows what appears to be a reasonable optimum stocking, viz. 120,000 head of mature stock, with 25% immatures, which is a reasonable ratio to maintain a healthy population. The small-stock and donkey figures are based on the previous census figures, which reveal the ratio which the Masai themselves like to maintain. It thus appears that a Masai herd of about 120,000 mature beasts is within the capacity of the Area, which the above analysis suggests is in the nature of 100,000 units, under prevailing methods of husbandry.

There are of course concentrations of stock which lead to degradation in certain areas, but in general it would appear that the Conservation Area is *not* overstocked and that if adjustments of distribution could be made the figure of 100,000 mature bovines could be maintained on a basis of sustained yield.

Let us assume that the Masai sell 6% of their stock and slaughter 4% for internal consumption (figures ascertained from careful counts and questionnaires) and on average lose 10% from natural causes, East Coast fever being one of the chief killers. This 20% decrease should maintain stability in the herds, though varying rainfall will naturally cause ups and downs. The 6% sold yields 6,000 head per year; at prevailing prices this means a cash income of £60,000, to be shared by some 8,500 people, plus of course £40,000 worth of meat consumed locally. This is a minute *per capita* income for people who have the capital – the cattle – the land, and the know-how to make so much more of their opportunities than they currently do. Estimates reveal that this cash income could be pushed up about 2½ times on present values, or 5 times if by better husbandry the value of the beast could be doubled.

This shows how far the actual utilisation falls short of the potential, but in what sphere does this shortfall not occur? Throughout most of agricultural Africa the same problem applies. Maize production in many areas is around 4 bags per acre, whilst by the application of modern science, yields could be pushed up to 40 bags. The same applies to cotton, groundnuts, or any agricultural produce one likes to name. So in comparison, the Masai return from the land they use is equal to or better than that of other land users.

Wildlife protection, and the legislation necessary to enforce this, is

13

a thread running throughout the British period. The first Game Pre-servation Ordinance came into operation in 1921 which demanded that hunting should be on licence for which fees were laid down: certain methods of hunting were prohibited, but no special regulations were applied to the Serengeti or Ngorongoro, which could be hunted over just as anywhere else. As lion were at that time classified as vermin, they could be shot without restriction.

In 1928 the Crater, bounded by the rim, was made a Complete Reserve, in which all hunting was prohibited. As about one third of the Crater floor was in private ownership – that of Sir Charles Ross – that area had to be excluded from the order, but there is no evidence that Sir Charles or any of his friends ever took advantage of this position of privilege: on the contrary he was one of the earliest to regard the Crater as a game sanctuary.

In the early 1930's the whole of the Loliondo sub-district and the Musoma district came under control, i.e. all the country from the Rift to Lake Victoria, from the Kenya border to the southern boundary of the Serengeti, inclusive of the Crater and the highlands. No one could enter this area for the purpose of hunting or photography without the written permission of the Provincial Commissioner. There is no record of a fee being charged for entry, nor that anyone was ever refused a permit. It did mean, however, that the authorities knew who was entering the area, and unsuitable types, e.g. persistent offenders against the Game Ordinance, would not have the effrontery to apply.

So far nothing had been done to limit the hunting activities of those who were permitted to enter what was then known as the Serengeti Closed Reserve but in 1935, following cases of the 'tame' Banagi lions being shot by 'sportsmen', the killing of lion was prohibited in the neighbourhood of Banagi and Seronera, and within a 15 mile radius of the Ngorongoro Rest Camp – now the Lodge. For some obscure reason the prohibition over the last-named area was removed in the following year. Although this represented a beginning, the Serengeti lion could be hunted throughout the rest of the Reserve, but only one per holder of a Resident's or Visitor's Full Game Licence. It was not till 1937 that a complete prohibition on the hunting of certain species was imposed throughout the whole of the Serengeti Closed Reserve: these were lion, cheetah, leopard, giraffe, rhinoceros, buffalo, roan, hyaena and wild dog.

That is how the matter stood till World War II when in spite of other preoccupations the Tanganyika Government enacted new game laws on 1 August, 1940 under which areas could be declared National Parks. The area of the previous Serengeti Closed Reserve was so declared, thus becoming Tanganyika's first National Park.

There had been no previous consultation about this with the Masai resident in the area – I can vouch for that as I was A.D.O. i/c Loliondo at the relevant time, but by a stroke of the pen some 10,000 inhabitants had their existing rights seriously diminished. The only people who could enter or reside in a national park were public officers, persons whose place of birth or immovable ordinary residence is within the park, people with property situated in the park, people travelling through the park, and the dependents and servants of the above. This meant that a Masai outside the park who habitually used the area for wet season grazing, or who wanted to visit a relative in the park was committing an offence if he failed to obtain a permit to enter. A further restriction was imposed, which made it unlawful wilfully or negligently to cause any bush or grass fire in a national park.

There is no record of action being taken under this legislation, which was replaced in 1948 by a National Parks Ordinance. This removed the control of National Parks from the Game Department and allowed for the setting up of a Board of Trustees to run the nation's parks. But it was not till May, 1951 that this ordinance was brought into force and a proclamation published defining the boundaries of the Serengeti National Park.

It was more than a year later, in August, 1952, that the park authorities moved in. Major Hewlett, the first park warden, built the house which was later converted into the Forest Resort (Dhillon's Lodge). He was introduced to the Masai by the District Commissioner who, in a speech still on record, told the Masai what the future held for them. He explained that the park was controlled by a Board of Trustees, of whom one was the Member for Local Government, a European responsible in the government for 'African interests', and one was an African, Chief Adam Sapi, now (1968) Chairman of the Board. The day-to-day affairs were in the hands of a local Board of Management of which he, the D.C., was a member.

The rights of the pastoralists, both Masai and Arusha, would be safeguarded, but only in respect of those who were living in the park when it was set up in June, 1951. No other Masai were allowed to move in and no more stock would be allowed than existed when the park was established: in fact it might be necessary to reduce the numbers of stock in the interests of conservation.

These conditions must have caused much consternation, but what followed was even more upsetting. No cultivation whatsoever was to be allowed in the park and all Arusha, Mbulu and other alien cultivators within the park would be required to leave. This statement blandly ignored the fact that Masai themselves might be cultivating at the time or might wish to do so in the future; and what was to be the position of the Masai with an Arusha wife who was engaged in cultivation?

Finally the Masai were told that to protect grazing all Masai within the park must follow any directions the park warden might give regarding the burning of grass or starting of fires.

This District Commissioner concluded with the following words:

> To summarise, Masai who are now in the Park, and their progeny, may stay in the Park, and a written acknowledgement of their rights to remain will be given them by the District Officer, Loliondo. The only difference is that they must follow the Park Warden's directions in the matter of grass burning; they must of course obey also the forest rules. Also, if it is found that they have too many stock for the carrying capacity of the land they must dispose of the surplus. They have lost no land; their only loss is the employment of non-Masai to cultivate *shambas*.

> The rights of the Masai are protected by law and cannot be abrogated. Government relies on the elders to co-operate with the Park Warden, to follow his direction and to keep the Park Laws.

All this sounded fine, but it contained seeds of dissension which speedily brought forth a goodly crop of complaints and controversy. Without going into detail, it soon became apparent that the basic principle of successful Park management, that all human rights must take second place, applied here as to the rest of the world. The Government took steps in this direction by moving the cultivators out of the Crater. It is not generally realised today that in 1954 there were about 50 cultivating households in the Crater, comprising 67 adult males, 57 females and 119 children. In addition to the village clustered round the old Siedentopf farm at Lerai – where the remains of the sisal hedges surrounding their fields can still be seen – settlements had sprung up at Koitoktok and the Lonyuki stream. Homes for these people were found outside the Area and they were assisted by government in their move. Likewise Empakaai crater was inhabited by 50 families, who were similarly moved, but infiltrated back again and in the period 1961 to 1965 presented a difficult problem to the Conservator, eventually solved by my successor, as described on p. 214.

The Serengeti controversy arose basically from the problem of human rights in national parks. It soon proved that park officials were not ideal administrators as far as the Masai were concerned. The first step taken to meet this situation was the posting of an Assistant District Officer to Ngorongoro in 1954: his house is now the Kimba Lodge. But this move may have aggravated rather than alleviated the situation. Certainly it is Dr Grzimek's view that the Masai skilfully played off the park authorities and the provincial administration against each other and that this divided control created more difficulties than it solved. Certainly within a year or two discussions started between government and the Park Trustees, which resulted in the publication of the notorious White Paper, *Sessional Paper No.* 1 of 1956.

This recommended a break-up of the Serengeti National Park into three smaller parks; the first, the Western Serengeti, which ironically included very little of the true Serengeti Plains but consisted mostly of the bush country running westward from the Serengeti edge to Lake Victoria, amounting to 1,400 square miles. Secondly there was proposed a Ngorongoro National Park, consisting of Ngorongoro Crater and the Northern Highlands Forest Reserve (450 square miles), and finally the Empakaai Crater Park (10 square miles). These parks were to be surrounded by a complicated system of areas under varying degrees of control, 'Special Game Areas', 'Game Reserves', 'Controlled Areas', and 'Partial Game Reserves'.

These proposals created a storm of protest. Looking back over the years, the exaggerated statements made by many of the parties concerned appear foolish in perspective, but at least they had the merit of causing the government of the day to reconsider its proposals. A high-powered three man Committee of Enquiry was appointed in July, 1956 consisting of Sir Ronald Sinclair, a colonial judge, as Chairman, with Sir Landsborough Thomson, Second Secretary, Medical Research

Council (Privy Council) and President of the Zoological Society, and Chief Humbi Ziota, M.B.E., a senior chief of the Nzega District and a Director of the Tanganyika Agricultural Corporation. In the event the Chairman was not available for this work and a new committee was set up with another judge, Sir Barclay Nihill, K.B.E., M.C., as Chairman. In addition to the two previously named members Mr. F. J. Musthill, O.B.E., late Conservator of Forests, Burma, joined the committee.

This delay had the advantage of allowing time for further enquiries to be made, and additional views to be aired. The American Wild Life Management Institute and the American Committee for International Wild Life Protection sent out a small group, led by Lee Talbot, then staff ecologist of the International Union for the Conservation of Nature and Natural Resources, and now on the staff of the Smithsonian Institute in Washington, who duly reported.

After discussions with the Colonial Office in London, the British fielded their team, a one-man show commissioned by the Fauna Preservation Society. Their choice of the late Professor W. H. Pearsall, D.Sc., F.R.S., Quain Professor of Botany at the University of London, had a profound effect on the course of events. For his report, issued after a two month visit to the area, November–December, 1956, in effect formed the scientific basis of the recommendations of the Committee which sat in July of the following year.

At that time I was down in Lusaka as Director of the Rhodes-Livingstone Institute, but was called back as a witness by the Tanganyika Government. The formal public meetings of the Committee were held in Arusha where an array of legal and ecological talent had been assembled. The Wildlife Societies of Kenya and Tanganyika (now unified into a single body) had briefed a Queen's Counsel, Mr Clive Slater of Nairobi, to represent them: the Tanganyika Government was represented by the Solicitor-General. Dr Leakey was there, the Chairman of Trustees and the Director of the Tanganyika National Parks, veterinary officers, forestry officers, water engineers, and of course Masai representatives. Certainly the Committee did not suffer from a lack of advice; they did a remarkable job of sorting out the plethora of ideas into a workable solution.

Though great weight was attached by the Committee to Professor Pearsall's recommendations, his practical suggestions were not wholly accepted; the eastern boundary of the suggested (in the White Paper)

Serengeti National Park was brought far to the east by Professor Pearsall (but with Masai grazing concessions in the park) only to be moved back westward by the Committee's Report, and even further westward on final adjustment. The Committee Report was, as far as I can ascertain, the first published document to propound the idea of a *conservation unit*. Subsequently, to explain the terminology used throughout this book, the phrase 'Conservation Unit' is applied to the government body responsible for the administration of the 'Conservation Area', i.e. the block of country so designated by Law.

It would be tedious to enumerate in detail the recommendations of the Committee, and the manner in which the government reacted to them. Very briefly the Committee recommended pushing the eastern boundary of the 'Sessional Paper Park' further eastward to cover the full extent of the plains migration. In the then-existing state of knowledge the boundary as suggested did not in fact do this. Subsequently, in view of Masai claims, the boundary was pushed back westward, with no regard for the wildebeest.

The Conservation Unit idea, propounded by the Committee, was fully accepted, and in fact extended, by the Government. Its proposed area was expanded to include the Dulen country and the high rough country lying above the Eyasi Scarp – a total of around 1,000 square miles. The two craters, Ngorongoro and Empakaai, recommended as 'Nature Sanctuaries' by the Committee, were included in the Conservation Area, but to be accorded special attention by the Authority. When I took over in September, 1961 I found that two years of 'special attention' had resulted in 31 rhino spearings, a heavy intrusion of domestic stock into the Crater and the re-establishment of squatter cultivation in Empakaai! All these matters were subsequently rectified, but the fact that they occurred certainly justified the public (and governmental) misgiving concerning the efficacy of the Authority, leading eventually to its replacement by the Conservator system.

As I have seen no published record of the Masai's agreement to vacate Moru and the western Serengeti, for the sake of future historians I record it here. It read :–

Agreement by the Masai to Vacate the Western Serengeti

We, the Laigwanak (elders) of the Ngorongoro and Loliondo Divisions of the Masai District, agree on behalf of all the Masai living in these areas to renounce our claim to all those parts of the Serengeti Plains lying within the Northern and Lake Provinces which lie to the west of the line shown to us by the District Commissioner, Masai, on the 13th and 14th March and the 20th April, 1958.

We understand that as a result of this renunciation we shall not be entitled henceforth in the years to come to cross this line which will become the boundary of the new Serengeti National Park and which will be demarcated. We also understand that we shall not be entitled to reside in or use in future the land lying to the west of this line, which we have habitually used in the past.

We agree to move ourselves, our possessions, our cattle and all our other animals out of this land by the advent of the next short rains, that is before the 31st December, 1958.

Then followed the signatures of 12 Masai elders and an explanatory note reading :–

The line mentioned above is that marked in brown pencil on the plan attached to P.C.'s minute No. CC1/9/135 of 21.3.58. The above boundary retains for the use of the Masai the wells in the lower Olduvai and korongos to the north thereof: the Ildashi wells: the Meiran'gwai wells: and the grazing adjacent thereto. Lake Lgarja in its entirety will remain within the new Serengeti National Park.

The document concluded with the signatures of the executive officer of the Masai Federal Council as interpreter and of the Provincial and District Commissioners as witnesses.

Looking back, I honestly do not think a more workable solution could have emerged. The 1956 Sessional Paper would have landed the Park Authorities with *three* parks to cope with. Besides presenting difficult problems of administration, they were all of doubtful ecological viability. Professor Pearsall's solutions would have produced a crop of troubles, arising from the grazing rights for the Masai which he proposed within the Park. The Committee's solution avoided most of the pitfalls, but in my view, both today and at the time, the Government did well to adjust the Committee's recommendations as they did.

The Masai lost Moru and the Western Serengeti, over which subsequently discovered evidence confirms their century-old claim. But in the course of that century, particularly in recent years, they have been shown the way to produce, without detriment to the habitat, more cattle from the land remaining to them than could have been produced from all the country they occupied in the past. They have, generally speaking, chosen to ignore such advice and so forfeit any sympathy that their loss might have engendered. Further, the Ngorongoro Masai weathered the 1960/62 drought with a minimum of loss and hardship, in spite of the loss of Moru.

The Parks lost Ngorongoro and Empakaai, but the nation did not. Ngorongoro *might* have developed better or more rapidly, from the tourist point of view, under the Parks than under the Conservator, but the record of the present system is impressive. Empakaai *might* have been 'opened up' but in my view once it had been cleared of agriculture it is best 'kept on ice' till such time as a demand justifies its development as a nature-trail-on-foot area.

The Forest Reserve maintained its *status quo*. Certainly more might have been done to protect the smaller clumps of forest lying outside the reserve, but whether by fire control or from natural causes, considerable areas of grassland are reverting to woodland.

The wildebeest lost nothing; they still hold the trump card of malignant catarrh, which drives the cattle off their grazing grounds just at the season the wildlife requires it.

The rhino, whose fate seemed so doubtful, have an assured future. Not only is poaching under control, but research has revealed a much brighter picture than was at one time feared.

So, in spite of the criticisms levelled at the Government's decision at the time, the outcome has not been unsatisfactory. Some of the weaknesses which revealed themselves have been removed. Adjustments in the administrative machine have been made: the 'Authority' has been replaced by the Conservator; the Unit has been absorbed into the Ministry as an integral part of the organisation; the staffing position seems with Canada's help to have a rosier future. Also adjustments in boundaries have been made on the Parks side, which safeguard areas previously susceptible to poaching and to encroachment. But this is anticipating the story of more recent events.

The Authority speedily demonstrated its uselessness in administration. On the organisational side the four professional and technical officers, all European, not all of wide experience or great tact, in their enthusiasm to do a new job well formed a pressure group to demand drastic action and sweeping changes in the land use pattern. This, as might be expected, caused the conservative Masai members to become more resistant to change than ever. With the situation thus polarised, the Chairman, a young District Officer, was in no position to persuade either his technical colleagues to display more patience or the Masai to accept some small measure of change. As a result the Authority ground to a halt: meetings were suspended, the last being on the 9 May, 1960, less than a year after the Authority had been set up.

It was at this juncture that the Tanganyika Government invited me to revisit the area and tender advice on the sociological aspects of the *impasse*. I had just resigned the directorship of the Rhodes-Livingstone Institute for Social Research in Lusaka, Northern Rhodesia, and agreed to undertake this task on an honorary basis. I spent four months, January to April, based in Arusha, frequently visiting Ngorongoro and Dar es Salaam for consultations. I completed my report on a voyage to England, my daughter acting as honorary typist, the main recom-mendations being the reorganisation of the Authority and the establishment of an Advisory Board. There were also many detailed recommendations concerning the improvement of relationships with the Masai, measures to encourage the tourist trade, closer cohesion amongst the 'team', further research, and so on.

On the subject of the 'Authority' I thought it worth while attempting to resuscitate this defunct body, with stronger professional representa-tion on the one hand and more and younger Masai on the other. To get more objective minds to bear on the problems, I suggested that the provincial officers from Arusha should replace the local forest, game, veterinary and water representatives. I also suggested that the Authority should be a statutory body, self-accounting in financial matters. It must be realised that at that time, 1961, the future of the organisation at Ngorongoro was completely uncertain. Not only capital funds but current expenditure was being drawn from the Colonial Development Welfare Grant of £182,000 which had been made to Tanganyika to enable the country to put into effect the recommendations of the Serengeti Committee. This meant that the salaries of the staff, my own included, came from this source: in the case of civil servants seconded from departments, forestry, game, etc. their salaries were reimbursed to the departments concerned. Where the money was to come from to continue these payments beyond June, 1964 when the grant expired, no one knew. One of the principles on which the Colonial Development and Welfare grants were given was that of 'pump-priming', i.e. the money was regarded as a means of getting a project off the ground and by the end of the period the recipient was expected to carry on alone with the scheme. I felt that if all sources of revenue were diverted into the Authority's coffers there would at least be enough to keep it running, but emphasised that funds would have to come from outside for capital development. Further experience and study have taught me that only in very exceptional circumstances do parks pay for themselves: their benefit lies not in direct revenue earning, but in the indirect revenue which they stimulate in the tourist industry, hotels, transport, sale of curios and so on. Further, the revenue from the firewood plantations was to prove very unreliable; due to various set-backs very little revenue has accrued from this source, or is likely to accrue for some time yet.

So in retrospect it was fortunate that my idea of a self-accounting Authority was turned down, although at the time no alternative was proposed. We just drifted along, drawing our funds from Colonial Development and Welfare: but this scheme was due to close on 30 June, 1964. When the deadline drew near, the Government of Tanzania (as it had then become) manfully accepted its responsibilities and agreed to carry the costs of the Conservation Unit.

This was a great step forward. It guaranteed the survival of an administrative machine to run Ngorongoro in perpetuity: just as there will always be a Forest Division or a Medical Department, so the Conservation Unit should always be there.

To return to my 1961 proposals, the other important suggestion was the establishment of an Advisory Board. This idea had already been put forward, unbeknown to me, by Sir Julian Huxley, in his report to UNESCO entitled *The Conservation of Wildlife and Natural Habitats in Central and East Africa*. Indeed the composition he suggested was much the same as mine, designed to ensure that the responsible Minister received the best advice possible. In addition to governmental representation I suggested that there should be a representative of local wildlife and tourism interests, an overseas representative covering the same ground, the Director of the East African Agriculture and Forestry Research Organisation at Maguga near Nairobi (then, as now, an East African Common or Community Service), the professor of zoology from Makerere College, Kampala, Uganda (at that time the University of East Africa with campuses at Kampala, Nairobi and Dar es Salaam had not been established).

The omission of the Director of National Parks was criticised, but I felt that tension between the park authorities and the Masai should be allowed to die down before such an appointment was made. Close informal liaison with the parks was of course maintained, particularly on research matters, and the link has now been formalised, as I always intended it should be at the appropriate juncture.

I felt that the Advisory Board should be a statutory body, i.e. appointed under the law, with a legally-defined composition, terms of reference and procedure. In the varying circumstances of modern government, many types of statutory body have emerged, with the Ministries exercising various degrees of control. In some cases the Minister is bound to consult the board on certain specified matters, and if he refuses the advice proffered, he must record in writing his reasons for so doing. In some cases a greater measure of freedom is given to boards to run their own affairs, e.g. the Board of Trustees of National Parks, but even then there is usually a 'small print' clause in the Act obliging the Board to fulfil any direction which the Minister may see fit to give it. And even if such clause does not exist, Government always has the whip hand for it can cut off the subsidy or other form of financial aid if the board does not behave itself.

However, the idea of a statutory board was rejected. One reason for this was a feeling held by some that it was an infringement on the sovereign rights of an independent state, such as Tanganyika became in December, 1961 to invest non-citizens with a legal right to advise a Minister as to his duties. This was not very valid as I proposed only three outsiders out of a total of 11 members. The present membership amounts to 19 of whom 11 are local, two from neighbouring Kenya and six from overseas. I revert to its future status in Chapter XI.

The Arusha Conference of September, 1961 called by the International Union for the Conservation of Nature and Natural Resources (I.U.C.N.) formed a convenient occasion for a review of my recommendations. It was attended by many leaders of thought in the conservation field, Sir Julian Huxley, Peter Scott, Bernard Grzimek, Dr Wasawo, Dr Worthington and several others, who were invited by the Tanganyika Government to advise on the current situation at Ngorongoro, which most of them also visited at that time. It was perhaps fortunate that Ngorongoro at that time presented itself as an 'all time low'. The drought was at its worst; rhino spearing had been heavy (see p. 93); intrusion of domestic stock was considerable, and the Authority was at a standstill. These conditions made it impossible for Government to ignore the complaints and advice of the assembled conservationists. Particularly was this so as Prime Minister Julius Nyerere, shortly to become first President of the Republic of Tanganyika, had, with his Ministers, just presented the 'Arusha Manifesto' to the conference. Although it has been frequently quoted, it certainly bears repetition in the present context.

> The survival of our wildlife is a matter of grave concern to all of us in Africa. These wild creatures amid the wild places they inhabit are not only important as a source of wonder and inspiration but are an integral part of our natural resources and of our future livelihood and well being.
>
> In accepting the trusteeship of our wildlife we solemnly declare that we will do everything in our power to make sure that our children's grand-children will be able to enjoy this rich and precious inheritance.
>
> The conservation of wildlife and wild places calls for specialist knowledge, trained manpower and money, and we look to other nations to co-operate in this important task – the success or failure of which not only affects the Continent of Africa, but the rest of the world as well.

How, in the light of this, could Government ignore the plight of the 'wild creatures amid the wild places they inhabit'? In the course of prolonged discussion, tactfully and skilfully presided over by Clive Mace, Permanent Secretary of the Ministry of Lands, Forests and Wildlife (so renamed following the Conference) there emerged the idea of a Conservator responsible through the Permanent Secretary to the Minister for the 'conservation and development' of the natural resources of the Conservation Area.

This idea was approved by the Cabinet, so, though I took office as Chairman of the Authority and functioned as such for several months, it was accepted that I would become Conservator, with changed responsibilities, as soon as the necessary legislation could be put through Parliament. The position was legalised in an amended Act which became law on 1 November, 1963. Besides defining the position of Conservator, the opportunity was taken to adjust several other points of weakness in the original ordinance.

For the next three years I was resident at Ngorongoro, but retained my house at Duluti near Arusha. In spite of the personal cost of maintaining two establishments I found that as much work was involved in dealing with provincial politicians and officials at Arusha as with the Masai and local problems at Ngorongoro. It was a difficult job, in which I was only partially successful, to weld a heterogeneous group of officials into a team, especially as one had no say in choosing them. Additionally they were seconded from other departments, and not unnaturally retained loyalty to their 'parent' department. Furthermore, by historical accident the residences of the senior officers were scattered over a distance of 17 miles along the Crater rim, the Assistant Conservator (Game) living in what is now Forest Resort (Dhillon's Lodge) and the Assistant Conservator (Forests) having his dwelling and his nurseries at the Old Boma, now Kimba Lodge.

Not unnaturally these individuals resented their homes and offices being concentrated at the Conservation Headquarters. I had 'inherited' two permanent houses and a permanent office built for the Authority by the P.W.D. on the present headquarters site. These were not ideal, either in design or position, but in the then existing circumstances one could not start from scratch but had to take over and possibly adapt the policies already inaugurated. Appreciating the fact that permanent buildings were undesirably near the road, I permitted no more in that vicinity, concentrating on timber structures which could be salvaged when replaced by other buildings on a new site. The erection of permanent official housing on the rim of the Crater has been criticized, but I continued to put up more houses on the site originally chosen. Having lived there for several years and gained both knowledge and inspiration from observing the Crater in its ever changing moods as season followed season, I saw no reason why future generations of senior officials should be denied a privileged view of the Crater which any tourist could obtain by hiring accommodation used as lodges. This policy is still maintained, though a 'staff village' is now under construction, well back from the rim but still commanding a good view of the crater, which will lead to the eventual removal of the wooden structures.

To pull all the threads of tourist development together into a connected narrative, it is necessary to collate stray pieces of information which appear from time to time in earlier chapters.

Ngorongoro could only be reached by foot until the first road was constructed from Oldeani (Kampi Nyoka) to the Crater rim and thence to the Balbal and the Serengeti in about 1932. Colonel Hallier, then Provincial Commissioner in Arusha, quickly realised the tourist potential of Ngorongoro and obtained funds – a meagre £400 – to build the first Lodge. Construction began in 1935 under the supervision of Gordon Russell, an Assistant District Officer. The idea of building in logs was suggested by an ex-naval man called Marks who was employed on the job, as also a farmer Prinsloo, who brought up a team of oxen from Karutu to haul the logs from the forest. The timber used is Pillarwood, *Cassipourea elliotii*, of which many fine specimens are to be seen from the road.

The Lodge was opened on a do-it-yourself basis, and remained so for 27 years till the present concessionaire took over in July, 1963. Everything was on a basis of strict economy: thatched roof – so pleasing to the eye and cheaper than corrugated iron or shingles. Lighting was by kerosene lamp, and water hand-pumped from the adjacent valley; water heating was by firewood under 44 gallon drums and sanitation by pit latrine. The mess hut was built at that time – later reception and office before it was burnt down in 1968 and replaced by the present larger office and shop – and two lines of huts, one along the Crater rim and the other up the valley.

The road was such that the Lodge could only be reached in dry weather: there was of course no motor access to the Crater and the visitor wishing to descend to the Crater floor had to do so by foot. Very shortly the war came along, which put paid to tourist develop- ment, but the Lodge was used by service men on leave from Kenya, Abyssinia and Aden. After the war development did not recommence till the park authorities took over in 1952. For the first time a European manager was installed, a shop opened where visitors could purchase their food, to be cooked by the camp attendants: some new huts were built, but again funds were a limiting factor and clapboard and corrugated iron roofing made their ugly appearance on the scene. The administrative camp and Masai dispensary which I had built in 1935–36 were taken over: I had never found out whether the Masai Treasury was compensated for the money they had put into the office and dispensary there.

By 1 July, 1959, when the park's jurisdiction came to an end at Ngorongoro, no alternative arrangements had been made for the running of the Lodge so the park staff remained till a private lessee took over in the following year. The Chairman of the Authority reported that the continued presence of uniformed park staff gave the Masai the impression that Government was not sticking to its agreement, and as a result the Masai were against approving land grants for Government building-land and for forestry plantations.

At the close of the park period visitors numbered about 3,000 per year. By 1961 the figure was 6,044, and since then numbers have continued to rise. The annual totals, now over 25,000, are plotted on Fig. 6, against a hypothetical gross rate of 30 % per annum, with the 1961 figure as the starting point.

At the present growth rate it appears as though the 1970 figure could reach 64,000, but only if certain conditions are fulfilled. Firstly there are several factors beyond local control. The economic health of the countries from which the tourists originate is of critical importance. For example, in the United States the tax on overseas airline tickets and on tourists funds exported in excess of a very modest *per diem* allowance is an unexpected blow which will hit the tourist trade very hard and against which the recipient countries have no redress. Again, any suspicion of insecurity in the country concerned or even in neighbouring countries is enough to divert the tourists elsewhere. It is not perhaps sufficiently realised locally what competition faces even such an attractive area as Ngorongoro. A visit to some of the more spectacular U.S. game parks, Yellowstone, Grand Taton, or Yosemite (as the author was privileged to make in 1964) brings home a realisation that Ngorongoro has by no means a monopoly in scenic grandeur. Admittedly the wildlife of those parks cannot compete with Ngorongoro, but that of the Kruger National Park in South Africa, Gorongoza in Mocambique, Chobe in Botswana or Luangwa in Zambia certainly can. Then it is not everyone who seeks a combination of wildlife and scenery. What about scenery and sophistication, as in the Asu caldera in Japan, Aztec or Aya ruins in the Americas, the cathedrals of Europe, the pyramids of Egypt, the temples and shrines of India, Ceylon and Burma? A choice of all these faces the potential tourist when he goes a-shopping to his travel agent.

So Ngorongoro has got to be good if it is to keep abreast of the current expansion trend.

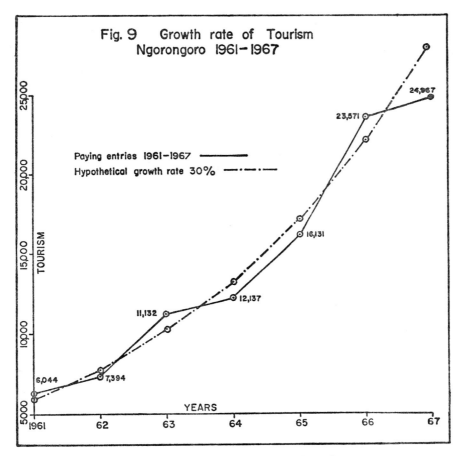

Fig. 9   Growth rate of Tourism
Ngorongoro 1961–1967

Paying entries 1961–1967 ————
Hypothetical growth rate 30% —·—·—·—

TOURISM

6,044   7,394   11,132   12,137   16,131   23,571   24,967

YEARS

Fig. 6 Growth rate of tourism 1961–1967

On present plans the position appears to be well in hand to cover a 30% annual rise till the end of 1970, when the entry figure should be around 64,000. For the bed capacity as recorded in the 1967 Annual Report is 228. Some of this is new accommodation and so not yet used to maximum capacity: some is austere and so not fully utilised. But the established Lodge, with 105 beds, runs at 54% capacity. Two new Lodges, assumed to be 200 beds in the first place, will bring the total accommodation up to 428 beds. Used at 50% capacity this would

14

provide 78,110 bed nights, which closely approximates to the anticipated total of visitors, adjusted to their estimated length of stay.

Standards must also rise, but a full range of accommodation should continue to be offered, from the luxury level to the do-it-yourself for the family and the youth hostel for the student. That was accepted as policy when I was Conservator and I am glad to note that my successor is following the same lines. As a result a new modern lodge is now under construction, with more modest accommodation available at Kimba – centred round the old District Officer's house – and a tented camp on the plains at Lake Ndutu. This last is a step in the right direction: accommodation in the Nasera-Doinyoogol area and at Olduvai will eventually follow, in spite of water difficulties. Nasera rock provides an attractive site on the plains, whilst Empakaai Crater must eventually provide accommodation for the nature-trail enthusiast – but no vehicles please!

These latter suggestions will all help to avoid over concentration, as also the policy which Government accepted in my time and which I hope will be continued, that no lodge should be allowed to grow beyond 100 beds. I am fully aware that the hotel trade considers that an uneconomic figure: they would prefer up to 200 to carry the overheads of management. But from the balance sheets I have seen, a hundred-bed lodge can itself earn a very handsome profit. If they exceed this, the concentration of people and transport completely spoils the tranquillity which is one of the most uplifting features of a visit to Ngorongoro. Similarly whilst every visitor should descend to the Crater floor, he should be encouraged to spend some of his time visiting the outlying attractions. For the Crater itself is bound to reach saturation point some time, but it is a long way off yet. A hundred square miles is a lot of country – the size of the original District of Columbia before Virginia reclaimed its contribution and brought the figure down to 68 square miles. One danger is overconcentration around a particular attraction, a pride of lions, a rhino, or wild dog on a kill, to which all vehicles are naturally attracted. The only way to avoid this is by training drivers and guides not to overcrowd their clients at one point, and by strict warden control if and when un-accompanied vehicles start using the Crater in considerable numbers, as is the case today in the Nairobi National Park. I pioneered the system of licensed guides – that is as far as East Africa is concerned – in 1962. I am glad to read (March, 1968) that an advance in this field has come from one of the largest tour operators, the United Touring Company of Nairobi, who have introduced comprehensive in-service training for its driver-guides and invited the Principal of the College of African Wildlife Management at Mweka, the Conservator, and National Parks representatives to sit on an examining panel.

In short, to keep the expansion continuing at the present rate, the accommodation must expand, the attractions be diversified and the amenities maintained. Another way of minimising the impact of increased numbers, and incidentally of increasing the revenue both of Government and private enterprise, is to spread the tourist load evenly throughout the year. East Africa is most favourably placed in this regard, as compared with, say, Switzerland, or the Yellowstone National Park, or the Kafue or Luangwa in Zambia. These are examples of tourist attractions which must inevitably have a closed season, due to snow, or paradoxically, lack of snow, or rain or some other feature. Not so Ngorongoro; though some months are admittedly better than others, with improved roads it has been possible to keep the Crater open all the year. I inherited a 'closed season' system, but succeeded in keeping the Crater open throughout the year for the first time in 1962. Since then the figures for the 'off season', April and May, have risen steadily from a monthly average of 138 in 1964 to 772 in 1965 and 1,191 in 1967. This last figure compares with an overall monthly average of 2,090. Analysis of the figures also reveals two peak periods, which arise from external circumstances. The August peak is due to school and university holidays, whilst the January–February–March peak corresponds to the period when people, after enjoying Christmas at home, are most anxious to exchange the cold damp winter of the northern hemisphere for the sunshine of Africa.

The coming of independence to Tanganyika, under a Governor-General from 12 December, 1961 and under President Nyerere from 12 December, 1962 coincides with the administrative changes at Ngorongoro. Let us here summarise what the British had to hand over to the new government at Ngorongoro. Firstly a legal and administrative machine which, given goodwill, suitable staff and sufficient funds could be made to work. These elements were forthcoming in varying degrees over the next few years and account for such success as was achieved.

Then there was a system of roads which enabled officials and tourists to get to and around the Conservation Area. The road from Arusha had been tarmac-ed for the first 50 miles and then straightened and gravelled to the base of the rift at Mto-wa-Mbu. Thereafter there were weak links through the red soil of the Mbulu highlands, but the climb up to the Crater and the run along the Crater rim and down to the Serengeti had been greatly improved. Up till 1961, this section had not been surfaced. It is impossible to imagine the difficulties of communication posed by the local soil conditions. A shower of rain made it impossible to go from the Conservation Headquarters to the Lodge, even in a four-wheel-drive, without fitting chains. A costly gravelling scheme remedied these conditions – later the section from the western foot of the Crater highlands to the National Park boundary was also gravelled.

Until the hand-over by National Parks mid-1959, access to the Crater floor had been by the circuitous route along the eastern rim which I had pioneered in 1940. During their regime the Park officials had begun the construction of a more direct route down the southern wall of the Crater. But the terrain presented such difficulties that this could only be constructed on a gradient suitable for four-wheel-drive vehicles, and not for saloon cars or mini-buses. Furthermore, so much sidecut into solid rock was necessary that it was uneconomic to make the road wide enough for vehicles to pass. It was therefore necessary to control traffic on a 'one-hour-down-and-one-hour-up' basis. This was obviously unsatisfactory if we were to attract large numbers of tourists: it was most tedious if one just happened to misjudge one's timing and in consequence had to hang around for an hour. If waiting to descend the tourist was impatient to see the highlight of his trip to Africa and resented wasting an hour of his precious day. Equally in the evening, after a tiring day in the Crater one wanted to get back to a bath and a drink without undue delay.

This problem was solved by utilising and improving the prehistoric tracks leading down from Malanja to the Seneto corner of the Crater. This was completed in a remarkably short time, for very little money, thanks to the efforts of the Assistant Conservator (Works), the late Gert Fourie, the Headman Isa Lonyoki and his labour gang. This was still a one-way track, with gradients of up to 1 in 4, but we avoided waiting and permitted a constant flow of vehicles into and out of the Crater by making one road the descent road, and the other the exit.

Within the Crater communications were also improved: but here there are dangers. If one makes the tracks too good, or too straight they encourage speeding and also look unsightly. What we aimed at was a single track gravel road which would enable a complete circuit of the Crater to remain open throughout the year, sufficiently well surfaced to obviate dust, good enough to attract traffic to use the road rather than cut across country, but twisting and narrow enough to discourage overtaking and to necessitate reduced speed when passing another vehicle.

A double track descent into the Crater was surveyed in 1965, but work was not started because the rupture of diplomatic relations with the United Kingdom led to the cessation of the British aid from which this scheme was to be financed.

The Lodge was the only accommodation available when the Conservation Unit took over. It possessed about 40 beds and no catering was available. As the Conservation Unit, unlike the Parks, was unwilling to run the Lodge itself, Government let it on concession at a remarkably low figure. It continued for some time on a do-it-yourself basis, but then a new company took over. 'A.B.' Fletcher from the United States provided the drive and energy to get new buildings up, whilst 'Ben' Benbow, an experienced British hotelier, brought in the know-how which got the catering off to such a good start. Though this team failed to survive, they laid such good foundations that by 1967, according to the Annual Report, the 105 bed Lodge provided 20,724 bed nights accommodation in a single year. This represents a 54% occupancy, a very high figure considering the seasonal nature of the business.

Further accommodation added during my period at Ngorongoro was the Forest Resort or Dhillon's Lodge, so named after the energetic and charming Sikh couple who were the first concessionaires, and the Youth Hostel to accommodate educational parties, with an annex to cater for hitch-hikers. Since I left further accommodation had been provided, so from about 40 bed spaces in 1961 there are now 248 available. The principle, already touched on, of catering for all tastes and pockets has been adhered to: it is essential that it should be maintained in future.

It would be tedious to record in detail the difficulties encountered in getting the Conservation Unit off the ground and developing it as a functioning machine capable of handling the increased intake of tourists, whilst at the same time conserving the natural beauty of the Area and coping with local development. Faced with conflicting interests the Conservator was in a position that he could not please everyone. It has been explained how it was decided to make Dulen the focus of agricultural development, and to resettle the outlying pockets of cultivation there. It was a three year battle to get the squatters out of Empakaai Crater: my successor eventually succeeded by going in with a posse of police and standing firm against the threats of a group of hysterical spearmen. At Dulen itself difficulties also arose in the form of elephants. Rather than have them shot I invested in bird scarers, a device activated by calcium carbide which exploded with a deafening bang at intervals. This was not successful – after a short period of effectiveness the elephant got used to the noise and ignored it. However, I thought it was worth trying, but the locals did not; the Regional Commissioner received the following indignant letter written on their behalf, translated below from Swahili to English.

> Greetings, Sir! With respect we write this letter to inform you of the damage which we have suffered in our farms which have been destroyed by elephants, also with reference to the letter of the Conservator of the 31st May, 1963 which prohibited the Game Scouts from shooting these elephants which are ruining the farms of the people of Dulen. We understand completely that poverty is one of the three enemies of Tanganyika. The people are cultivating in order to get rid of the enemy of poverty but we people of Dulen are supporting this enemy by following the letter of the Conservator which said that these elephants should not be shot . . .
>
> Your Excellency, this order of the Conservator displays the cruelty of a he-goat such as we have never seen in Tanganyika, but only in South Africa where our African brothers are treated thus by the Boers. Further, we say straight out that the Conservator is not here at Ngorongoro to help the Masai, but to hurt them and keep them down in their previous state . . .

And so on in similar vein. Which shows that the Conservator just cannot win!

Without further facts and figures I shall endeavour to sum up the period of my Conservatorship. I feel I can claim some credit for having established a sound foundation for development on a basis of multiple land use. Rhino poaching was contained and a system of publicity set up – annual reports, newsletters, bulletins, press handouts, etc. – to ensure that this and other achievements received notice. By this means world-wide misgivings concerning the partition of the Serengeti National Park were to some extent allayed.

Tourism went ahead by leaps and bounds. The overseas factors giving rise to this were of course beyond our control, but the Unit managed to keep facilities expanding at a rate sufficient to cope with the influx.

Poaching or illegal killing of wildlife other than rhino was main-tained at a minimal level. By several accidents of history and geography the wildlife of the Serengeti is as safe, if not safer, in the Conservation Area as in the National Park; when this point was got across to the public much of the opposition to the Conservation Unit died down.

Research went ahead both through workers directly associated with the Area – Goddard and Estes – and several visitors from the Serengeti Research Project (later Institute), Klingel, Kruuk and others. These workers not only added greatly to our knowledge of the species they studied, thereby facilitating management; they also provided reassuring figures concerning wildlife numbers. In particular, Goddard's counts of the rhino population of the Crater and Olduvai, duly publicised, did much to reassure public opinion and to refute the wilder statements of over-ardent conservationists.

Following the tensions of the National Park period and of the brief reign of the Authority, relationships with the Masai improved. The elders became more co-operative in the matter of investigating rhino killings and in producing the culprits. The same attitude was not apparent in the matter of forest trespass, but this time-honoured offence has been going on in spite of heavy fines ever since the Masai were denied free access to the forest. Whilst the damage so caused is serious it is less so than the heavy attrition of the rhino population which with Masai co-operation is now under control.

In the field of animal husbandry the situation was contained but little positive progress made. Excessive grazing on the Crater floor was kept well under control. Stock numbers throughout the Area fluctuated, but by Act of God and not due to imposed control: firstly famine reduced the cattle population, and when a return to good rainfall

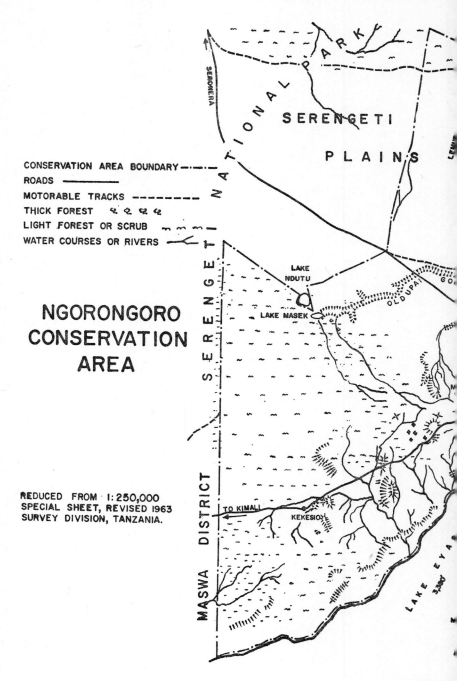

CONSERVATION AREA BOUNDARY ---·--
ROADS ————————
MOTORABLE TRACKS --------
THICK FOREST ৫ ৫ ৫ ৫
LIGHT FOREST OR SCRUB ~ ~ ~ ~
WATER COURSES OR RIVERS

NGORONGORO
CONSERVATION
AREA

REDUCED FROM 1:250,000
SPECIAL SHEET, REVISED 1963
SURVEY DIVISION, TANZANIA.

SERENGETI PLAINS

NATIONAL PARK

SEROMERA

SERENGETI

MASWA DISTRICT

LAKE NDUTU

LAKE MASEK

OLDUPAI

TO KIMALI

KEKESIO

LAKE EYASI

3380

Fig. 7 The Ngoron

TO LOLIONDO

Senjor R.

LAKE
NATRON
1950'+

ANGATA SALE

DOINYOOGOL

ANGATA KITI

LENGAI
(Active
Volcano) 9,650'+

KERIMASI
8,550'+

10,700'+ EMPAKAAI
CRATER
7,350'+

ENGARUKA

Sand Dunes

Broken Hilly Country

BULBUL
DEPRESSION

OLMOTI
10,168'

SIRUA
C.10,900' LOLMALASIN
12,000'+

TEPPES

MALANJA

Kimba
Lodge

NGORONGORO
CRATER

Crater Lodge
Wildlife Lodge

OLDEANI
10,460'

Dhlom's
Lodge

MBULUMBULU

OLDEANI

KARATU

GREGORY

RIFT

MTO WA MBU

Manyara
Hotel

TO ARUSHA

TO MBULU

MANYARA NATIONAL PARK

L. MANYARA
3150'

4 3 2 1 0   5   10   15   20 MILES

N

Conservation Area

conditions led to a rise in numbers, East Coast fever stepped in and brought the population down again. Sales in the markets fell, but this was due to circumstances prevailing throughout the region and not just locally in the Area. The implementation of schemes for improved ranching methods broke down against a wall of Masai indifference.

11 Can Ngorongoro Survive?

Can Ngorongoro survive? This sounds a simple question, capable of a straight answer, but in point of fact it raises several complicated issues.

In the first place what do we mean by Ngorongoro? The Crater, or the ecosystem of which the Crater is the hub? Or the Conservation Area of 3,200 square miles, artificially defined and containing in whole or in part several different ecosystems?

Then in what form do we envisage its survival? Just as it is at present, or, in terms of the legislation which safeguards it, 'conserved and developed' in the interests both of the nation and of the local inhabitants?

But what if the national interests and those of the local inhabitants clash? This has already happened at Olduvai, where it is in the interests of the Masai to graze and water in the Olduvai gorge, but nationally, and indeed on a world-wide basis, it is in the interests of science to preserve the gorge and its archaeological treasures from indiscriminate trampling.

Such problems can only be solved if the principles of optimum land use are applied. What, in all the circumstances, is the best use to which an area of land can be put? It may not, in fact it seldom will, be a single use – agriculture, or forestry, or wildlife, or tourism. So the second principle of multiple land use must be considered, encouraging the compatibles, reconciling areas of friction between closely allied types of land use, and eliminating one or other of those that are entirely incompatible. A third principle must also be constantly borne in mind, namely the principle of sustained yield, which in turn involves the conservation of the resource concerned, be it water or forest, wildlife or pasture.

If these principles are applied to the management of the Area,

Ngorongoro will surely survive. But there is much room for planning the form in which it should survive. To analyse this problem it seems simplest to start at the centre, the Crater, and then work outwards.

The Crater itself permits of no argument. Its optimum use is for wildlife and tourism; I can detect no body of public opinion that thinks otherwise. But such a happy situation has not happened by accident. It will be recalled how the Germans leased out the Crater as ranchland, how the early British administration realienated it to Sir Charles Ross; then how it permitted the intrusion of peasant agriculture and finally how, in response to pressure, it finally committed itself to preserving the Crater for wildlife, tourism and Masai pastoralism. This was the position when the independent government of Tanganyika took over, and this is the position the government has maintained to date. There is every hope that as this has proved itself the most appropriate and profitable form of land use, no future government will wish to alter the *status quo*. But there is no room for complacency; future governments will have to face tremendous problems and pressures arising out of the increasing population of the nation: for this reason the policy of keeping government and the public informed of the value of Ngorongoro to the whole country must be maintained. The annual reports and bulletins which I inaugurated have been kept up and improved by my successor. Misconceptions are still common which require correction. As late as 1967 in his book *Great National Parks*, Richard Carrington wrote of the Crater: 'The black rhino still exists there although its numbers have diminished over the last ten years.' He also implies that the wildlife numbers have diminished from what we now know was an exaggerated number when he wrote: 'early explorers estimate the number of herbivores it [the Crater] contained at certain seasons at no less than 100,000.' The same author also encourages bad tourist behaviour by writing that rhino 'can be teased into charging by any driver with the skill and nerve to get away'! So the same old lessons must be repeated again and again, even at the expense of boring the well-informed.

A particularly valuable innovation is the introduction of Swahili in addition to English into the Units publications. As prosperity increases so will the number of Tanzanian citizens who visit Ngorongoro: every facility must be provided to encourage such visitors, particularly the provision of accommodation at prices they can afford. This will avoid the impression that a trip to Ngorongoro is the privilege of the rich overseas visitor, and do much to build up a body of public opinion intent on ensuring the survival of Ngorongoro.

There will of course be many management problems to be met in the Crater; one concerns the position of the few Masai pastoralists still living in the Crater – should they be gradually eliminated or should they remain with their cattle, conforming to an overall management plan? The present policy aims at this eventual removal. Another problem concerns a suitable burning system, and another the method of cropping to be employed should an increase in wildlife numbers necessitate this. There is also the control of tourists to consider, both in numbers and in behaviour. But all these are problems of management which can be solved, provided the overall framework is secure.

But the survival of the Crater is not enough. It is part of a larger ecosystem. Hydrologically it is dependent on the surrounding areas. The Lerai springs with their minimum flow of a million gallons of crystal-clear water a day are dependent on the Oldeani forest. The Koitoktok springs doubtless draw their water from the East Rim forest, whilst the Munge river has it sources in the Olmoti caldera. It should not be difficult to convince posterity of the necessity to preserve the Oldeani forest as part of the Northern Highlands Forest Reserve, for not only the Crater but the development areas of Oldeani, Karatu and Mbulumbulu are equally dependent on the continued existence of this catchment forest. But the Olmoti catchment presents a situation which requires watching.

Zoologically also the Crater is part of a larger ecosystem. It is not subject to wholesale migration – teeming with wildlife one month and empty the next; the year-round display of animals is indeed its greatest strength as a tourist attraction. None the less, nearly every significant species migrates in considerable numbers at some season of the year. Although a particularly localised animal, the rhino certainly make use of the Crater rim, whilst there are of course many more elephant and buffalo in the surrounding forest than in the Crater itself. Without the surrounding reservoir it is doubtful if the stocks in the Crater would survive. Likewise with eland and waterbuck – the former being particularly mobile; should the Crater stock meet with some disaster, from whence would reinforcements be drawn if the surrounding areas were denuded of wildlife? Some wildebeest migrate to the Balbal and the eastern Serengeti – perhaps up to one third of the population being absent at any one time, whilst large numbers of Crater zebra are to be seen at Malanja and indeed in the semi-forested area adjacent to the Conservation Headquarters at certain times of the year. As far as the carnivores are concerned, the natural restocking of the Crater by immigrant lion following the *stomoxys* plague has been recorded, whilst wild dog, such an attraction when in the Crater, are extremely mobile in their habits.

Thus there is obviously no future in the Crater as a glorified Whipsnade Zoo, with a fence, literal or metaphorical, round the rim. But just how much of the peripheral area is it necessary to preserve to conserve the Crater itself? As explained above the Northern Highlands Forest Reserve which safeguards the eastern and southern flanks is a must. But is the Lake Eysai trough, the broken upland country to the west of the Eyasi scarp, and indeed the Dulen area?

In the long term I would regard this southern area as expendable from the wildlife and tourism angle, best used as a development area for agriculture and pastoralism. It was not in the original Serengeti National Park so there is no 'breach of faith' to the world by permitting ex-parkland to revert to agricultural use. Further, it seems likely that there will eventually be a direct road link between Lake Victoria and the railhead at Arusha. This would be in lieu of a rail link and thus designed to carry heavy traffic. It could either follow the present road line along the rim of the Crater – but heaven preserve both the tourist and the truck driver from the presence of 20 ton lorries and trailers, on the tortuous climb up to the Crater: or it could follow the obvious alignment through the Oldeani area, then slip between the foot of the mountain and the north shore of Lake Eyasi, and thence up the scarp and along the southern margin of the Serengeti – well below the limit of the wildebeest migration. It would be premature to mark this route on the map on pp. 216–7 as 'proposed road', but the reader can trace it out for himself.

If and when this road is made it will be an incentive to development and surely provide the answer to the problem of the Masai who wishes to take up agriculture or modern ranching. The Dulen area on the southern slopes of Makarut mountain is a most suitable area for crop production – provided the policy of keeping agriculture out of the water-conserving forest is maintained: all it lacks is adequate access to markets, which the proposed new road would provide. Likewise the Kakesio area has great possibilities for improved ranching which would also benefit from improved communications. It would be a matter for study, based on up-to-date ecological knowledge, to determine the best boundary on the south of the Conservation Area. Then the road alignment should be sited well to the south of such boundary to permit development on both sides of the road, without infringing upon the migratory herds of wildlife.

Continuing clockwise in our study of the peripheral areas we now come to the western boundary of the Area, where it marches with the eastern boundary of the National Park. It is obvious that the present boundary is a compromise. It twists to the east to ensure that Lake Ndutu (Lagarja) falls within the Park, then ten miles westwards to include certain wells in the Conservation Area for use by the Masai. As a matter of interest the Masai claim to these wells has been recently substantiated by an early map published by the Royal Geographic Society in 1882 giving the name and approximate location of these wells under the same name as they are known by today.

However imperfect this boundary may be, the essential point is that it provides a workable compromise. The Masai can and indeed do argue that they keep their cattle to their side of the boundary, whereas the Park authorities cannot restrain the wildebeest to the confines of the Park. The answer is that it is impossible to construct a fence at an economically tolerable cost, to hold back the wildebeest migration. In any case it would be most undesirable to interfere with this migration, both ecologically and because it would deprive the world of the last spectacular migration in existence. It would be equally undesirable to move the boundary eastward, depriving the Masai of their ancient rights, as to do this would forfeit their goodwill in conservation matters. As pointed out in Chapter V, p. 80, the wildlife is as safe in the Conservation Area as in the Park, largely due to Masai tolerance. If the eastern Serengeti were an area capable of intensive ranching development, a head-on clash between pastoralism and wildlife would be inevitable. But in fact the rainfall is so low, the grass yield so small and the light volcanic soil so liable to wind erosion that there is no economic future in the development of the area by the provision of water supplies, fenced ranches and so on. Even on the western slopes of Makarut mountain it was of doubtful wisdom to build dams in compensation to the Masai for the loss of the Moru area, handed over to the Park in perpetuity (see p. 199).

In all these circumstances it seems best from all angles to leave the western boundary of the Area untouched. This then brings us to the northern boundary, running in a straight line from a point west of Soit Oyaya on the road to Loliondo to the tip of Kerimasi mountain, which is then linked to the northern tip of the Forest Reserve. This is one of those boundaries having no relation to tribal claims, to ecological considerations, or following a natural feature such as an escarpment or a river. It is a straight line 56 miles long between two easily discernible geographic features, an outcrop of rock on the west and an extinct volcano on the east. Here there is certainly a need for revision, as this artificial boundary cuts across the Masai grazing pattern, and equally excludes certain scenic features from the Conservation Area which could in future well repay development from the tourist angle.

Earlier (p. 38) I described my pipedream of a road through the Northern highlands, down to the Sale Plain, thence to the Engare Sero gorge and Lake Natron, around the active volcano Lengai and thence to the rich prehistoric site at Engaruka. If this should ever come about, it would obviously be desirable to have all these tourist attractions under the same control as Ngorongoro. At this juncture I would hesitate to suggest the precise line of the boundary, but no insuperable difficulties appear to prevent adjustment.

Thus for the survival of the Area as a viable unit I suggest the eventual discarding of some 800 square miles in the south, and the acquisition of some 300 square miles in the north. This would leave a total of 2,700 square miles lying within meaningful boundaries, unlikely to be bones of contention in the future.

Stable boundaries require a stable administration. How is this to be secured? It has been explained (p. 203) how the Conservation Unit was started from a development grant, but is now established as a division in the Ministry of Agriculture and Co-operatives. In passing, it is regrettable that the word 'wildlife' has been dropped from the name of the Ministry: its inclusion was announced and received with much acclaim at the Arusha Conference of 1961. Now integrated into the establishment, the Unit appears to have an assured future within the Ministry, but is that enough? My experience leads me to answer, definitely not! It has been explained (p. 203) how the Minister has set up an Advisory Board to guide him in his decisions, but he is in no way bound to follow such advice. I recommended, and still feel most strongly (as also does my successor), that *the Advisory Board should be given statutory status* and its terms of reference clearly defined. No Government can permit itself to be bound absolutely by the decisions of the boards it sets up: it must retain ultimate control, if only by keeping control over the purse-strings. But when a number of well-respected citizens and world-renowned experts agree to serve on such a board, great weight should be attached to their advice. This candidly does not appear to have happened in the past. One has sensed a feeling in the Ministry that 'the Board is only advisory and we are free to accept or reject the advice as we see fit'. It should at least be laid down that *the Minister either accepts the advice, or explains to the Board why he has rejected it.* This is a minimum courtesy to pay to those willing to give time and thought to the problems of Ngorongoro. A clearly defined constitution for the Board would encourage members, disappointed with results to date, to continue to serve. So this is a second step to survival.

A third essential is continuity of policy. This can best be achieved by the formulation of a management plan, and this task has indeed been undertaken. It was first attempted in 1960, and then when I took office as Conservator in 1961 I undertook a revision. Since then Mr Derschl has submitted a further revision. In formulating such a plan a nice balance has to be maintained between rigidity and flexibility. Obviously no one person or no body of men can be so farsighted as to be able to lay down a *plan* for decades ahead: on the other hand they can lay down *principles* which can be adhered to. Then in the light of changes in circumstances and of additional knowledge acquired by research, the application of those principles can be adapted within the framework of the plan. Indeed, more than one plan is necessary: firstly an overall one to cover the whole Area, and then sub-plans for the sub-units. These latter would cover such areas as the Crater floor, the Dulen area – unless and until it hives off, and the Northern highlands – rounded off by including the whole of the massif up to the shores of Lake Natron. The Northern Highlands Forest Reserve already has its plan: that for the Eastern Serengeti has been worked out in conjunction with the National Park authorities, as it forms part of the Serengeti ecosystem, the bulk of which lies within the Park.

Finally, adequacy and continuity of staff to carry out the plan is required. One must face the fact that there are insufficient Tanzanians to fill the necessary posts, ecologists, foresters, botanists, wildlife experts, road engineers, and so on. This situation is likely to prevail for many years to come, for although professionally-qualified Tanzanians will become available in increasing numbers, the demands for their

15

services in a vast developing country are unlimited. We cannot expect more than our fair share at Ngorongoro. It is therefore a great relief to know that the Canadian External Aid Office has virtually 'adopted' Ngorongoro. The first Canadian to work with us, John Goddard, was assigned to Tanzania to work in the woodland area south of Tabora. But prevailing conditions in that area at the time of his arrival prevented him from commencing work there, and when it was suggested that he might work at Ngorongoro, I jumped at the chance. The second Canadian was Mr H. J. Derschl charged with the revision of the Management Plan. His report re-enforced Canada's interest in Ngorongoro and by June 1968 they had three experts in the field, with a further eight under recruitment.

These then I see as the four basic essentials for survival; realistic and stable boundaries, a stable administrative machine including an effective Advisory Board, continuity of policy incorporated in a management plan, and an adequate stabilised staff. But behind all this, the nation itself must have the will to ensure Ngorongoro's survival. It certainly possesses this will at the moment: public opinion, led by President Nyerere, and reinforced by a steady stream of information about Ngorongoro in particular and National Parks and wildlife conservation in general, would strongly resent any major change in the *status quo* of Ngorongoro. But an apparently stable situation can be subject to erosion by small insidious steps. Each in itself looks innocuous, but trends may set in which are difficult to reverse when their import is finally understood. All interested parties, the Government, voluntary agencies such as the East African Wildlife Society and similar societies overseas, the tourist interests and most of all the Masai themselves must therefore be constantly alert. All must subordinate their sectional interests and pool their knowledge, resources and goodwill in a combined, continuing effort to ensure the survival of Ngorongoro.

Postscript

Two and a half years have passed since this book was written. During that time various changes have taken place at Ngorongoro. In the first place my successor Solomon ole Saibull has moved on to a more important post in the conservation sphere, namely Director of National Parks of Tanzania. I like to think that the period we worked together, followed by the years during which he ran the Conservation Unit so efficiently, provided a profitable apprenticeship which enables him to carry his present responsibilities more easily.

There have also been top level organisational changes. The Conservation Unit has been removed from the portfolio of the Minister of Agriculture and Co-operatives to the newly formed Ministry of Natural Resources and Tourism. This brings the Unit into closer association with National Parks, Wildlife, Forestry and other natural resources and so should lead to a more co-ordinated policy in the sphere of multiple land use which is the keynote of the Unit's policy.

In the years since I left Ngorongoro there has been much talk of reducing the size of the Unit, by transferring all but the two Craters, Ngorongoro and Empakaai and their immediate environment, to the control of the Range Management Commission. This is of course directly contrary to the concept of maintaining a viable ecological unit around the Crater to ensure that it does not become a glorified zoo in need of restocking from time to time. It appears that the prospect of carving up the Area has, happily, receded. Why all the fuss, one is tempted to ask, when the basic concept of the Range Management legislation is identical with the Ngorongoro Conservation Act; in fact large sections of the former are copied word for word from the latter. The Range Management Act goes further, in legislating for the creation of group ranches, called Ranching Associations.

Such ranches seem the ideal way of bringing about Masai development; they are already established, but on a slightly different basis, in Kenya. In Botswana, where I am now serving, similar legislation is under considera-tion. The aim in all cases is to place responsibility for a specific area of range land in the hands of a specified group of cattle owners, who are empowered by law to control stock numbers and the utilisation of grazing, water and soil. This is a great step forward compared with the 'free for all' position in the past, where everybody's business was nobody's business, so that stock numbers rose and grazing productivity decreased.

It therefore seems wholly admirable that these principles should be applied to those parts of the Conservation Area which, under the overall land use plan, have been designated for ranching, *provided* the Range Management Commission and the Ranching Associations which it encourages, controls and supervises, act within the scope of the overall land use plan, and accept the control of the Conservator in the utilisation of natural resources. Such an approach would ensure on the one hand that the local Masai did not feel that their development was being inhibited in the interests of wildlife and tourism: they would be taking their own decisions in such matters as range management, disease control, marketing and the like. On the other hand they would not be able to erect dips, dairies or fences in situations which might be in conflict with the overall land plan. So it is to be earnestly hoped that a compromise solution on these lines, currently under discussion, can be speedily finalised.

Adequate political and legal backing is essential to Ngorongoro's survival, but such support will only be forthcoming if the Crater plays and is seen to be playing its part in national development.

This fortunately is the present situation, with tourism expanding by leaps and bounds, and Ngorongoro absorbing its fair share of the expansion. When I was writing this book, about three years ago, I was rash enough to forecast that by the end of 1970 the entry figure of tourists would reach 64,000, a figure which many people thought unduly optimistic. I maintained that, provided facilities continued to expand, this figure could be achieved. Facilities have expanded, particularly by the provision of an additional Lodge, with a result that the 1970 figure was in the region of 70,000, well in excess of my optimistic estimate.

What is the impact of such expansion on the wildlife and on the general atmosphere of the Crater? Let me describe a return visit I made to Ngorongoro last Easter. At this time, if any, one would expect overcrowding to be most apparent, with both Lodges and the Forest Resort full to capacity. On Easter Sunday morning, having spent some time visiting the Lodges and other facilities on the rim, I descended the Crater about 11.30 and inspected the prehistoric site where the potsherds left by previous inhabitants can be seen. I then visited a grave cairn, another manifestation of earlier dwellers in the Crater, and then photographed the flamingoes on the Lake, present in quantities I have never before observed in my 37-year acquaintance with the Crater. During the whole of this period I did not see another vehicle— so much for overcrowding! It was now lunch time. I went to the Lerai

Forest where a close-cropped turfed glade is an authorised picnicking place, now discreetly provided with flush sanitation. Here I saw fresh evidence of a phenomenon I have observed over the years, the wonderful way in which wildlife tames down on closer acquaintance with man. With half a dozen Land-Rovers scattered around, there were weaver birds and starlings picking up crumbs from the rugs of one group of picnickers, a kite catching in mid-air scraps of food thrown up to it, and a vervet monkey standing begging by a Land-Rover. A happy scene of man at one with nature, though difficulties will arise unless some control is maintained, for kites can cause a nasty wound when they swoop to grab a sandwich from the hand of an unsuspecting picnicker, and monkeys, and even more so baboons, can be most destructive if encouraged to look for food inside vehicles.

An afternoon tour round the Crater was a continuing delight, with the taming-down process obvious in the larger mammals as well. I only had a small borrowed camera with me, but was able to take photos of waterbuck, bull eland and a pair of mating lions which completely filled the frame and would have done credit to an expensive camera with a telephoto lens. The general stock of wildlife seemed much as before, and the grazing situation was satisfactory.

Altogether a memorable day, concluding with dinner in the new Wildlife Lodge, which is to me a dream come true. The last occasion on which I visited the site we had been choosing the exact location of the proposed lodge: now it is there, with all modern amenities, yet blending in with the landscape in a most unobtrusive manner. Over dinner we discussed the key question 'Can Ngorongoro survive?' and came to the happy conclusion that, if present trends in policy and administration continue, it will indeed survive for posterity.

26 *July*, 1971, Gaborone, Botswana.

Bibliography

ADAMSON, G. A. G., 1964, Observations on lions in Serengeti National Park, Tanganiyka. *E. African Wildl. J.*, 2 : 160–161.

ANDERSON, G. D. and TALBOT, L. M., 1965, Soil factors affecting the distribution of the grassland types and their utilization by wild animals on the Serengeti Plains, Tanganyika. *J. Ecol.*, 53 : 33–65.

ARBUTHNOT, T. S., 1954, *Grand Safari*, William Kimber, London.

ARRIANUS (attributed), *Periplus of the Erythrean Sea, Travel and Trade in the Indian Ocean by a Merchant of the First Century.* Translated from the Greek and annotated by Wilfred H. Schoff, A.M., Longmans, Green and Co., New York, 1912.

BARNS, T.A., 1923, *Across the Great Craterland to the Congo.* Ernest Bonn, London.

BAUMANN, C., 1894, *Durch Masailand zur Nilquelle.* Part translated in *Ngorongoro's First Visitor* by G. E. Organ and H. A. Fosbrooke, East African Literature Bureau, 1963.

BEARD, P. H., 1966, *The End of the Game*, Paul Hamlyn, London.

BROOKS, PAUL, 1965, The Golden Plains of Tanganyika, *Horizon*, 7(1) : 80–89.

BROWN, LESLIE, 1966, *Africa, A Natural History.* Hamish Hamilton, London.

CARR, A., *et al, The Land and Wild-life of Africa.* Time-Life International (Nederland) N.V.

CARR, N., 1962, *Return to the Wild*, Collins, London.

CARRINGTON, RICHARD, 1967, *Great National Parks*, Weidenfeld and Nicholson, London.

CLOUDSLEY-THOMPSON, J. L., 1967, *Animal Twilight*, Foulis & Co., London.

COLE, SONIA, 1963, *The Pre-History of East Africa*, 2nd Edition.

COWIE, M., 1966, *The African Lion*, Arthur Barker, London.

CRITCHLEY, R.A., 1966, Wild dogs Lechwe Hunt, *Black Lechwe*, 5(3) : 15.

CULLEN, A., AND DOWNEY, S., 1960, *Saving the Game*, Harrolds Publishers, London.

DUGMORE, A. R., 1925, *The Wonderland of Big Game*, Arrowsmith, London.

EGGELING, W. J., 1962, *The Management Plan for the Ngorongoro Conservation Area and its Implementation*. Duplicated official report.

ELLIOTT, H. F. I., and FUGGLES-COUCHMAN, N. R., 1945, An Ecological survey of the Birds of the Crater Highlands and Rift Lakes, Northern Tanganyika, *Ibis*, 90 : 394-425.

EMERY, LIEUT., 1833, Short account of Mombas and the neighbouring Coast of Africa, *J. Royal Geog. Soc.*, 3 : 280–282.

ESTES, R. D. and GODDARD, J., 1967, Prey Selection and Hunting Behaviour of the African Wild Dog, *J. Wildl. Mgmt.*, 31(1) : 52–70.

ESTES, R. D., 1967, Predators and Scavengers, *Natural History*, 76(2) and, 76(3).

ESTES, R. D., 1967, The Comparative Behaviour of Grant's and Thompson's Gazelles, *Journal of Mammalogy*, 48(2).

FARLER, J. P., 1882, Native Routes in East Africa from Pangani to the Masai Country and the Victoria Nyanza, *Proc. Royal Geo. Soc.*, New Series 4 : 713.

FOSBROOKE, H. A., 1948, An Administrative Survey of the Masai Social System, *Tanganyika Notes and Rec.*, 26 : 1–50.

FOSBROOKE, H. A., 1963, The stomoxys plague in Ngorongoro, 1962, *E. African Wildl. J.*, 1 : 124–126.

FOSBROOKE, H. A., 1963, *Ngorongoro's First Visitor*, Ngorongoro Conservation Area Booklet No. 1, E.A.L.B., Nairobi.

FOSBROOKE, H. A., 1965, Success Story at Ngorongoro, *Oryx*, 8(3).

FOSBROOKE, H.A., 1967, Book Review *S.O.S. Rhino* by C. A. W. Guggisberg, *Black Lechwe*, 6(3) : 26–27.

FOSBROOKE, H. A., 1967, Correspondence re Hyaena, *Black Lechwe*, 6(3) : 29–31.

FOSBROOKE, H. A., 1968, Elephants in the Serengeti National Park : an Early Record, *E. Afr. Wildl. J.*, 6 : 150–152.

FOURIE, A. P., de K., c.1946, *Autobiography*, MSS. in possession of his son, P. Fourie.

GODDARD, J., 1966, Mating and courtship of the black rhinoceros (*Diceros bicornis* L.), *E. African Wildl. J.*, 4 : 69–75.

GODDARD, J., 1966, *Ngorongoro's Bird Life*, Ngorongoro Conservation Area Booklet No. 3, Conservator, N.C.A. Arusha.

GODDARD, J., 1966, *Ngorongoro's Animal Life*, Ngorongoro Conservation Area Booklet No. 4, Conservator, N.C.A. Arusha.

GODDARD, J., 1967, The validity of censusing black rhinoceros populations from the air. *E. African Wildl. J.*, 5 : 18–23.

GODDARD J., 1967, Home range, behaviour and recruitment rates of two black rhinoceros populations. *E. African Wildl. J.*, 5 : 133–150.

GRANT, H. ST. J., 1954, *Report on Human Habitation in the Serengeti National Park*, Tang. Nat. Parks.

GRANT, H. ST. J., 1956, *Masai Mode of Life*, Tanganyika Govt., D.S.M.

GRZIMEK, B. & M., 1960, *Serengeti Shall Not Die*, Hamish Hamilton, London.

GRZIMEK, B. & M., 1960, A study of the Game of the Serengeti Plains, *Z. Saugetierk*, 25 : 1–61.

GRZIMEK, B., 1964, *Rhinos Belong to Everyone*, Collins, London.

GUGGISBERG, C. A. W., 1962, *Simba, the Life of the Lion*, Bailey Bros. and Swinfen, London.

GUGGISBERG, C. A. W., 1963, *The Wilderness is Free*, Howard Timmins, Cape Town.

GUGGISBERG, C. A. W., 1966, *S.O.S. Rhino*, Andre Deutsch, London.

GUILLIAN, M., 1856, *Documents sur L'histoire, La Geographie et Le Commerce de l'Afrique Orientale*, Arthus Bertrand, Paris.

GUNZERT, THEODOR, 1907–1916, Memoirs of a German District Commissioner in Mwanza, translated by Joyce Hutchinson, edited with introductory notes by Ralph A. Austen, *Tanzania Notes and Rec.*, 66 : 174.

HALLET, J. P., 1965, *Congo Kitabu*, Hamish Hamilton, London.

HOEHNEL, L. V., 1894, *Discovery of Lakes Rudolf and Stefanie*, London.

HOLLIS, A. C., 1905, *The Masai: Their language and folklore*, Clarendon Press, Oxford.

HOLMES, F. R., n.d., c.1929, *Interviewing Wild Animals*, Stanley Martin, London.

HUNTER, J. A., 1952, *Hunter*, Hamish Hamilton, London.

HUNTINGFORD, G. W. B., 1953, *The Nandi of Kenya*, Routledge and Kegan Paul, London.

HUXLEY, ELSPETH, 1964, *Forks and Hope*, Chatto and Windus, London.

HUXLEY, Sir JULIAN, 1961, *The Conservation of Wildlife and Natural Habitats in Central and East Africa*, UNESCO, Paris.

JAEGER, FRITZ, 1911–1913, Das Hochland der Riesenkrater, *Mitt. a.d. deutsch. Schutzgebieten*, Erganzungsheft 4, 1911 u. 8, 1913.

JOHNSON, H., 1886, *The Kilimanjaro Expedition*.

KEARTON, CHERRY, 1941, *Cherry Kearton's Travels*, Robert Hale Ltd., London.

KLINGEL, H., 1964, Beobachtungen am Stefpenzebra (*Equus quagga boehmi* Matschie), Proceedings of the meeting of the German Zoological Society at Kiel, 1964.

KLINGEL, H., 1965, Notes on the biology of the Plains Zebra, *Equus quagga boehmi* Matschie, *E. African Wildl. J.*, 3 : 86–88.

KLINGEL, H. and KLINGEL, U., 1965, Notes on tooth development and ageing criteria in the plains zebra, *Equus quagga boehmi* Matschie, *E. African Wildl. J.*, 3 : 127–129.

KLINGEL, H. and KLINGEL, U., 1966, The Rhinoceroses of Ngorongoro Crater, *Oryx*, 8(5) : 302–306.

KRUUK, H., 1966, Clan-system and feeding habits of spotted hyaenas (*Crocuta crocuta* Ersleben), *Nature*, 209 (5029) : 1257–1258.

KUHME, W., 1965, Communal food distribution and division of labour in African hunting dog, *Nature*, 205 (4970) : 443–444.

LAMPREY, H. F., GLOVER, P. E., TURNER, M. I. M., and BELL, R. H. V., 1967, Invasion of the Serengeti National Park by elephants, *E. African Wildl. J.*, 5 : 151–166.

LEAKEY, L. S. B., 1965, *Olduvai Gorge* 1951–61, Vol. I, Cambridge University Press.

LEAKEY, M. D., 1966, Excavation of Burial Mounds in Ngorongoro Crater, *Tanzania Notes and Rec.*, 66 : 123–135.

LEDGER, H. P., 1963–64, Weights of some East African animals, *E. African Wildl. J.*, 1 : 123–124 and 2 : 159.

LIVERMORE, NORMAN B., 1923–24, *Diary of African Trip*, MSS in possession of his son H. Putnam Livermore of San Francisco.

MEINERTZHAGEN, R., 1957, *Kenya Diary* 1902–1906, Oliver and Boyd, Edinburgh and London.

MOORE, AUDREY, 1938, *Serengeti*, Country Life, London.

MOORE, M., 1947, Two Good Rhino Trophies, *Tanganyika Notes and Rec.*, 24 : 46.

NGORONGORO CONSERVATION UNIT, 1962–1965, *News Letters*, 1 – 8, series closed.

NGORONGORO CONSERVATION UNIT, 1962– , *Bulletins*, 1 – 15, series continues.

ORR, D. J. C., and MOORE-GILBERT, S. M., 1964, Field immobilization of young wildebeest with succinylcholine chloride. *E. African Wildl. J.*, 2 : 60–66.

ORR, D. J. C., and MOORE-GILBERT, S. M., 1964, Long-term Marking of African Game Animals by Branding, *E. African Wildl. J.*, 2 : 161–163.

PATTERSON, J. H., 1904, Report from East Africa, *J. Soc. Preserv. Fauna Emp.*, London.

PATTERSON, J. H., 1907, *The Man-Eaters of Tsavo*, Macmillan and Co., London.

PEARSALL, W. H., 1957, Report on an ecological survey of the Serengeti National Park, Tanganyika, *Oryx*, 4 : 71–136.

PERISTIANY, J. G., 1939, *The Social Institutions of the Kipsigis*, G. Routledge, London.

PICKERING, R., 1968, *Ngorongoro's Geological History*, Ngorongoro Conservation Area, Booklet No. 2, Conservator, N.C.A., Arusha.

PLOWRIGHT, W., 1963, The role of game animals in the epizootology of rinderpest and malignant catarrhal fever in East Africa, *Bull. epiz. Dis. Afr.*, 11 : 149–162.

RECK, H., 1926, Prähistorische Grab-und Menschenfunde und ihre Beziehungen zur Pluvialzeit in Ostafrika, *Mitteilungen aus den deutschen Schutzgebieten*, B. and XXXIV Helf, 1, Berlin.

RECK, H., 1933, *Oldoway*, F. V. Brockhaus, Leipsiz.

SASSOON, H., 1966, Engaruka: Excavations during 1964. *Azania*, 1 : 79–99, Nairobi, Kenya.

SCHILLING, C. G., 1906, *With Flashlight and Rifle*, Hutchison and Co., London.

SEIDENTOPF, A. R., 1947, *The Last Stronghold of Big Game*, Hodder and Stoughton, London.

SHANTZ, H. L., and TURNER, B. L., 1958, *Vegetational Changes in Africa over a Third of a Century*, University of Arizona.

SIMON, N., 1962, *Between the Sunlight and the Thunder*, Collins, London.

SMITH, A., 1963, *Throw Out Two Hands*, George Allen and Unwin Ltd., London.

SUTTON, J. E. G., 1966, The Archaeology and Early Peoples of the Highlands of Kenya and Northern Tanzania, *Azania*, 1 : 49–57.

SWYNNERTON, G. H. and HAYMAN, R. W., 1951, A check list of the land mammals of the Tanganyika Territory and the Zanzibar Protectorate, *Journal of the East African Natural History Soc.*, Vol. XX No. 6 & 7 : 274–392.

TALBOT, L. M., 1960, *A Look at Threatened Species*, Fauna Preservation Society for I.U.C.N., London.

TALBOT, L. M., 1964, The Concept of biomass in African wildlife research, *Mammalia*, 28(4) : 613–619.

TALBOT, L. M., and TALBOT, M. H., 1963, *The Wildebeest in Western Masailand, East Africa*, Wildlife Monograph No. 12, The Wildlife Society, Washington, D.C.

TALBOT, L. M., TALBOT, M. H., and LAMPREY, H. F., 1961, *An Introduction to the Landscape*, Govt. Printer, Nairobi.

TANGANYIKA GOVERNMENT, 1956, *Sessional Paper No. 1 of 1956*, G.P., Dar es Salaam.

TANGANYIKA GOVERNMENT, 1957, *Report of the Serengeti Committee of Enquiry*, G.P., Dar es Salaam.

TANGANYIKA GOVERNMENT, 1958, *Government Paper No. 5 of 1958*, G.P., Dar es Salaam.

TANGANYIKA GOVERNMENT, *Annual Reports of the Ngorongoro Conservation Unit*, 1959 July – Dec., 1960, 1961 (duplicated) 1962, 1963, Ministry of Lands, Forests & Wildlife, Dar es Salaam.

TANZANIA, *Annual Reports of the Ngorongoro Conservation Unit*, 1964, 1965, 1966, 1967, Ministry of Lands, Forests and Wildlife, Dar es Salaam.

THEAL, G. MCC., 1898–1902, *Records of South Eastern Africa*, 9 Vols., Capetown, reprint Amsterdam, 1965.

THOMSON, JOSEPH, 1885, *Through Masailand*, Sampson Low, Marston, Searle and Rivington, London.

TURNER, M., and WATSON, M., 1964, A census of game in Ngorongoro Crater, *E. African Wildl. J.*, 2 : 165–168.

WALTHER, FRITZ, 1961, The Mating Behaviour of Certain Horned Animals, *Inter. Zoo Yearbook*, Vol. 3.

WALTER, von FRITZ, R., 1964, Einige Verhaltensbeobachtungen am Thomson-gazellen (*Gazella Thomsoni* Gunther, 1884) im Ngorongoro – Krater, *Zeitschrift fur Tierpsychologie*, 21(7) : 871–890.

WALTER, von FRITZ, R., 1965, Verhaltensstudien am der Grantgazelle (*Gazella granti* Brooke, 1872) im Ngorongoro, *Zeitschrift fur Tierpsychologie*, 22(2) : 167–208.

WAKEFIELD, T., 1870, Routes of Native Caravans from the Coast to the Interior of Eastern Africa, *J. Royal Geo. Soc.*, 40 : 303–338.

WARD, ROWLAND, 1962, *Records of Big Game*, 11th Ed. (Africa) Rowland Ward, London.

WATSON, R. M. and TURNER, M. I. M., 1965, A count of the larger mammals of the Lake Manyara National Park: results and discussion, *E. African Wildl. J.*, 3 : 95–98.

WILLIAMS, JOHN, 1963, *A Field Guide to the Birds of East and Central Africa*, Collins, London.

WILLIAMS, JOHN, 1967, *A Field Guide to the National Parks of East Africa*, Collins, London.

WILLIAMS, JOHN, and FENNESSY, R., 1966, *Birds of Africa*, Collins, London.

WILLOUGHBY, J. C., 1887, *East Africa and its Big Game*, Longmans, Green and Co., London.

WILSON, G. M., The Tatoga of Tanganyika, *Tanganyika Notes and Rec.*, 33.

Index

Adamson, George, 114
Adamson, Joy, 29
Age-set system, 32, 160–1, 165, 186
Allison, H. C., 177
Amboseli, 94
Anderson, F. J., 110
Anderson, Dr G. D., 46, 77
Antelope, 85–6
Arning, Dr, 148
Arusha, town of, 19, 142, 164, 174, 185, 198, 202, 206, 222
Arusha Conference, 51, 139, 204–5, 224
Arusha people, 19, 20, 159, 173, 189, 195, 196

Babati, Lake, 54
Baboon, 86
Bageshawe, Mr, 23
Balbal depression, 77, 85, 115, 142–3, 221
Bamboo, 44
Barabaig people, 157
Barkhaus, 49
Barns, T.A., 26, 27, 53, 89, 107–8
Bat, 77
Bau game, 150–1
Baumann, Dr, 25, 52, 98, 107, 156, 174
Beard, P. H., 119
Benbow, 'Ben', 213
Bere, Rennie, 29
Bernhard, Prince, 126, 133
Bigalke, Dr R., 134
Biomass, 74–6, 91
Boma, Masai dwelling unit, 166–7
Boma la Ngombe, 169
Bongo, 87
Buffalo, 48, 84–5
Buffalo Ridge, 47, 84
Burials. *See* Graves
Bushbuck, 48, 84
Bush-pig, 86–7

Caldera, 35–6
Cape Chestnut, 58

Caracal or African lynx, 134
Carr, Norman, 119
Carrington, Richard, 220
Cattle, 52, 53, 61, 66, 67, 69, 74, 94, 130, 145, 146; trade in, 183–7, 190; stocking problems, 190–3
Cattle tracks, prehistoric, 151
Cedar forest, 57, 70
Chagga people, 101, 159–60, 173, 189
Cheetah, 133–4
Climate, 41–2
Conservation Unit, 25, 68, 69, 70, 93, 145, 191, 199, 201, 203, 213–4, 227–9
Cowie, Mervyn, 29
Critchley, Colonel, 123–4
Crotelerea, 58

Derschl, H. J., 225, 226, 228
Doinyoogol Hills, 32, 79, 84, 86
Doole, Peter, 96
Dorobo people, 55, 142, 155, 156
Duck, 138
Dugmore, Major, 26, 27, 89, 108
Dulen, 48, 214, 222, 225
Duluti, Lake, 19

Eagles, 138
East Tsavo National Park, 62
Ecological unit, Serengeti, total of animals in, 87–8
Eland, 74, 81
Elephant, 48, 60, 62–3, 64, 75, 91–3, 214
Elliott, Sir Hugh, 39
Eltz, Herr von, 97
Elusine, 61, 62
Empakaai, crater, 35, 37, 53, 136, 137, 197, 199, 210, 214
Engare Nanyuki, 156
Engare ol Motonyi, 159
Engare Sero gorge, 139, 224
Engaruka, 38, 142, 143, 152, 153, 224
Engaruka river, 152

Erosion, 49–53, 64
Estes, Dick, 78, 121, 124, 129–30, 132, 215
Eucalyptus tree, 47, 48
Eyasi, Lake, 34, 35, 40, 86, 105, 137, 152, 157, 171, 222
Eyasi Man, 153
Eyasi Rift, 21

Fever-tree, 54, 64–5
Fire, 55–7, 59; control of, 59–61, 71
Fischer, A. G., 39
Flamingo, 137
Fletcher, 'A.B.', 213
Flooding, 54; control of, 54–5
Forest hog, 87
Forest Resort, 83, 84, 195, 206
Fourie, Gert, 212
Fourie, A. P. de K., 28
Fox, 134

Gazelle, 82–3
Geese, 138
Gelai, mountain, 20, 38
Giraffe, 73
Glover, Dr, 61
Goats, 74
Goddard, John, 76, 96, 99, 100–1, 117, 121–5, 133, 136, 139, 215, 226
Gogoland, 189
Grant's gazelle, 41, 82–3
Grassland types, 46–7
Graves, in Ngorongoro, 148–9
Gregory Rift, 21, 34, 35
Greenway, Dr P. J., 54
Groundnut Scheme, 56, 68
Grzimek, Dr Bernard, 25, 77, 82, 87, 89, 93, 107, 111, 117, 124–7, 174, 197, 204
Grzimek, Michael, 47, 139, 177
Guggisberg, C. A. W., 29, 96, 97, 101

Hadza people, 55, 142, 155–7
Hallet, Jean Pierre, 118
Hallier, Colonel, 27, 207
Hamman, John, 177
Hanang, Mount, 157
Hartebeest, 83–4
Hewlett, Major, 195
Himo, 159
Hippo, 105–6
Hippo Pool, 55, 105
Holmes, F. Radcliffe, 27
Homo habilis, 143, 144
Honey hunting, 55
Howe, Eric, 178–180, 183
Hunter, J. A., 28, 108–9
Hurst, Captain G. H. R., 27, 89, 177
Huxley, Elspeth, 44, 96, 100
Huxley, Sir Julian, 139, 203, 204

Hyaena, 91, 116, 123, 127–32
Hygenea abyssinica, 57–8

Impala, 73, 85
Iramba tribe, 169
Iraqw or Mbulu people, 22–4, 64, 142, 169, 172, 196

Jaeger, F., 25
Jackal, 123, 134
Jackson's widow-bird, 140

Kainam, 142
Kalenjin ethnic group, 31–2
Karatu, 142
Kattwinkel, Professor, 143
Kerimasi, mountain, 21, 224
Keshei Hill, 135, 150
Kikuyu grass, 61–2
Kilimanjaro, Mount, 19, 20, 136, 139, 159, 169, 189
Kipsigis people, 31, 157
Kissongo people, 170
Kitati Hill, 36, 82, 84, 134, 137
Kitete Settlement Scheme, 64
Kitumbeni, mountain, 20, 38
Klingel, Dr Hans, 80, 101, 215
Klipspringer, 84
Kluver, Hans, 130–2
Koironyi island, 71, 188
Koitoktok, 27, 64, 65, 150, 197, 221
Koitoktok Springs, 37, 55
Kolb, Dr, 97
Kondoa, 28; rock paintings, 152, 153
Kruuk, Dr Hans, 128–9, 130, 215
Kudu, 86
Kung rocks, 37
Kuria people, 32

Laiboni, Masai prophet or seer, 161
Lairrataat stream, 70
Lammergeyer, 136, 139
Landslides, 53–4
Larsen, Dr Kohl, 152
Leakey, L. S. B., 77, 142, 143, 145, 146, 148, 149, 150, 152, 154, 198
Leakey, Mrs, 142, 143, 146, 148–9
Lengai, volcano, 20–1, 38–40, 44, 49
Leopard, 132–3
Lerai forest, 27, 42, 54–5, 62, 64, 70–1, 82–3, 86, 91–2, 100, 106, 132, 139, 176, 178, 221
Lettow-Vorbeck, General von, 125
Lion: tawny-maned, 48, 114; and cattle, 69; photography of, 110; struck by *Stomoxys* pest, 111, 113; increase of population, 113–14; and tree-climbing, 114–15; predators on, 115–16; Masai methods of hunting, 116, 118–19; flight reaction,

116–17; and man-eating, 117–18; poor hunters, 119–21
Livermore, Norman B., 28, 108
Locust, 160, 168
Loirobi grasslands, 140, 151
Lol Kisale, granite insulberg, 20
Loliondo, 29, 178, 186, 194
Lolmalasin, mountain, 21, 30, 39, 44
Lonyoki, Headman Isa, 212
Lonyokie stream, 71, 151, 197

Mace, Clive, 205
Magadi, Lake, 40
Makarut, mountain, 21, 30, 37, 53, 57, 70, 222, 223
Makat, Lake, 188
Malanja, 178, 222
Malanja depression, 81
Malignant catarrhal fever (Snotsiekte), 78–9
Manduusi plant, 60
Manduusi Swamp, 55, 60, 114
Mangati tribe, 115
Manyara, Lake, 20, 21, 32, 40, 109, 137
Manyara, town, 30, 31, 64, 105
Manyara National Park, 21–2, 29, 75, 76, 114–15, 136
Masai people, 23, 25, 50, 56, 58, 82, 83, 86, 87, 133, 142, 146, 156, 157, 202; and place-names, 20, 22, 31, 32, 39; pastoralism, 52–3, 60–2, 65–9, 188–90; livestock, 74, 76; and wildebeest, 78, 79; and rhino, 93–4, 96, 98, 101, 103–5, 201, 215; and lions, 111, 113, 115–19; their *bau* game, 150; history, 158–60, 168–70; markets, 158–9; social and political organization, 160–3; attempts to improve their dress and hygiene, 163–5; social consequences of breaking down age-set system, 165; the women, 165; transhumance and its social consequences, 165–8; loss of land, and agricultural problems, 171–3; and cattle, 183, 185–7; and their rights in Serengeti, 195–7; agree to vacate Moru and Western Serengeti, 199–201; question of their future, 219–24
Masailand Range Management Commission, 227–8
Mbulu, 137, 174, 185; District, 157, 158, 167; highlands, 212
Mbulumbulu, 23, 64; settlement scheme, 71
Meinertzhagen, Colonel, 87, 122, 124, 134
Meru, Mount, 19, 87, 136, 169, 173, 189
Meru land case, 171
Meru people, 19, 20, 173, 189
Migration routes, 63–4, 92–3
Missionaries, 24–5
Monduli, 110, 229

Monduli, mountain, 20, 169
Monkeys, 86
Moore, Audrey, 109, 127–8
Moore, Monty, 109
Moore-Gilbert, Bill, 96, 105, 106, 120
Moran, Masai warrior, 116, 161, 165
Moru, 199, 201
Moshi, 169, 185
Mosquito, 22
Mto-wa-Mbu, village, 21–2, 38, 65, 212
Munge river, 107, 132, 176, 221
Murchison Falls National Park, Uganda, 62
Murray-Smith, T., 127, 128
Musoma district, 194
Musthill, F. J., 198
Mwakangata, A. W., 163

Nainokonoka, 130
Nairobi National Park, 94, 210
Nandi people, 31, 157
Nasera Rock, 84, 146, 148, 154, 210
Natron, Lake, 38, 40, 224, 225
Ndutu, Lake, 142, 210, 223
Newbury, Andrew, 28
Ngurdoto, crater, 37
Nihill, Sir Barclay, 198
Nolkaria hills, 36
Northern Highlands Forest Reserve, 174, 189, 192, 197, 201, 221–3, 225
Nyerere, President, 174, 205, 211, 226

Oldeani, mountain, 20–1, 30, 35, 42, 44, 87
Oldeani, town of, 64, 207
Oldeani coffee plantations, 98–9, 101, 110
Oldeani farms, 71
Oldeani forest, 221
Oldeani View, 31
Olduvai gorge, 25, 34, 40, 96, 100, 101, 142–6, 153, 210, 219
Olgeju lol Munge, 180
Olmoti, mountain, 35, 221
One Trough Pass, 37, 38
Oryx, 85–6
Ostrich, 136

Pastoralism, 52–3, 60–2, 65–9, 188–90, 223
Patterson, J. H., 118
Pearsall, Professor W. H., 198, 199, 200
Pelican, 137
Pickering, Dr, 32, 34
Pigs, 86–7
Pluchea monocephala, 59
Pottery, 150, 152
Purku, Masai sub-tribe, 169, 170

Queeney, E. M., 118

Ranching Associations, 227–8
Range Management Act, 227–8
Rainfall, 42, 112
Rangi people, 50
Reck, Professor Hans, 26, 143, 148, 176
Red safari ant, 92
Reedbuck, 48
Reid, Neil, 177
Rhino, 44, 59, 74, 144; hunting of, 93–8, 101–2, 205, 215; range of, 99–101; population, 100–1; trade in their horn, 101–2; the Masai and preservation of, 103–5, 201, 215
Rinderpest, 25, 160, 168
Roads, 211–13
Rock paintings, 152, 153
Rodentia, 77
Ross, Sir Charles, 26–8, 107–8, 170, 176, 194, 220
Russell, Gordon, 207

Saibull, Solomon ole, 227
Sale plains, 34, 38, 39, 44, 139
Salt lakes, 40
Sanjan gorge, 34, 139
Sanya Plains, 171, 173
Sapi, Chief Adam, 195
Satiman, mountain, 39
Scott, Peter, 204
Segi, Masai leader, 25
Seneto, 42, 84, 113
Serengeti Closed Reserve, 194–5
Serengeti National Park, 63, 70, 77, 79–80, 86, 93, 109, 127, 136, 142, 215, 222, 223; wildlife census, 87–8; controversy about, 197ff.
Serengeti Plains, 25, 29, 30, 46, 49, 77, 83, 142, 144, 155, 156, 157, 166, 169, 197
Serengeti Research Institute, 74, 78
Seronera, 114–15
Serval, 134
Share-cropping, 171
Sheep, 74
Shifting Sands, 49, 140
Siedentopf, A. R., 99
Siedentopf brothers (Adolph and Friedrich Wilhelm), their farms, 25–8, 47, 53, 86, 107, 138, 143, 148, 169, 170, 176, 177, 180, 197
Silalei Hill, 36, 121
Simon, Noel, 190
Sinclair, Sir Ronald, 197
Sirua, mountain, 21, 30, 39, 44, 81
Sisal hedges, 47, 197
Sitete swamps, 38
Slater, Clive, 198
Smallpox, 160, 168
Soda lakes, 40

Sonjo tribe, 86, 152, 172–3
Spathodea or Nandi flame, 58
Spoonbill, 138
Stock routes, 187–8
Stomoxys pest, 111–13, 114, 115
Storks, 136–7
Sukuma, 185
Sukumaland, 52, 189
Sun-bird, 136, 140

Taita wild cat, 134
Talbot, Dr Lee, 46, 77, 102, 198
Tamura, Professor, 35
Tarosero, mountain, 20, 38
Tatog people, 31, 32, 157–8, 169
Teleki, Count, 97
Thomson, Joseph, 97–8
Thomson, Sir Landsborough, 197
Thomson's gazelle, 82–3
Topi, 86
Tourism, 38, 68, 144, 153, 206–11, 228–9
Transhumance, 65, 165–8
Trevor, Dr, 148
Tsavo National Park, Kenya, 62, 91, 101, 173
Tsetse fly, 22, 114, 173
Turaco, 140
Turner, Myles, 126
Tussock grass, 61

Ulyate, R. R., 110, 177

Volcanic activity, 34–5, 49
Vultures, 138–9

Walther, Fritz, 93
Wart-hog, 86–7
Wasawo, Dr, 204
Waterbuck, 48, 83
Watson, Dr, 78, 87
White rhino, 96–7
Wild dog, 121–7
Wildebeest, 64, 69, 75–80, 89, 124–5, 127, 129–30, 201, 221
Wildlife census, 87–91
Wildlife protection, 193–7
Willoughby, Sir John, 97
Worthington, Dr, 204

Yellow-barked acacia, 65, 91

Zebra, 64, 76, 79, 80–1, 221–2
Zimbabwe creeper, 58–9
Zinjanthropus (now called *Australopithecus boisei*), 143–4
Ziota, Chief Humbi, 198

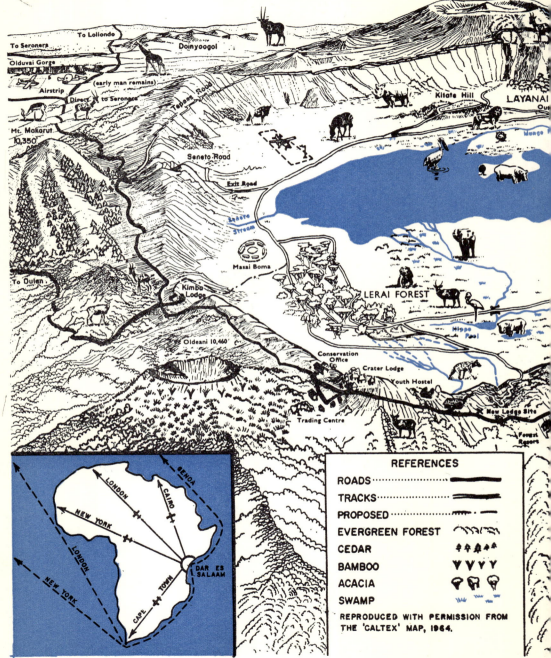

THE NGORO

Olmoti 10,160'

To Seronera
To Loliondo
Doinyoogol
Olduvai Gorge
Airstrip
(early man remains)
Direct rt to Seronera
Mt. Makarut 10,350'
Seneto Road
Exit Road
Seneto Stream
Masai Boma
To Duian
Kimba Lodge
Oldeani 10,460'
LERAI FOREST
Conservation Office
Crater Lodge
Youth Hostel
Trading Centre
New Lodge Site
Forest Resort
Kitote Hill
LAYANAI
Mange
Hippo Pool

GENOA
LONDON
CAIRO
NEW YORK
LONDON
NEW YORK
DAR ES SALAAM
CAPE TOWN

REFERENCES

ROADS	━━━
TRACKS	━━━
PROPOSED	▬▬
EVERGREEN FOREST	
CEDAR	
BAMBOO	
ACACIA	
SWAMP	

REPRODUCED WITH PERMISSION FROM THE 'CALTEX' MAP, 1964.